Your Majesty

Your Majesty

THE LIFE & REIGN OF ELIZABETH II

Graham & Heather Fisher

ROBERT HALE · LONDON

© Graham & Heather Fisher 1985
First published in Great Britain as *Monarch* 1985
Second edition 1992

ISBN 0 7090 4736 3

Robert Hale Limited
Clerkenwell House
Clerkenwell Green
London EC1R 0HT

Photoset in Linotron Bembo by
Rowland Phototypesetting Limited
Printed in Great Britain by
St Edmundsbury Press Limited, Bury St Edmunds, Suffolk
and bound by WBC Limited

CONTENTS

List of Illustrations   vii
Authors' Preface   ix
Biographical Details   xi
Prologue   1

1   The Queen Today   5
2   Birth of a Princess   24
3   Lilibet   34
4   Heir Presumptive   50
5   Wartime Princess   61
6   Princess in Love   76
7   The Young Bride   92
8   Her Father's Deputy   107
9   The 62nd Monarch   118
10 Mother Again   144
11 Great Going, Liz   160
12 Granny Queen   174

Books Consulted   203
Index   205

ILLUSTRATIONS

Between pages 52 and 53
1   A Princess in Piccadilly: Elizabeth at the age of two
2   With Margaret Rose outside the Welsh playhouse in the grounds of Royal Lodge
3   An official engagement: the pit pony display at the 1939 Royal Show
4   The Little Princesses at Buckingham Palace
5   Broadcasting to the children of the nation
6   A royal performance: *Old Mother Red Riding Boots*
7   Wartime training in the ATS
8   Victory!: with Churchill on VE Day
9   With General Smuts and her family in Natal's beautiful National Park
10   Elizabeth married Lieutenant Philip Mountbatten in November 1947
11   The young royal family at Clarence House, their first home
12   A portrait of baby Anne and her mother
13   The Coronation
14   Leading home Carrozza, winner of the Oaks at Epsom in 1957
15   Her first Christmas Day television speech
16   Cheered by Australian children at Northam

Between pages 100 and 101
17   Like any mother Elizabeth keeps a tight grip on Andrew near water
18   Waiting for the Balmoral train
19   A meeting with the Mounties
20   New Zealand walkabout
21   The investiture of her eldest son as Prince of Wales

22 A Silver Wedding portrait
23 With the Duchess of Windsor in Paris
24 At her daughter's wedding
25 Silver Jubilee walkabout
26 At the Cenotaph on Remembrance Sunday
27 With King Khalid of Saudi Arabia
28 The family gathers at Lord Mountbatten's funeral
29 The Head of the Commonwealth with her High Commissioners, 1984
30 Trooping the Colour

Between pages 140 and 141
31 Lunch with King Hassan of Morocco
32 Prince Andrew's ship, HMS *Invincible*, returns from the Falklands
33 With her eldest grandchild Peter Phillips
34 At Charles and Diana's wedding
35 The Queen met Indira Gandhi on her tour of India
36 At the D-Day Celebrations in Normandy, 1984
37 The Queen has always loved horses: Royal Windsor Horse Show, 1984

Between pages 188 and 189
38 The Queen and her corgis
39 Walkabout in Bracknell, 1990
40 As Colonel-in-Chief of the Welsh Guards
41 40 years a Queen

PICTURE CREDITS

The Hulton Picture Library: 1–3, 5–8, 10–37.
Camera Press: 38–41.

AUTHORS' PREFACE

A definitive biography of Her Most Excellent Majesty Queen Elizabeth the Second must necessarily wait upon the future, upon that point in time when her successor accords some privileged biographer access to her personal papers and the royal archives of her reign. This book makes no claim to be a definitive biography. It is an account of her life and reign to date, an interim portrait of a woman who, like her father before her, had no desire to be Monarch, but through force of circumstances finds herself fulfilling a role which had its origins in the Saxon England of eleven and a half centuries ago.

G. & H. Fisher

FOR
James, Robert, Joanna and Pendaran

Her Most Excellent Majesty
ELIZABETH
THE SECOND

NAME

Elizabeth Alexandra Mary Windsor

TITLE

Elizabeth the Second, by the Grace of God of the United
Kingdom of Great Britain and Northern Ireland and of Her other
Realms and Territories Queen, Head of the Commonwealth,
Defender of the Faith★

BORN

17 Bruton Street, London, 21 April 1926

FATHER

Albert Frederick Arthur George, Duke of York and later
King George VI (died 6 February 1952)

MOTHER

Elizabeth Angela Marguerite, Duchess of York, previously
Lady Elizabeth Bowes-Lyon and later Queen Elizabeth. Now
Queen Elizabeth the Queen Mother (born 4 August 1900)

SISTER

Princess Margaret Rose (born 21 August 1930)

★ The wording differs slightly in the seventeen other Commonwealth countries
of which she is also Queen, but the essence is the same. These other countries are:
Canada, Australia, New Zealand, Jamaica, Barbados, Mauritius, Fiji, Bahamas,
Grenada, Papua New Guinea, Solomon Islands, Tuvalu (Ellice Island), St Lucia, St
Vincent and the Grenadines, Belize, Antigua and Barbuda, St Christopher and
Nevis. Of these, only Canada and New Zealand also recognize her as 'Defender of
the Faith'.

Westminster Abbey, London, 20 November 1947

Philip, Duke of Edinburgh, Earl of Merioneth and Baron
Greenwich, previously Prince Philip of Greece, naturalized
British as Lieutenant Philip Mountbatten RN. Now
Prince Philip, Duke of Edinburgh

SUCCEEDED TO THE THRONE
6 February 1952

CROWNED
Westminster Abbey, 2 June 1953

HEIR APPARENT
Charles Philip Arthur George, Prince of Wales and Earl of
Chester, Duke of Cornwall and Duke of Rothesay, Earl of
Carrick and Baron Renfrew, Lord of the Isles and Great Steward
of Scotland (born 14 November 1948; married Lady Diana Frances
Spencer July 29, 1981; has issue – Prince William of Wales, born
21 June 1982; Prince Henry of Wales, born 15 September 1984)

OTHER CHILDREN
Anne Elizabeth Alice Louise, Princess Royal (born 15 August
1950; married Captain Mark Phillips 14 November 1973;
separated August 1989; has issue – Peter Phillips born 1977,
Zara Phillips born 1981)

Andrew Albert Christian Edward, Duke of York
(born 19 February 1960; married Miss Sarah Ferguson 23 July
1986; has issue – Princess Beatrice, born 8 August 1988,
Princess Eugenie, born 23 March 1990)

Edward Antony Richard Louis (born 10 March 1964)

PROLOGUE

But for a quirk of fate Elizabeth Alexandra Mary Windsor, forty years a queen on 6 February 1992, would never have become Elizabeth II. Like her father and grandfather before her, she was not born in direct line of succession to the throne. Her grandfather became King George V only because his elder brother, Albert Victor, Duke of Clarence, died of pneumonia at the youthful age of twenty-eight. Her father, in turn, became King George VI only because his eldest brother, King Edward VIII, vacated the throne once it became apparent that he could not have both it and the twice-divorced American from Blue Ridge Summit, Pennsylvania, he had hoped to see crowned as his Queen Consort. With her father's unexpected accession to the throne, Princess Elizabeth of York, as she had been until then, became Heir Presumptive. Not Heir Apparent. Only a son could have been that, and one might yet have been born to supplant her. But there was to be no baby brother, and with her father's death in 1952, when she was still only twenty-five, she became Queen.

There were many ways in which fate might have ordered things differently. The Duke of Clarence might have lived to marry the girl to whom he was already betrothed at the time of his death (and who would later marry his brother and become Queen Mary); lived to become King Albert Victor, with a child to succeed him. Her uncle, King Edward VIII, might have fallen in love with someone the nation would have been happy to accept as Queen Consort and might equally have had a child to succeed him. Her parents' second child might have been a boy instead of another girl who, because sons take priority over daughters, would have assumed precedence on the ladder of succession. Or there might have been a third child – a son – born later, as Prince

1

Philip was born at a time when his parents already had four daughters.

How different life would have been for her had any of these things happened. Without the unseen burden of future monarchy, her childhood would have been more private, less constrained. No need for her father and her grandmother to concern themselves that she should be adequately prepared to ascend the throne when her time came. She might still have fallen in love with and married Philip, might still have become the mother of four children, though not necessarily princes and a princess. Until her father altered his own father's earlier edict, royal titles could be handed down only in the male line. And even then, her father restricted the extension to the children of his elder daughter, the one who would one day be Queen. Which is why the children of Princess Margaret and Princess Anne are not princes and princesses. Princess Margaret's children, because their father accepted the Snowdon earldom, have subsidiary titles which stem from him, while Princess Anne's children, because their father has preferred to remain simply Captain Mark Phillips, are without titles.*

Conscientious and dutiful as she is by nature, Elizabeth, had she never come to the throne, would doubtless have fulfilled her obligations as a royal princess. But it would have been a minor role, a lighter burden, leaving her more time for the personal side of life, for her family, her horses, her dogs, affording her a greater degree of privacy. The glare of the public spotlight, more intense today than it has ever been in royal history, would have been turned in another direction.

For Princess Elizabeth of York, as she then was, the subtle process of change which would turn her into Queen Elizabeth II began when she was a child of four. That was in 1930, when her favourite uncle, the Prince of Wales and future King Edward VIII, went to a party given by Thelma, Lady Furness, one of the two married women who shared his princely favours at the time. Both were quickly to find themselves replaced in the future King's affections by yet another married woman who was also at that fateful party, an American, Wallis Simpson, already once divorced

* Princess Margaret's children are Viscount Linley and Lady Sarah Armstrong-Jones while Princess Anne's are simply Master Peter Phillips and Miss Zara Phillips.

2

and subsequently to divorce her second husband in expectation of yet a third marriage which would make her Queen Consort. The marriage came off, but not the expectation of becoming Queen Consort. In order to marry her, the Queen's uncle was forced to abdicate the throne, and the wife who had thought to be Queen Wallis became no more than Duchess of Windsor.

The four-year-old Princess knew nothing of her uncle's involved love-life of course. Even at the age of ten, on that historic day when her uncle abdicated, her father became King George VI and she herself was suddenly Heir Presumptive, she still did not understand the full significance of what had happened or why.

Over the next few years, as she grew from girlhood to womanhood, the strain of monarchy, especially during the stressful years of World War II, was to tell more and more on her dutiful, conscientious father, compounding his health problems and shortening his life. With his premature death at the age of fifty-six, his elder daughter was proclaimed Queen Elizabeth II, a role to which, at the youthful age of twenty-five, she brought all the freshness of youth and which she continues to fulfil all these years later with dignity and charm.

1 THE QUEEN TODAY

The Queen was a girl of ten that December day in 1936 when her Uncle David abdicated the throne, her father took over and the probability of future monarchy first loomed on the horizon of her life. The memoirs of her governess, Marion Crawford, paint a portrait of a responsible, conscientious child, serious beyond her years and occasionally quick-tempered. Over half-a-century later, with her sixty-fifth birthday and forty years of monarchy behind her, a grandmother six times over, and with two of her grandchildren already older than she was herself on that historic day when she became Heir Presumptive, she remains as responsible and conscientious as ever, perhaps more so. Gloomy predictions made in the early years of her reign that her health would suffer if she did not ease up have happily gone unfulfilled. Indeed, she has seemed to thrive on a work-load such as no previous British monarch can have known, travelling further and more frequently than was ever envisaged in that pre-jet era when she succeeded to the throne. Over her years of monarchy she has been really ill only twice and in hospital only once. That was for the extraction of a wisdom tooth. Another minor operation, for sinusitis, was carried out at Buckingham Palace under local anaesthetic. Those two occasions apart, she has suffered from nothing more than head colds, sometimes bad, and the upsets of pregnancy during her years as Monarch.

Her good health is perhaps due as much as anything to the moderation of her lifestyle. She does not smoke; never has. She drinks more orange squash, Malvern water, barley water than ever she does wine. A single glass of wine will last her through an entire state banquet. Plenty of light exercise helps, brisk walks round the 39-acre Palace gardens during the week, longer walks and horse riding during her weekends at Windsor Castle and really long walks, as much as seven miles or more, with her dogs when on holiday at Balmoral Castle or Sandringham. While she may not actually diet, she eats lightly and sensibly. Plenty of salads, fresh vegetables and fruit. She avoids porridge and cereals, pies, puddings and pastries. Except when entertaining guests, there is no soup or other starter for either luncheon or dinner. Instead, it is straight on to a main course of lean meat, chicken or fish served with a few vegetables and a side-plate of salad. Instead of a sweet course, she has a little cheese at luncheon. At dinner, the main course will be followed by another light savoury dish instead of anything sweet, with some fresh fruit to conclude. She takes both tea and coffee without sugar.

The result is a figure which has changed little since she first ascended the throne as a young wife and mother. Her eyes, blue with a hint of green, are still perhaps her best feature. She makes no secret of her need to wear glasses when reading a speech or perusing official papers (unlike her husband who prefers to keep his glasses tucked away in his pocket until he is away from the public gaze). A grandmother several times over, it is inevitable that there should be times when she looks her age, and at such times she bears a striking resemblance to her imperious grandmother, Queen Mary. But equally there are other times, especially when she smiles, when the years roll away and she exudes the same radiance as she did when she opened her first Parliament at the age of twenty-five and a fortunate photographer captured a picture of a young, smiling Queen which went round the world.

Monarchy has obliged her to do many things which are not really in her nature; to adopt a curiously contradictory lifestyle. By nature she is a reserved, intensely private person. Yet her life has been more and more lived out in the glare of the public spotlight, more blinding than it has ever been in these days when television cameras can zoom in to record every gesture and facial expression. A woman who is far happier in casual, time-tested clothes, she is constantly obliged, in the words of her eldest son and Heir Apparent, to 'dress up and queen it'. A fabulously wealthy woman with a strongly economic, even frugal, streak. A woman who sometimes finds it difficult to adhere to the royal maxim her grandmother drilled into her in childhood: *Never show your emotions in public.* Indeed, there have been times when it has been almost impossible for her to observe the rule; occasions when she has had to choke back or blink away tears. Her Coronation and, years later, her Silver Jubilee were two occasions when her emotions briefly got the better of her. So, for a totally different reason, was the occasion of her 1966 visit to the Welsh mining village of Aberfan in the wake of the coal-tip disaster which claimed so many young lives. If a radiant royal smile will sometimes convey the pleasure she derives on some public occasions, deeper emotions, equally, are sometimes concealed only with difficulty behind a face so serious as to appear almost grim. But that same impression of grimness may also sometimes hide a temptation to giggle at something so pompous it strikes an amusing note. In public, desirous of maintaining the dignity of both monarchy and the occasion, she seldom permits herself to discard the mask of royal impassivity, unlike her daughter-in-law. The Princess of Wales will joke with people, let herself be held and hugged (though she does not like to be kissed), take small children in her arms or lift them on to her lap. Neither the shyness of the Queen's nature nor her deeply ingrained sense of regality will permit her to do the same. Yet away from the public gaze, in the privacy of the family circle, she can be every bit as uninhibited as her daughter-in-law, playing happily with her grandchildren, exchanging quips with Prince Philip, lapsing into some delicious piece of mimicry, human enough even, on one occasion at least, to have slammed a door in anger.

Fear, fortunately in this age of violence, is an emotion almost foreign to her nature. She does not so much overcome it as not know it. A former prime minister, Harold Macmillan, even if he was quoting words used by Elizabeth I, can hardly have endeared himself to feminists by attributing to the Queen 'the heart and stomach of a man'. Nevertheless, his words sum up the Queen's reaction to the increased threat of violence which has characterized much of her reign. If she is no longer called upon to lead her troops into battle – George II was the last British monarch to do that* – she sees it as her clear duty to set an example of courage and calmness, a task in which she is helped by her deeply held religious

* In 1743 at the Battle of Dettingen, when he led a cavalry charge against the French.

convictions and a sort of disbelief in the idea that anyone would really wish to harm her. Even the mock assassination attempt which punctuated the 1981 Trooping the Colour ceremony* startled her only momentarily. Once she had her horse under control again, she was more concerned for the safety of her husband and eldest son than for her own. Satisfied that they were unharmed, she continued with the ceremony as though nothing had happened and is said to have returned to Buckingham Palace 'totally relaxed'. However, the intrusion of Michael Fagan into her bedroom the following year penetrated her emotional defences as well as her Palace. She was unsettled for several weeks after.

Punctuality was another of the rules drilled into her in childhood. As Queen it has been necessary for her to live by both the clock and the calendar, her programme of public engagements methodically planned months ahead. Her daily routine is timed to the minute, and it fidgets her if things show signs of running late. Her day starts when one of her personal maids tiptoes into the royal bedroom to draw the curtains before going through to the adjoining bathroom and dressing-room to run the Queen's bath and lay out the clothes she will be wearing that day. Prince Philip has his own bathroom and dressing-room, the latter equipped also with a single bed with which he makes do (to avoid disturbing the Queen) if he is late back from an official engagement or wishes to be up and away early, which is what happened the morning the Queen awoke to find Michael Fagan in her bedroom.

Except when preparing to leave for some official engagement, the Queen is not one to linger overlong at her dressing-table with its array of silver-gilt accessories which were among her wedding gifts. Her fine complexion is inherited, but aided also by the application of preparations made specially for her and by the consumption of home-made barley water. She employs the same degree of beauty aids as most women, a liquid foundation and matching face powder, sometimes a little rouge, some mascara, lipstick and clear nail varnish.

* 'Trooping the Colour' is the popular name for what is more formally styled 'the Queen's Birthday Parade', of which it forms the most important part. An army custom dating back to the seventeenth century at least, it was first linked to the monarch's birthday in the reign of George II. Today it takes place on Horse Guards' Parade in London each June, usually on the second Saturday (though the Queen's birthday is actually in April).

Her toilet complete, the Queen goes through to her private dining-room with its oval-shaped mahogany table which can be extended to seat more people when they have guests to dinner. Usually she and Prince Philip have breakfast together, both busily flicking through the day's newspapers as they eat. Plates and cups alike are adorned with the Queen's EIIR cypher. Cutlery and condiment sets are of solid silver. So that they can converse freely and privately, no servants wait on them. Instead, they help themselves from an array of covered dishes kept warm on hotplates. The Queen also likes to brew her own pot of tea, for which purpose she uses an antique silver kettle which her inventive husband has adapted so that it now works by electricity instead of a spirit lamp.

Breakfast over, the Queen adjourns to the large bay-windowed sitting-room overlooking Constitution Hill which serves her also as a study. While Prince Philip's study, a few doors further along the royal corridor, is efficiently masculine, the Queen's is rendered feminine and more homely with flowers, a drinking bowl for the corgis and a handsome Hepplewhite cabinet, another wedding gift, on which is displayed her collection of glass and porcelain horses. Family photographs – of Prince Philip, herself and Philip on honeymoon, the children, her parents and her grandmother, Queen Mary – jostle with telephones, blotter, paper-rack, lamp, clock and calendar for space on the flat-topped Chippendale desk which was her father's before her. A devoted daughter as well as a conscientious monarch, the Queen's first task is to pick up one of the two telephones and have a brief chat with her mother just down the road at Clarence House.

That done, the Queen sets about what is perhaps the most important of her royal duties and yet, paradoxically, a side of her work of which the vast mass of her subjects are totally unaware. She calls it 'doing my Boxes'. They are in fact leather-covered despatch boxes from the prime minister's office in Downing Street, from the Foreign Office and other government departments, from the many Commonwealth countries of which she is also Queen, each containing a fresh batch of paperwork to be read and digested. The first of the Boxes – still labelled 'The King' because there had not yet been time to effect a change – was already waiting her attention at Clarence House that day in 1952 when she flew back from Kenya as Queen. They have continued to pursue her since every day of her reign, following her even to Balmoral or Sandringham when she is on holiday, their contents air-lifted out to her when she travels abroad. On tour, she will tackle her paperwork in the so-called 'rest' intervals between public engagements. On holiday she may come through to breakfast dressed for riding, but riding itself must wait until she has first dealt with the papers contained in the latest Box. With her, there is no skipping. Every document, every scrap of paper, is studied thoroughly and diligently, and more than one prime minister has been embarrassed to realize that the Queen was better informed that he was on a particular political or international issue.

During the course of the morning the Queen will ring for one or more of her Private Secretaries. They arrive bearing wicker trays containing yet more documents and correspondence. Except for the very trivial and the 'cranky', the Queen likes to see every letter sent to her. And every sensible letter is answered in her name, though not by her personally. For the most part, only relatives and close friends receive letters written in her own, hurriedly scrawled, handwriting, though there are occasional exceptions. Ian Smith was one at the time of his unilateral declaration of independence in Rhodesia. In an attempt to head him off, the Queen wrote him a personal letter reminding him of his allegiance to the Crown. He took no notice.

With the help of her Private Secretaries, the Queen plans her future programme of public engagements at home and visits overseas. Prince Philip must be consulted to ensure that there is no clash between them. He has the tricky task of fulfilling his own schedule of engagements, more onerous than his wife's these days, while still leaving himself free to accompany the Queen on her major public engagements at home as well as on state visits to foreign countries and tours of the Commonwealth. A Commonwealth tour, in particular, is a complicated planning process of maps and timetables which may take as long as eighteen months to bring to fruition. Rather than make a clean sweep of the clutter on the Queen's desk, maps are often spread out on the floor, with Her Majesty, His Royal Highness and their senior aides crawling around them on hands and knees.

For the most part, the Queen's visits to foreign, as distinct from

Commonwealth, countries reflect Britain's foreign and economic policies. She goes where it benefits Britain, and in 1980 this found her obliged to accept the high-handed treatment meted out to her by King Hassan of Morocco because a large steel contract depended upon the King's goodwill. She has been several times to the United States in the furtherance of Anglo-American relations as well as entertaining US presidents on their state visits to Britain. On the other side of the coin, she has never been to the Soviet Union, though she told President Gorbachev when he lunched at Windsor Castle in 1989 that she hoped to do so 'in due course'. Unlike her foreign visits, her Commonwealth tours require no approval or otherwise from the British Government. She goes to some Commonwealth countries as their Queen – Queen of Canada, Queen of Australia, Queen of New Zealand, as the case may be – and to others, with their own monarchs or republican presidents, as Head of the Commonwealth. But whatever her overseas destination, she does not require a passport, though Prince Philip does. Since British passports are issued in her name, it would seem ridiculous for her to carry one. The Queen is secretly proud of the fact that she is easily the most travelled monarch in Britain's history. While no one has apparently thought to keep an exact record of her global mileage, which is a pity, an expert guess estimate puts it at close to a million miles.

Her Boxes, paperwork and planning dealt with, it is time to move on. The Queen reaches for her handbag, touches up her make-up and makes for her Audience Room, a handsome apartment on the same floor as her private rooms and overlooking the gardens to the rear of the palace. Here, for the next ninety minutes, she receives people 'in audience' – ambassadors and judges, bishops and field marshals, governors and governors-general – allotting an average of ten minutes to each. Alternatively, perhaps twenty times a year, this time of day will involve a meeting of her Privy Council, a hangover from the days when Britain's monarchs *ruled* as well as reigned. Today, it is a curious anomaly of Britain's system of constitutional monarchy that while only the Queen can do certain things – declare war, for instance – equally she must do what Parliament ordains or the prime minister of the day formally advises. The anomaly is resolved by having every Cabinet minister sworn in as a member of the Privy Council. As appointment to the Privy Council is for life, this creates the further problem that at any one time the Queen has several hundred Privy Councillors. This problem is resolved in turn by having only a small handful attend each session, the business of the day traditionally (and perhaps in the interest of the Queen's timetable) being conducted standing. Like her Boxes, Privy Council meetings tend to pursue the Queen wherever she goes. They have been held at Balmoral or Sandringham when she has been on holiday there, aboard the royal yacht and, at the time of the Suez crisis, at Arundel Castle, seat of the Duke of Norfolk, when she was attending the races at Goodwood.

Sometimes the last visitor of the morning will be invited to stay for lunch. Prince Philip may or may not be present. His busy programme includes frequent luncheon engagements, and the Queen, in consequence, often lunches alone. From time to time the Queen will give what is known as 'an informal luncheon party'. Designed to help her keep in touch with what is going on beyond the railings of Buckingham Palace, the guest list over the years has included politicians and trade unionists, civil servants and businessmen, academics, ecclesiastics and scientists, even the occasional sporting celebrity or pop star. Prior to the Queen's appearance, royal footmen hand round apĕritifs, and royal aides do their best to ease the guests' nerves. Then the Queen joins the gathering accompanied usually by Prince Philip and perhaps others of the Royal Family, the Queen Mother or the Prince of Wales, as well as the inevitable corgis and dorgis. (The 'dorgis', so-called, are the result of a romantic interlude involving one of the Queen's corgis and a dachshund belonging to Princess Margaret.)

The Queen and accompanying members of the Royal Family circulate among the guests, conversing briefly with each in turn, until the announcement: 'Luncheon is served, Your Majesty.' The Queen then leads the way into the adjoining room and takes her seat at the dining-table. Usually, she and Prince Philip do not sit at each end of the table but midway along, facing each other, the better to join in the lunchtime conversation (which is, after all, the real purpose of such functions) and keep it flowing. The corgis and dorgis take up positions under the table, with the Queen slipping them the occasional titbit. Also out of sight under the table, suspended from a specially shaped hook she carries with her, is her handbag. Compared with most women's handbags, it contains only a few essential items, a handkerchief, her glasses, her gold fountain pen and a combination powder compact-lipstick case which, like her tea kettle, was designed for her by her inventive husband. Except when she goes to church on Sundays, she never carries money.

Unlike the Queen's private lunches, which are limited to two courses, luncheon parties stretch to four. A typical menu will start with prawn cocktail or melon followed by roast lamb or veal. Then comes a light sweet such as apple meringue with cheese and fresh fruit to conclude. There is a choice of white and red wines with the various courses, and brandy and liqueurs are served with the coffee. Cigarettes and cigars are also on offer, though neither the Queen nor Prince Philip smokes.*

The pattern of the Queen's afternoons varies, though not by all that much. Some afternoons bring a sprinkling of public engagements in or close to London. Others may include sessions with the Keeper of the Privy Purse or the Master of the Household, for the Queen is a housewife as well as a monarch. She may not do the cooking or wash the dishes at Buckingham Palace (though she has been known to help with both when on holiday), but she is quick to keep her finger on the pulse of the palace's domestic life. There is even a book in which any breakages are carefully recorded and which is produced regularly for her inspection. Part of Monday afternoon is always reserved for her hairdresser, though she no longer goes to a salon as she did when she was a young naval wife in Malta; these days the hairdresser comes to her. Other afternoons, if there is a Commonwealth tour or state visit in the offing – and 1960, when Prince Andrew was born, is the only year when there was not – can involve sessions in her dressing-room with her shoemaker, milliner or one or other of her three main fashion designers as yet another travel wardrobe is put together.

In her younger days as monarch it was not unknown for the Queen to jib at the mass of regal finery she is sometimes required to wear. 'One did not feel she was really interested in clothes', the late Sir Norman Hartnell, for long her principal fashion designer, once said of her. In recent years, however, particularly since the

* Prince Philip did smoke in his younger days but gave it up at the time of their betrothal.

13

Princess of Wales' delight in clothes began to rub off on her, she has been more fashion-conscious. But she still has her unwritten rules which those who design for her know they must observe. Because a quick change is often necessary, clothes must be easy to slip on and off. There must be plenty of arm movement. What a gift it would be to the photographers if a seam split as the Queen waved to the crowd. There must be nothing to snag or catch if she tours a factory or building site; no possibility of embarrassment when she descends stairs or climbs onto a platform. For this reason, the Queen makes only the very slightest concession if fashion dictates a shorter length for skirts. Shoes usually have three-inch heels to afford added height to her five feet four inches on public occasions. Hats must be small so that her face is not in shadow; handbags mum-ish to be suspended from the wrist. A shoulder-strap bag was once suggested as a variation but proved awkward in practice. Colours must be sharp and bright for the most part so that she can be clearly seen even by those at the very back of the crowd.

The Queen continues to observe the traditional custom of afternoon tea. On holiday at Sandringham or Balmoral, surrounded by family and guests, tea-time becomes a minor feast of bread and butter, cucumber and other sandwiches, cakes of various varieties, large and small. But though there are sandwiches and cake equally available on weekdays at the palace, the Queen seldom has more than a cup of tea. The corgis fare better. Tea-time is also their feeding time. Wielding a silver spoon and fork with experienced dexterity while the corgis push and pummel around, the Queen mixes quantities of chopped-up meat, dog biscuit and hot gravy into a canine feast which she ladles into the feeding bowls arrayed along the crimson-carpeted corridor outside her sitting-room. It is time also to think of her own meals for tomorrow. Suggested menus for the next day's meals reach her in a leather-covered folder. There are three choices of menu for each meal, with the Queen required only to delete those she does not want. Only very occasionally will she delete all three and, instead, pen some suggestion of her own in hastily scrawled writing quite unlike her flourishing formal signature.

Tea-time on Tuesdays is usually followed by a visit from the prime minister, with whom the Queen discusses affairs of state. If the Queen has less real power than any monarch before her –

certainly far less than Queen Victoria who, according to her ministers, suffered from 'the delusion' that she was the author of Britain's foreign policy – she still has the right, as her great-great-grandmother had, 'to be consulted; to encourage; to warn'. While no one can know for certain what passes during these highly confidential meetings between Monarch and prime minister, the Queen's character is such as to suggest that she exercises what is perhaps her sole surviving right to the full, seeing herself as a link between one government and the next. Over her years of monarchy, she has so far had dealings with nine different prime ministers, from Sir Winston Churchill to John Major. Thanks to the conscientiousness with which she combs through the contents of her Boxes, her knowledge of both domestic politics and international affairs is profound, and both Churchill and, years later, Harold Wilson were surprised in turn to realize that she was better informed on at least one issue than they were themselves. Harold Wilson has himself confessed to being caught out soon after he became prime minister when the Queen asked him about a new town to be built near Bletchley. He had not done his paperwork on that and felt rather like 'a schoolboy who hadn't prepared his lessons'. The new town, of course, was Milton Keynes. Inevitably, her relationship with individual prime ministers has varied, though never dramatically so. Churchill, in the early years of her monarchy, was inclined to treat her rather like a favourite granddaughter, while the youthful Queen, for her part, was perhaps a little in awe of the grand old man who was so largely responsible for victory in World War II. It was mainly on his advice that she reverted to her maiden name of Windsor soon after ascending the throne, a change she might not have made in later years when she had matured in her role of Queen. Indeed, though she has never gone back on the change in regard to herself, she has since, in fairness to her husband, incorporated his name in the Mountbatten-Windsor surname of her descendants.

Churchill's successor, Anthony Eden, prime minister for only fifteen months between 1955 and 1957, was hardly in power long enough – and a sick man for much of the time – for a true working relationship to be established. It was with Harold Macmillan (prime minister 1957–63) that she matured into the Queen she is today. She saw Macmillan as 'a guide and instructor', though jibbing at his advice in 1961 that it was unsafe for her to visit Ghana. While she is duty-bound to take the advice of the prime minister of the day, she takes the view that such advice may be tendered to her only in her role as Queen of the United Kingdom and not in her capacity as Head of the Commonwealth – a subtle distinction. She enjoyed working with Alec Douglas-Home during his brief period of office (1963–4) and, to many people's surprise, with the Labour leader, Harold Wilson, who was twice Britain's prime minister (1964–70 and 1974–6). She found Wilson surprisingly helpful when her divorced cousin, the Earl of Harewood, sought her formal permission (required under the Royal Marriage Act of 1772) to marry his former secretary. Personally, she had no wish to prevent her cousin marrying again. As Supreme Governor of the Church of England, however, consent might be seen as countenancing divorce. With Harewood no higher than eighteenth in line of succession, the issue was hardly a constitutional one, but Wilson, to help the Queen out, elected to treat it as such. Churchill and Eden, in the earlier case of Princess Margaret, had both advised against giving consent. Wilson's formal advice, in the case of Harewood, was to consent. Coming from her prime minister, it was advice the Queen was both willing and constitutionally bound to follow.

By the time Edward Heath (1970–4) became her prime minister, the Queen had been on the throne for eighteen years. She was now not only a mature Monarch but one with views of her own, and Heath's procrastination over resigning when his government was brought down by the 1974 miners' strike, though constitutionally proper, is said not to have been to her taste. When he did eventually resign, she sent again for Harold Wilson. Politically, he was the obvious choice, but she saw him also as the one man who might clear up the industrial chaos of that time.

Wilson's successor, James Callaghan, was impressed by her knowledge of and enthusiasm for Commonwealth affairs. If Elizabeth II is no longer the all-powerful Empress her great-great-grandmother was, she finds her role as Head of the Commonwealth every bit as satisfying, perhaps more so. She was especially enthused when Canada's Pierre Trudeau invited her to Ottawa in 1972. It was the first time she had opened a Commonwealth Conference held outside Britain and she has opened every one since . . . even that held in Zambia in 1979. Margaret Thatcher, the eighth prime minister of her reign, advised initially against the Queen going because of fighting on the Zambian border, though she was going herself. As with Macmillan, this raised the question of how far the Queen is duty-bound to accept the advice of her British prime minister on matters of Commonwealth. She was, she said, prepared to accept Mrs Thatcher's advice only 'as a last resort'. However, it did not come to that, and both women, Queen and prime minister, went to Lusaka for the conference.

The Queen undertakes fewer evening engagements these days, perhaps a small concession to the medical fears of her early reign. Prince Philip has more, but there are still many evenings when they are free to be together in private. Unless they are entertaining guests, they no longer change into evening dress for dinner, though the Queen Mother, clinging firmly to the traditions of an earlier and more gracious age, continues to do so at Clarence House even if she has no more than the television set for company. As at breakfast, the Queen and Prince Philip prefer to dispense with servants and serve themselves. So only they can know what they talk about in the privacy of their dining-room and, later, in the adjoining sitting-room. It is unlikely to be horse-racing, a topic which bores Philip almost as much as it enthuses the Queen. About their children and grandchildren no doubt, as parents and grandparents are apt to do. About what they have each been doing that day, equally doubtless. Affairs of state? Perhaps. It is often said, and indeed Prince Philip himself has said it, that constitutionally he does not exist. He is simply, as it says in the Civil List, 'husband of the Queen'. Unlike Prince Albert in Queen Victoria's day, he is not permitted to be present when the Queen and her prime minister confer on Tuesday evenings. He is not permitted to see the contents of those never-ending Boxes, though the Prince of Wales, as Heir Apparent, is. He is not permitted to 'advise' the Queen in the official sense of the word, as the prime minister does, but it is surely not unreasonable to suppose that there must be times when the Queen turns to him, if not for 'advice', at least for a considered opinion. He is, after all, not only her husband but a much-travelled man, meeting more and a greater variety of people than the Queen herself does, well-informed on many issues through his travels and the people he meets. He is also among the longest-serving of her Privy Councillors, an office to which he

17

was appointed by her father before she was even Queen. So if conversation over dinner should sometimes hinge on some troublesome affair of state, it is hardly to be wondered at.

The dining-table is set in some style. There is a silver table centre, silver cutlery and condiment sets, crystal goblets and gold-rimmed plates. The only time a servant is seen is when Prince Philip rings for the coffee. But the page who serves it withdraws immediately after, and they are again undisturbed until another ring signals that they are moving into the next-door sitting-room and the table can be cleared.

The sitting-room is the same one which serves the Queen also as a study, and she goes first to her desk to deal with anything which has come in since she was last there. That done, she nudges off her shoes and relaxes on a settee with her feet up. She may watch television if there is something she especially wants to see. She particularly enjoys any programme which has to do with horses, major sporting events (like the Olympic Games) in which Britain is participating, fact-fiction programmes about her royal predecessors, from *Henry VIII* to *Edward and Mrs Simpson*, or a good comedy show. If there is nothing which interests her on television, she will chat with her husband or settle down to tackle a crossword puzzle. And if the puzzle is still unfinished at bedtime, seldom later than half-past ten, she will take it through to her bedroom with her.

Weekends, from Friday afternoon to Monday morning, are spent usually at Windsor, where she and Prince Philip have contrived a pleasantly comfortable apartment for themselves in one of the towers of the largest surviving castle in Europe. Weekends at Windsor, and occasional weekend visits to Sandringham, her home in Norfolk, afford her the opportunity for the riding and brisk walking which are her favourite forms of exercise. Sunday mornings, whether at Windsor, Sandringham or elsewhere, are a time for church-going, while later in the day, on those Windsor weekends, may find her driving to Highgrove to visit her eldest son and his children or to Gatcombe Park to see Princess Anne and hers.

The circumstances of the Queen's work require that she lives by the calendar as well as by the clock. The same traditional ceremonies crop up on her engagement diary this year, next year and the year after that. There is, each year, the distribution of the Royal Maundy, when she hands out specially minted silver coins to as many old men and old women as the years of her age, in pursuance of a royal custom dating back to Edward the Confessor. There are, every year, garden parties and investitures. There is Remembrance Day, when she stands, black-clad and solemn, at the Cenotaph in Whitehall, a solitary figure symbolizing a nation's remembered sorrow. There is, at Windsor, the annual procession to St George's Chapel of the Knights of the Garter, Britain's highest order of chivalry, when the Sovereign and her Knights dedicate themselves afresh to 'Christ's faith, the liberties of the Church and the just and necessary defence of them that be oppressed and needy'. There is her Birthday Parade, when she rides side-saddle to take the salute at the military ceremony of Trooping the Colour. There is the State Opening of Parliament, when she dons her crown, mounts her throne in the House of Lords and summons the members of the House of Commons to attend upon her as the wise men of the land first attended upon the monarch nearly a thousand years ago. In those days it was the monarch who had the main say. Today things are very different. The 'Speech from the Throne', as it is called, may still be couched in personal terms, but it is in fact written by the prime minister of the day, and the Queen is obliged to read it word for word as written. This age-old ceremony takes place in the House of Lords because the Queen is not permitted to enter the House of Commons. No monarch has been allowed in there since King Charles I swooped on the place with his guards and arrested five of the members. At least not officially, though the Queen and her father, in the days when she was Princess Elizabeth, were unofficially permitted to inspect the chamber so that they could see how it had been rebuilt after the damage it suffered during World War II.

The combination of horse-racing and high fashion known as Royal Ascot is surely the hardy annual the Queen enjoys most.★ For her, it is both a public engagement and a personal pleasure.

★ Ascot racecourse is the property of the Queen. It was originally laid out on the orders of Queen Anne, and the first race was run there in 1711. George IV instituted the present royal procession. Today it is run for the Queen on a non-profit basis by a board of trustees known as the Ascot Authority. Profits are used to provide further prize-money and improve the amenities.

The personal side takes the form of a large house party at Windsor Castle, with the guests taking it in turns to share the privilege of accompanying the Queen on the ceremonial drive along the course which precedes each day's racing. The Queen has always been mad on horses. As a child she collected toy horses with the sort of enthusiasm other small girls devote to dolls. Her first racehorse was a wedding gift from the Aga Khan. She gave it the appropriate name of Astrakhan. However, it won only one race for her before being retired on account of weak forelegs. A half-share with her mother in a jumper named Monaveen brought more victories, though a hoped-for success in the Grand National did not materialize. With her father's death, she inherited his small string of racehorses along with the traditional racing colours of the Sovereign – purple, gold braid, scarlet sleeves, black cap with gold tassel. It was a major disappointment to her when the unpredictable Aureole, which she had first seen as a week-old foal in the royal stud, was pipped at the post in the Coronation year Derby, a failure atoned for with a series of victories the following year. The Queen was leading owner that year and again in 1957, when she was also second in the list of winning breeders. In 1977, when her filly Dunfermline won the Oaks and St Leger, she was again second in the list of winning breeders. She has won the One Thousand Guineas (with Highclere) and the Two Thousand Guineas (with Pall Mall). But the Derby has continued to elude her, and it remains her big ambition to win it, as her great-grandfather, Edward VII, did, with a horse bred in the royal stud.

Her passion for horses is the one thing that can tempt her from the ordered pattern of her life, as when she flew to Kentucky in 1984 in the hope of finding fresh blood among the stallions there which might lead to that elusive Derby winner. For the most part, she is as traditional in her personal life as monarchy requires her to be in public. She likes doing the same things, going to the same places, at the same time of year. She likes seeing the New Year in at Sandringham (where she also spent her Christmases until others of the family jibbed at its remoteness) as her father, grandfather and great-grandfather all did before her. She likes spending Easter at Windsor, as her forebears did. She likes spending her summer vacation at Balmoral, that Disney-like castle in Scotland which

Prince Albert devised for Queen Victoria, with its Victorian furnishings, wallpaper and carpeting. Most of all, family woman that she is, she likes spending Christmas (at Windsor these days) with her family around her.★

In an age when family unity is not what it used to be, the Queen has contrived to keep her family close-knit. She is close both to her children and to her mother. In an era when divorce has counted even her sister, Princess Margaret, among its victims, her own marriage stands out as an unqualified success. Given the uniqueness of her position, it might easily have been otherwise. Even a generation before she might have found herself a partner in an arranged marriage, as the marriage of her Aunt Mary, the Princess Royal, was arranged for her. But the Queen's parents were of different calibre from her paternal grandparents; concerned more for their daughter's future happiness than the wealth or standing of the man who became their son-in-law. Prince Philip was, of course, eminently suitable in every respect except wealth, theoretically a Greek prince, in practice one whose formative years were spent in British schools and the Royal Navy. Even so, far from 'arranging' the marriage, her father, at least, was concerned to delay it, worried that his daughter had not had sufficient opportunity to meet other young men. It was the daughter who pestered to be allowed to marry the man for whom she had first developed a girlhood 'crush' at the tender age of thirteen.

That 'crush' has matured into a happy and lasting marriage. Inevitably, it has not all been smooth sailing. There was a period of a few years immediately following the Queen's accession to the throne when her involvement with monarchy was to cause a succession of marital hiccups. It was a period when, as a new young Queen, she had too much to do, while Prince Philip, a dominant, energetic man, had too little to do of real consequence. For a man of his temperament, it was no easy task to reconcile himself to being merely second fiddle in the royal orchestra, and there were times when he was considerably frustrated, even

★ Windsor Castle, like Buckingham Palace, belongs to the nation. Balmoral Castle and Sandringham are the Queen's private property. Queen Victoria bought the Balmoral estate for £31,500 in 1852, and the castle, designed by Prince Albert, was built 1853–5. The Sandringham estate was bought in 1861 for £220,000 by the Prince of Wales who later became King Edward VII.

depressed. But their attachment to each other was strong enough to weather the passing storm.

With a degree of give and take on both sides, marriage achieved a fresh stability and a new level of happiness. The Queen, as a young woman, had once said that her ideal was a family of four children, 'two boys and two girls'. With the births of Prince Andrew and Prince Edward that youthful dream was close to fulfilment, even if one of the hoped-for girls turned out to be a third son.

Family woman that she is, the Queen is never happier than on those occasions when she has all her family around her. Weddings and christenings are just such occasions, but there are not too many of those. Christmas, on the other hand, comes round every year, and every Christmas, at Windsor, the Queen surrounds herself with as many of the family as can be prevailed upon to join her, husband and children, son-in-law and daughter-in-law, grand-children, her mother and her sister and her sister's children, her cousins and their children, a family party of perhaps thirty or more in all. The late Duke of Windsor once described the family gathering as 'a Dickensian Christmas in a Cartier setting'. He was speaking of an earlier generation, of course, but things have changed little with the years. It is certainly still Dickensian in its traditionalness, a Christmas decked with holly and mistletoe, complete with tall Christmas tree and brightly coloured crackers, plump turkeys (it takes two large birds to fill so many stomachs), plum pudding and hot mincepies. The grown-ups of the family exchange their gifts on Christmas Eve and go to church on Christmas morning. The Queen fills old stockings with small knick-knacks as Christmas stockings for her grandchildren. Econ-omically minded as she is, she does not think that shop-bought Christmas stockings always represent good value for money. There are home-made stockings too for the corgis and dorgis, filled with such doggy delights as chocolate drops, dog biscuits, rubber balls and artificial bones. Christmas lunch, with its brace of turkeys from Sandringham and a brandy-flamed plum pudding, is an occasion for festive fun which the Queen can enjoy to the full now that she is no longer obliged to dash away, her meal half-finished, to appear on television. These days her Christmas message to the Commonwealth is video-taped in advance. There is a brisk walk through the grounds after lunch to settle the digestion. So that those grandchildren not yet of an age to lunch with the adults may not miss out altogether on the festivities, afternoon tea takes on the guise of a children's Christmas party complete with mince pies, small chocolate cakes and a large Christmas cake. And so that royal servants can have time off for their own festivities, the evening meal these days takes the form of a serve-yourself buffet. Then comes the Christmas party. Charades is a favourite game. The Queen's children are the fifth generation of the Royal Family to have played it, dressing up in caps, aprons and coats, flourishing pipes, walking-sticks and riding-crops as they act out the words. And so to a late-night singsong round the piano, a medley of carols, old-time favourites, musical comedy numbers and contemporary pop songs.

Members of the Royal Family pride themselves on their long memories. Prince Charles claims he can remember his nanny wheeling him around in his pram. But it is highly unlikely that the Queen can remember her first Christmas. The family gathering was held at Sandringham in those days. Her grandfather, George V, of the apple-red cheeks and booming quarter-deck voice, was King Emperor and head of the family. Her parents, the Duke and Duchess of York, would shortly be compelled to leave their baby daughter behind while they undertook a royal tour of Australia. She was just eight months old, Princess Elizabeth of York.

2 BIRTH OF A PRINCESS

It had been raining earlier, and more rain was forecast for later, but for the moment it was dry. Bruton Street had been crowded earlier with people eagerly awaiting news of the baby's birth and would be crowded still more a few hours hence, but at that hour of the morning the crowds had gone and the handful of reporters whose jobs would not yet let them go home to bed had the street to themselves. In an age when there was more rapport between royalty and reporters, the prospective father suggested they come inside, out of the cold, for coffee and sandwiches. The house they trooped into was No. 17, a double-fronted mansion of Georgian aspect. That once elegant mansion has long since been reduced to rubble, and only a slate plaque at the entrance to the bank which now occupies the site records the historic event which took place there in the early hours of Wednesday, 21 April 1926.

> The house which stood on this site was the London home of the Earl of Strathmore. From this house his daughter, Lady Elizabeth Bowes-Lyon, was married to H.R.H. Prince Albert, Duke of York, later King George VI. Here was born on April 21, 1926, their daughter, The Princess Elizabeth, who was to become Queen Elizabeth II.

Prince Albert, Duke of York, was the second son of King George V, the bearded father-figure who reigned over not only the United Kingdom but the whole vast globe-encompassing expanse of what was then the British Empire. Married a little under three years, the Prince was at this time a man of thirty, shy, self-conscious and with a tendency to stammer, nervous of his father almost to the point of being frightened of him, in awe even of his mother, Queen Mary. Nevertheless, it was to his mother

24

that he had confided his feelings after a visit to Glamis Castle in the autumn of 1920 where he met the youngest of the Bowes-Lyon girls, Lady Elizabeth. She was twenty that year, and he was captivated by her. Eager to see at least one of her four surviving sons married and perpetuating the royal line, Queen Mary encouraged him in his pursuit of a potential bride. Indeed, when he visited Glamis in 1921 for the third time, she went with him, anxious to see for herself the young lady who might become her daughter-in-law. As things turned out, the royal visit came at a time when Lady Strathmore was convalescent. So the daughter was obliged to deputize for her mother as hostess, and Queen Mary was considerably impressed by the way she did so. But if the Queen saw her as a future daughter-in-law, Lady Elizabeth, for her part, did not at that time visualize Queen Mary as her future mother-in-law. Nor did King George V rate his son's chances in that particular direction very highly. Before proposing, the Duke was obliged to seek permission from his father under the Royal Marriage Act★. Giving it, the King expressed the view that his son would be lucky if the lady accepted him.

Initially at least the King's doubts were to seem more than justified. The Prince proposed – and the lady turned him down! It was by no means the first proposal of marriage she had rejected, though for very different reasons. Other suitors had been rejected because they did not match up to her own high standards of morality and loyalty. The Duke of York could certainly not be faulted on those scores. He was a man very different in character from his more rakish, though publicly popular, brother, the Prince of Wales, who had a reputation for going to bed with other men's wives. The Duke of York, in contrast, had to bolster all his courage merely to touch the hand of the young lady he sought to marry, while the act of actually proposing to her was a tremendous ordeal for him. The reason for her initial rejection was based on her horror of becoming a member of the mighty Royal Family with all the constrictions she felt that would entail.

★ The Royal Marriage Act was passed in 1772 at the behest of King George III after two of his brothers had made what he thought were undesirable marriages. Still law today, it lays down that no descendant of George II (other than the issue of princesses who have married into foreign families) may marry without the consent of the reigning Sovereign.

Queen Mary was disappointed when she heard what had happened. Lady Elizabeth's mother, Lady Strathmore, if not disappointed, was sorry for the Duke who she saw as a man who would be 'made or marred' according to the quality of his wife. While this was to prove an accurate assessment, there were depths to the Duke's character (revealed later when he unexpectedly found himself King) which were not immediately apparent on the surface. Shy and uncertain as he undoubtedly was, he was also obstinate, tenacious, persevering. He saw that first rejection and a second not long after simply as temporary defeats in minor skirmishes, with the war itself still waiting to be won.

Yet again he contrived an invitation to stay with the Strathmores, this time at St Paul's Waldenbury, their home in Hertfordshire. On a Sunday morning in January, 1923, while the rest of the family were at church, the Duke and the girl he sought to make his wife took a stroll in the woods. For yet a third time, he proposed, and this time, to his delight and amazement, his proposal was accepted. Acceptance came 'almost as much of a surprise to me as it was to him', the young woman who is now the Queen Mother would reveal later.

But if her acceptance was born of the impulse of the moment, it was also one which she never had a moment's cause to regret, then or later. As for the Duke, he was overjoyed and promptly sent off a cryptic telegram to his royal parents: 'All right – Bertie'. They knew what it meant and both were delighted, though the King, according to a letter of congratulation which he wrote to his son, seems to have viewed his future daughter-in-law more as a new partner in the royal firm. Even so, he could have had no idea of how strong that partnership would prove in the years ahead; of the sacrifices his son and daughter-in-law would be called upon to make. And certainly not the slightest notion that it would be through them that the line of succession would lie.

With no expectation that their firstborn child would one day be Monarch, there was no occasion, as there would be with the birth of Prince Charles a generation later, for the birth to take place at Buckingham Palace. Nor were the royal grandparents-to-be as sentimentally inclined about such things as their second son and his wife would be when they became grandparents in turn. So, still lacking a proper home of their own despite nearly three years of marriage, the young Duchess of York – she was now twenty-five – had chosen to have her baby in the London home of her parents. The baby she was expecting would be the King's third grandchild but would rank ahead of the other two, the Lascelles sons of Princess Mary,* in succession to the throne. So the birth was supervised by two eminent physicians, Sir Henry Stimson and Walter Jagger. Because the birth was not completely straight-forward, as a medical bulletin would reveal later, they also decided to call into consultation Sir George Blacker, obstetric physician at University College Hospital.

The baby who is now Queen Elizabeth II was born at twenty minutes to three in the morning. Told that he had a daughter, the Duke went eagerly to see her. So did the Home Secretary of the day, Sir William Joynson-Hicks, whose duty it was under the custom prevailing at the time to ensure that no changeling was introduced into the royal line. It was a custom the Duke found highly embarrassing, and years later, when he became King and his daughter was expecting her first child, he was to bring it to an end. The future Queen, only a few minutes old, felt no such embarrassment, of course. She merely yawned.

News of the baby's birth was sent immediately to Windsor Castle, where the King and Queen were in residence. Becoming grandparents was not a new experience for them, but this baby was different. Their two existing grandchildren, George and Gerald, because they were descended from the King through a female line – his daughter, Princess Mary, was married to Viscount Lascelles, heir to the Harewood earldom – were not princes. The new baby, however, descended through the male line, sired by the King's second son, would be a prince or princess, according to sex. So the King, retiring to bed the previous night, had left strict instructions that he was to be informed immediately there was news from Bruton Street, whatever the hour. In accordance with those instructions, the duty equerry at Windsor, Captain Reginald Seymour, awoke the royal couple between three and four o'clock in the morning to tell them that they had a granddaughter.

An official bulletin, issued shortly after the baby's birth, was brief in the extreme: 'Her Royal Highness the Duchess of York

* The King's only daughter, later created Princess Royal, had married in 1922 and given birth to sons in 1923 and 1924.

was safely delivered of a Princess at 2.40 this morning. Both mother and daughter are doing well.'

It was a second, slightly longer bulletin issued a few hours later which would start speculation which has continued to this day. This second bulletin began reassuringly enough. 'The Duchess of York has had some rest since the arrival of her daughter. Her Royal Highness and the infant Princess are making very satisfactory progress.' Then came the somewhat ambiguous wording which was to create so much speculation. 'Previous to the confinement a consultation took place at which Sir George Blacker was present and a certain line of treatment was successfully adopted.'

Wording could hardly have been devised more calculated to whet the appetites of the newspapers. There was a barrage of enquiries. What did it mean? What was the 'certain line of treatment'? Had the baby been born by Caesarean section? An authoritative statement issued by the Press Association the following day was designed to answer such queries. It ran: 'The wording of Wednesday morning's bulletin appears to have given rise to some misunderstanding and natural, but absolutely unnecessary, anxiety. The phrase "a certain line of treatment" led to considerable speculation from which the possibility of a Caesarean or other operation was not excluded. Nothing of the kind was intended to be implied or was the case in fact.'

The newspapers of the day also drew attention to how the baby's birth had changed the line of succession. In the succession to the throne, sons always rank ahead of daughters (even if the daughters are older than the sons), and grandchildren rank according to the succession seniority of their royal fathers or mothers. A glance at the line of succession as it stood before and immediately after the birth of the new baby may clarify.

Before the birth of the baby the order of succession was:
1. King George V's eldest son, the Prince of Wales
2. The King's second son, the Duke of York
3. The King's third son, the Duke of Gloucester
4. The King's fourth son, the Duke of Kent
5. The King's only daughter, Mary, Viscountess Lascelles (though she was in fact older than two of her brothers)
6. Mary's elder son, George Lascelles
7. Mary's younger son, Gerald Lascelles

But now the baby daughter born to the Duke of York interposed herself between her father and those who came after him. So that the order of succession following the baby's birth had become:

1. The Prince of Wales (later Duke of Windsor)
2. The Duke of York
3. The unnamed infant Princess who was the Duke of York's daughter
4. The Duke of Gloucester
5. The Duke of Kent
6. Mary, Viscountess Lascelles (later Princess Royal)
7. George Lascelles
8. Gerald Lascelles

In the years ahead, as others of the Royal Family married and had children, as those children married and had children of their own, the order of succession would change again and again. By 1984, with the birth of a second child to the present Prince and Princess of Wales, it had changed to such extent that Princess Mary's elder son, once sixth in line, would no longer rank even in the first two dozen.

Not that anyone in 1926 seriously expected that the baby girl born to the Duke and Duchess of York would one day succeed to the throne. Well, hardly anyone. The exception was the newspaper editor who saw fit to place on record, with strangely prophetic insight, the thought that 'the baby who was the chief topic of conversation throughout the Kingdom yesterday could conceivably become Queen of England.' Perhaps he simply devised it as a nice turn of phrase, not really believing what he wrote. It seemed, at the time, an unlikely prediction. The baby might be third in line, but the line through which she was descended was not the direct one. That ran through her father's elder brother, the Prince of Wales. Not yet thirty-two, there was still plenty of time for him to marry and have children. Even if he did not, the Yorks themselves might yet have a son or sons to rank ahead of their baby daughter.

The world into which the York baby was born was very different from that of today. One-fifth of the world map was still coloured red with the land-mass of the British Empire. George V was not only King but Emperor. Britain's Navy was perhaps the most

29

formidable in the world. Air power, like air travel, was in its infancy. Radio too was in its infancy, and television was still in the future. In the 'kinemas' of the day 'pictures' would not become 'talkies' for another year. On the dance floor the Charleston was all the rage. In London and other cities high-bodied automobiles threaded their way between horse-drawn drays and carriages, while in the quiet residential squares of the capital hurdy-gurdy men still cranked out tunes for pennies, and muffin men rang their bells and cried their wares. But there were tensions beneath the surface of national life. Unemployment was dropping from the two million mark it had touched earlier (though it would rise again later), but the figure was still frighteningly large in an era when far fewer women worked and the overall labour force was consequently much smaller than today. The short-lived General Strike would erupt within days of the baby's birth.

The Royal Horse Artillery serenaded the birth of the infant Princess with a twenty-one-gun salute. Among the first to see the newcomer was the baby's aunt, Princess Mary, mother of the Lascelles boys. At Windsor Castle, by a curious quirk of fate, the baby's paternal grandparents were entertaining a trio of guests, a coincidence so remarkable that it would surely seem far-fetched even in one of today's television soap operas. The King's luncheon guests at Windsor Castle that day were Princess Andrew (née Alice) of Greece, her sister, Louise, the Crown Princess of Sweden, and their mother, the Dowager Marchioness of Milford Haven, respectively the mother, aunt and grandmother of a four-year-old Greek prince named Philip.

Luncheon over and their guests gone, the King and Queen drove to London in the royal Daimler to see their latest grandchild. The crowds were back in Bruton Street and cheered them loudly. But were the royal grandparents perhaps a shade disappointed that while their daughter had given birth to two sons, their daughter-in-law had managed only a daughter? Certainly the baby's father seemed to think it necessary to write to his mother the following day in almost apologetic vein. He hoped, he wrote, that she and Papa were delighted to have a granddaughter 'or would you sooner have had another grandson?'

That slightly apologetic note had its roots in the childhood memories of a nervous small boy subject to the hectoring of a disciplinarian father. Even as a grown man, the Duke remained always a little frightened of his father. Not so the Duchess. Nor had she the same reason to be. The family martinet of earlier days had begun to mellow by the time she arrived on the royal scene and her relationship with him was different. She found him both dependable and kind.

The baby Princess was breast-fed for the first few weeks. Her mother's old nanny, Mrs Clara Knight, known to the children of two generations as Alla, now became her nanny, taking her to the small railed-in garden of Berkeley Square for airings in one of those large-wheeled, high-bodied baby carriages which were fashionable at the time. Such outings attracted curiously little public attention, certainly far less than if a royal baby was taken out similarly today. It was an era when reporters and photographers were far less intrusive; editors more respectful. So much so that one must rely upon the remembered snippets of royal relatives and friends to know what the future Queen was like in that early stage of babyhood. 'Quiet and contented' were among the phrases used to describe her. Also remembered are her 'large blue eyes', 'tiny ears', 'well-shaped head' and a mass of fair, almost flaxen, hair which the Duchess encouraged into curls with the aid of a silver-backed brush. That brush was to be treasured over the years as a family keepsake and brought into use afresh a generation later when the baby Princess of 1926 herself became the mother of a baby Prince.

Two days after the baby's birth the Duke again wrote to his parents, to his father this time, cautiously seeking approval to the names he and his wife had picked: Elizabeth Alexandra Mary. Mary was the name of the Duke's mother and Alexandra the name of his grandmother, widow of King Edward VII, who had died only the previous November at the age of eighty-one. Elizabeth, of course, was the name of the baby's mother, though the Duke did not think, he wrote to his father, that this would cause any confusion.

If the King approved the names, the baby would be Princess Elizabeth of York, which the parents thought sounded 'nice'. It was also – though whether the parents realized this is not apparent – the name and title of the fifteenth-century bride of King Henry VII from whom the baby's mother was descended.

That there was need for caution in the Duke's approach to his father over the question of names was revealed by the King's first reaction. He was concerned that the name Victoria was not included. For three generations it had been almost obligatory for a daughter in each branch of the family to bear that honoured name. Queen Victoria herself passed the name on to her eldest daughter. Five of her granddaughters were also given it, while a sixth was christened Helena-Victoria. George V himself had married a Princess Victoria, daughter of one of the old Queen's cousins, and had passed the name on in turn to his own daughter. So many Victorias already abounded that there was danger of confusion. So much so that the Victoria the King married was known by the second of her eight names and became Queen Mary, while his daughter was similarly called by the last of her four names, Princess Mary. In any event, Queen Victoria's family tree was now fast-spreading into its fourth generation and she herself had been dead for a quarter of a century. So the King, on further reflection, contented himself with writing back that he thought Elizabeth 'a pretty name'.

But if Queen Victoria was not remembered in the baby's names, her memory was still honoured at the christening ceremony in Buckingham Palace on 29 May. The christening robe of Brussels lace in which the baby Princess was draped was one Queen Victoria had had made for the christening of her own children. The gold lily font at which the Archbishop of York, Dr Cosmo Lang, performed the christening ceremony was the one designed by Queen Victoria's husband, the Prince Consort; and one of the baby's six sponsors was the old Queen's last surviving son, Arthur, the seventy-six-year-old Duke of Connaught. The other sponsors were the baby's royal grandparents, King George V and Queen Mary, her maternal grandfather, the Earl of Strathmore, and an aunt from each side of the family tree, the Duke's sister, Princess Mary, and the Duchess's eldest sister, Lady Elphinstone. Among the other relatives present at the ceremony was the Duke's eldest brother, the Prince of Wales, whose abdication, unthinkable at that time, would one day bring the newly baptized Elizabeth of York within a heartbeat of the throne.

The baby who was to become the most-travelled Queen in Britain's history began her travels early, though in modest fashion.

Her parents took her with them on a visit to Glamis Castle, her mother's ancestral home, to be admired by Scottish relatives and friends. Christmas was spent with the King and Queen at Sandringham. Shortly after came the first spell of separation. Australia wanted one of the King's sons to open the first Parliament to be held in the new federal capital of Canberra. The eldest of those sons, the Prince of Wales, felt that he had already done his fair share of royal touring, with prolonged visits to Canada and the United States, Australia and New Zealand, India and Japan, South Africa and South America. The King agreed. It was time for his second son to do his share.

Neither that son nor his wife relished the prospect, though both saw it as their duty. The outward journey alone, aboard the battleship *Renown*, in those days before air travel became commonplace, would take the best part of two months. With visits also to be paid to other parts of the Empire, to Jamaica, Fiji and New Zealand, they would be away altogether for some six months. If the Duke, because of his nervous stammer, was horrified at the prospect of the speeches he would have to make, the Duchess was distressed at the thought of leaving her baby daughter. The idea of taking the baby with them, as another Prince of Wales and his Princess would take their baby son two generations later, did not occur to them. And even if it had, it is highly unlikely that the Duke's father would have countenanced it.

3 LILIBET

The baby Princess was eight-and-a-half months old when her
parents sailed for Australia in January, 1927; and into her fifteenth
month by the time they returned. She was looked after in their
absence by her nanny and shuttled to and fro between her maternal
grandparents at St Paul's Waldenbury, where the Duke had successfully proposed to his Duchess, and her royal grandparents at
Buckingham Palace. The presence of a small granddaughter about
the Palace wrought a considerable metamorphosis in the King. If
Queen Mary remained as inhibited over the baby as she had been
with her own children, the King did not. He became a very
different man, a doting grandfather, writing frequently to the
baby's parents as to how she was coming along. She now had four
teeth, he reported in one letter, which he thought was 'quite good'
at eleven months. He played with her in a way he had never played
with his own children, spoiled her and was quickly subservient to
her every whim. 'Sweet little Lilibet' he styled her when she first
began to talk and her baby attempts to say her own name emerged
in this fashion. The name stuck and from then on she was Lilibet
rather than Elizabeth to everyone in the family circle, a fact which
was also useful in distinguishing between her and her mother.

In her parents' absence, arrangements went ahead for them to
move into 145 Piccadilly, a four-storey Victorian mansion close
to Hyde Park Corner. A terrace house, nothing much like a royal
residence to look at, 145 Piccadilly was actually far larger than was
apparent at first glance. Inside, it boasted a library as well as a
drawing-room, dining-room and some twenty-five other rooms,
was equipped with such luxuries as an electric lift and double
glazing – this in 1927! – and, most important to a small, growing
girl, had access at the rear to a small private park known as

Hamilton Gardens. The baby and her nanny moved in a week before her parents were due back from their six-months' tour. For the next ten years it was to be Lilibet's home, her father having arranged to take it on a ten-year lease which, in curious fashion, was timed to lapse coincidentally with a totally unforeseen move into Buckingham Palace.

On 27 June Lilibet was taken again to Buckingham Palace, this time to await the return of her parents. Her royal grandparents had gone to Victoria Station to welcome the couple back, and her uncles, the King's other sons, to Portsmouth to see the *Renown* dock and escort their brother and sister-in-law to London. Almost the first question the Duchess asked was, 'How is my baby?' 'Thriving,' her father-in-law told her.

A vast crowd had gathered outside the palace to witness the Royal Family's return. Whose idea it was to take Lilibet out onto the balcony is not known, but the King must have approved or it would never have been done. So the London crowd obtained its first real glimpse of the baby Princess, held fondly in her mother's arms under the shelter of an umbrella, and the future Queen her first experience of public ovation. It was an experience which was to be repeated later in the day, several times, at the Yorks' new home in Piccadilly which also had its balcony and its welcome-back crowd.

It was at 145 Piccadilly that the future Queen grew from babyhood to girlhood. Gradually toddling became walking, and words were strung more and more into sentences. Imaginary telephone conversations were among her favourite games.

It was also at 145 Piccadilly that Marcus Adams took those early photographs which made her, young as she was, a national celebrity. It is curious, looking back, to recall how much more public interest there was in her than ever there was in her Lascelles cousins, the only other royal children of the period. Almost as though they knew that fate would one day take a turn which would make her Queen, newspaper editors published everything that could be garnered about her. Almost as though the public sensed the same thing, people avidly collected the picture postcards of her which were on sale everywhere.

Of this public interest she herself was totally unaware. Her small world was limited to the nursery of 145 Piccadilly and the sooty shrubs of Hamilton Gardens at the rear. The nursery was on the top floor. It lacked both plumbing and central heating. Coal for the nursery fire and hot water for the tin tub in which she was bathed had to be laboriously hauled up from lower down. This was a task for the nurserymaid, Margaret MacDonald, a young auburn-haired Scots lass, daughter of a railwayman, who had previously worked as chambermaid at a small Highland hotel. Even more than Nanny Knight, she doted on the baby Princess and was in her element on the rare occasions when she was permitted to take over and give Lilibet her bedtime bath. There was a brief period, with Mrs Knight ill with influenza, when the young nurserymaid temporarily took control of the nursery. Her joy knew no bounds as she bathed her charge, fed her, took her for outings in the carriage which the King sent round from Buckingham Palace and played with her in Hamilton Gardens. Hide-and-seek was a favourite game. Margaret MacDonald would hide among the shrubs and Lilibet would seek. The nurserymaid would spring out of her hiding place with a cry of 'Boo!' Lilibet would clap her small hands in delight. 'Boo-boo', she would cry back.

So Margaret MacDonald became 'Bobo' to her small charge and, indeed, to all members of the family. It marked the start of an unusual relationship between Princess and nurserymaid which was to grow deeper following the birth of Princess Margaret. With Nanny Knight obliged to devote most of her energies to the younger sister, Bobo took sole charge of Lilibet and has been with her ever since, by turns nurserymaid, nanny, personal maid and dresser. And always a very special confidante. Over half a century later, now well beyond the normal age of retirement, she is with the Queen as this book is being written, still known to her by that childhood nickname of Bobo, a very special servant with her own three-room apartment at Buckingham Palace and with two assistant dressers to help her in the task of master-minding the Queen's wardrobe.

The loves of Lilibet's young life were her parents, her sister later, Alla and Bobo, and her paternal grandfather, the King. She was the apple of the King's eye. Later she would become close to Queen Mary too, though in different fashion. Queen Mary could no more unbend with her grandchildren than she had done with her own children, and it was not until Lilibet was older, with her grandmother seeing her as the Heir Presumptive rather than merely a granddaughter, that the two of them would be drawn together. Earlier both Lilibet and the sister not yet born were intimidated by their formidable grandmother almost to the point of being frightened of her. Margaret, indeed, would always be a little frightened of her.

Unknown to the bulk of his people, who viewed him as an all-powerful monarch who would reign for ever, the King was often in pain, the heritage of a visit to France during the Great War of 1914–18 when his horse reared and rolled on him, fracturing his pelvis. Then in 1928, when he was sixty-four and his granddaughter was two, came the first signs that his health was beginning to fail. It started with what, in his bluff fashion, he dismissed at first as no more than 'a beastly cold'. But the 'beastly cold' turned into a pleural abscess which resulted in toxaemia. For ten months he was seriously ill. Recovering (or so it seemed, though there were to be two relapses later), it was 'sweet little Lilibet' he asked to have with him for company when he went to convalesce at Craigweil House, near Bognor. She would toddle alongside as he was pushed round the grounds in his wheelchair, and on Easter Monday 1929, as Lilibet neared her third birthday, they ventured out together on a stroll to the sea-wall. Dr Cosmo Lang, who had now been appointed Archbishop of Canterbury, visited the King during this period of convalescence and was astonished, as any of the King's subjects would have been, to find the King-Emperor crawling around on his hands and knees, playing the part of a pony, while Lilibet led him along by his beard. Toddler though she still was in many ways, she had already started riding lessons, and for her birthday her grandfather gave her a Shetland named Peggy, her first pony. Horses of any sort – riding ponies, carthorses, cavalry mounts – fascinated her from an early age, and her favourite excursion, on visits to Sandringham, was to go with her grandfather to the stables, with him picking her up so that she could feed sugar lumps to each horse in turn. Back in London following the King's spell of convalescence at Bognor, grandfather and granddaughter developed a daily ritual. Immediately after breakfast each morning Lilibet would stand at one of the topmost windows of her Piccadilly home and her grandfather at one of the windows of Buckingham Palace, some five hundred yards away, and they would wave 'Good morning' to each other. Later they improved upon this daily game with the addition of a pair of binoculars each.

If her parents could have been granted their dearest wish, not even the Abdication would have resulted in Lilibet growing up to be Queen. By then she would have had a small brother who, though younger, would have ranked ahead of her in the line of succession. Indeed, the Duke and Duchess had so convinced themselves that their second child would be a boy that the birth of another daughter found them totally unprepared in the matter of names.

Because the Duchess wished to have her second child born in Scotland, in Glamis Castle, her old home, there were to be problems over the anachronistic custom of the Home Secretary being present to authenticate the birth. Before the family left for Scotland, the Duke informed the Home Secretary – J. R. Clynes now held the post – that he would let him know in good time when the baby was due. However, this was not good enough for the conscientious Clynes. Instead of waiting upon the Duke's summons, he did his own pre-natal calculations and set out for Scotland of his own accord, arriving at Glamis, to the Duke's irritation, some two weeks too soon. He was promptly packed off to spend those two weeks at Cortachy Castle, the nearby home of the Dowager Countess of Airlie. He was just sitting down there to dinner at eight o'clock on the evening of 21 August 1930 when a telephone call alerted him to the fact that the baby was about to be born. He drove through a downpour of rain to Glamis, arriving there around nine o'clock. The baby was born at 9.22, but whether as a result of the Duke's distaste for the whole business or for some other reason, the Home Secretary did not get to see the new arrival until after ten o'clock. Time enough for half-a-dozen babies to have been smuggled through in warming-pans, as rumour had it happened in the distant days of James II. If the Duke was perhaps seeking to demonstrate how foolish the whole business was, he undoubtedly succeeded.

With the Prince of Wales, to his mother's regret, seemingly still in no hurry to marry and have children, the new baby, another girl, as yet unnamed, ranked fourth in the line of succession. Her parents thought first of calling her Ann Margaret. They felt that Princess Ann of York and Princess Elizabeth of York were names and titles that went well together. However, the King, driving over from Balmoral to see his latest grandchild for the second time, grumbled that he did not particularly care for the name Ann. His opinion being tantamount to a royal command, his son and daughter-in-law talked over the matter of names again. They toyed with the idea of simply reversing the proposed names and calling the baby Margaret Ann. But in the end they decided upon Margaret Rose. Lilibet, now four, inspecting her baby sister in her cot, did not see her as a Rose, however. 'I shall call her Bud,' she decided.

The birth of Margaret Rose brought a change in the nursery regime, with Margaret MacDonald promoted to the position of assistant nanny and given charge of Lilibet. By royal standards, the Yorks ran a comparatively modest establishment, and their way of life was a quiet one compared to the more gadabout standards of the Duke's eldest brother, the Prince of Wales. Even so, they felt the pinch of the times in a nation which had never recovered from the debilitating economic effects of the 1914–18 war with Germany. It was a period of further industrial depression, with unemployment again rising above the two million mark, and the early 1930s found the Duke obliged to forgo his hunting with the Pytchley and sell off his six hunters. In the interests of the national economy, his father surrendered £50,000 of his annual allotment under the Civil List, while the Prince of Wales donated half of his revenues from the Duchy of Cornwall to the Treasury.

At 145 Piccadilly family meals, for the most part, were built around Scottish dishes favoured by the Duchess, though she was careful also to ensure that her husband stuck to the diet he had been obliged to follow since being invalided out of the wartime Navy with duodenal ulcers. Public engagements apart, husband and wife seldom went out of an evening except for an occasional sortie to the cinema at Marble Arch to see the latest 'talkie', with the Duke making a nightcap of cocoa for them both when they got back. Other evenings were spent listening to the wireless and, when Lilibet and Margaret were old enough, in hilarious family card games of Snap and Happy Families. Lilibet and Margaret too once she was old enough were dressed in 'sensible' clothes, pleated skirts, Fair Isle jumpers and velvet berets. The Prince of Wales –

'Uncle David', as Lilibet called him – was an occasional visitor, saying how much he envied his younger brother's quiet, contented family life, though himself showing no inclination to discard his mistresses in favour of a wife and children. Royal engagements frequently required the Duke and Duchess to leave their daughters for short periods, though there was to be no repetition of that long parental absence of 1926–7. When he was at home the Duke would sometimes join the girls and their nannies in Hamilton Gardens, demonstrating his prowess at the game of hopscotch. Because of his long-time involvement with the boys' camps which bore his name,* he also taught his elder daughter the words of such rollicking camp-fire songs as 'Under the Spreading Chestnut Tree'. She never forgot them and years later, as Queen, would briefly astonish everyone by joining in the singing of another camp-fire favourite, 'Susannah's A Funniful Man'. Occasional visits to or by her Lascelles and Elphinstone cousins afforded her some degree of younger company. For pets, there was a parrot called Jimmy which her parents had brought back from Australia and, a little later, some rabbits and the first in the long line of royal corgis.

In 1931, when Lilibet was five, her grandfather decided that his York grandchildren needed more open space and fresh air than was available in Hamilton Gardens. Accordingly he offered his son a weekend retreat in the form of a run-down royal residence on the edge of Windsor Great Park. Known as Royal Lodge, a name amply justified today as the elegant weekend residence of the Queen Mother, it was anything but elegant in those 1930s days when her husband first took her to view it. Built in the days of George II, used as a country retreat by George IV, partly demolished by his brother, William IV, it had been uninhabited ever since and was fast mouldering into decay. But the Duke and Duchess saw possibilities in it, took it over, and the work of restoration and extension was put in hand. New wings were built on, and the grand saloon restored to its former glory. If the bulk of this work was necessarily carried out by architects, builders and decorators, the Yorks themselves undertook the onerous task of turning the surrounding sixteen acres of wilderness into a proper

* The Duke of York Camps, as they were known, started in 1921. Between then and the outbreak of World War II, the Queen's father attended all but one and would have attended that but for illness.

garden. Friends and relatives who came to visit were roped in to help. So were pages and footmen, chauffeur and detective. While the Duke slashed away with a billhook, clearing the overgrowth, the Duchess lopped and snipped, and Lilibet staggered back and forth with the debris, piling it into heaps which, under parental supervision, became large smoky bonfires. 'Bud', as yet, was still too young to help.

Aspects of education were not forgotten. Even before Margaret was born, the Duchess was already teaching the elder daughter to read with the aid of Beacon primers from America. She was taught piano by a music teacher called Mabel Lander, a name which quickly had the young Lilibet referring to her as 'Goosey'. There is some question as to what constituted her first public appearance (other than that on the balcony of Buckingham Palace at the tender age of fourteen months). She appears, though unofficially, to have 'taken the salute' at a march-past by the Scots Guards at Windsor Castle on her fourth birthday, and there is reference to her being presented with a bouquet at a children's concert which she attended around the same time. Certainly at the age of five, on the suggestion of Queen Mary, she was deemed old enough to attend the Trooping the Colour ceremony for the first time, sitting with her parents in an open carriage while her grandfather took the salute.

Riding lessons continued under the supervision of a bowler-hatted groom named Owen. Lilibet hero-worshipped him, as small girls will. She was constantly talking about him – Owen this and Owen that. Her frequent references to him were inclined to fidget her father. 'Don't ask me; ask Owen,' he retorted on one occasion when she put some question to him.

At five, her parents felt, it was time to start her education proper. She might perhaps go to university later, they thought (though World War II was to prevent the thought being brought to fruition), but the idea that she might go to school never seems to have occurred to them. Schooldays for royal children would not come about until she was a mother herself and would be influenced by Prince Philip in the matter of royal education. She herself had only a governess. Marion Crawford was in her early twenties, a progressive young woman with an interest in child psychology who had become a sort of freelance governess to the children of well-to-do families in the Dunfermline area, among them the

41

young daughter of Lady Rose Leveson-Gower, a sister of the Duchess. Having met her at the Leveson-Gower house, Lilibet's parents invited her to come to them on a month's trial. She proved satisfactory and stayed for seventeen years.

Neither of Lilibet's parents seemed to have any very clear idea of what form their daughter's education should take. Her royal grandfather stipulated one thing only. 'Teach Margaret and Lilibet to write a decent hand, that's all I ask,' he boomed at the new governess. 'None of my children can write properly. I like a hand with some character in it.' Queen Mary was the one who took an intelligent interest. Studying a copy of the proposed educational syllabus, she expressed the opinion that there were too many lessons in arithmetic, a subject a Princess was hardly likely to need. On the other hand, she suggested including more lessons in history, geography and religion. And for Lilibet to learn poetry, she said, would be useful in training her memory. 'Crawfie', as the Princess was soon calling her governess, promptly revised the suggested timetable in accordance with Queen Mary's comments and so the pattern of the future Queen's education took shape.

Somewhat to the dismay of the new governess, the pattern was often disrupted because the Princess was called away from her lessons by one or other of her parents. The garden room, its furnishings reinforced by the addition of a blackboard, a world globe, some maps and a dictionary, served as a schoolroom. Lessons started at half-past nine and continued until eleven o'clock, the session being parcelled into half-hourly periods devoted to Bible reading, arithmetic (four periods a week), history (four periods), grammar (two periods) and a single weekly period each of geography, writing, literature and poetry. Though it is not shown in the original timetable, there were also French lessons given by a visiting mademoiselle. Eleven o'clock brought an hour's break for play in Hamilton Gardens. The remainder of the morning, until lunch at one o'clock, was devoted to reading. *Black Beauty*, because it concerned a horse, was naturally a great favourite. Other favourite books included *Peter Pan*, the *Doctor Doolittle* stories and Thackeray's *The Rose And The Ring*. Lilibet also enjoyed following the adventures of such newspaper cartoon characters as Pip, Squeak and Wilfred and became a regular reader of the *Children's Newspaper*. After lunch, which she ate with her parents, came drawing, music, singing and dancing lessons with various visiting instructors. Queen Mary would sometimes intervene in her granddaughter's education, her interest in her growing as the Princess grew older, and take her off to see round some museum or art gallery which she thought of educational interest. Lessons continued as usual on Saturday mornings at Royal Lodge, Windsor, with a riding lesson in the afternoon.

For the most part the Princess tackled her lessons with that same degree of concentration which today, as Queen, she brings to bear on the contents of her Boxes. Not all subjects came easily to her, and the result was a spate of nail-biting which, despite the admonitions of her governess and others, persisted for some years. And her behaviour in class, on one occasion at least, was hardly in the tradition of a fairy-tale princess. Frustrated at being set to write out long columns of French verbs, she brought the lesson to an abrupt halt by the messy expedient of up-ending her silver inkpot.

As yet there were no television sets around which so many present-day families sit of an evening like so many zombies. Instead, there was, each evening, a playtime session with her small sister and their parents. Playtime continued with splashing games in the bathroom and pillow fights in the bedroom, with an anxious Alla worried that the two small Princesses would never be able to get to sleep for all the excitement. There were also occasional outings with her parents, to the Horse Show at Olympia, to the Royal Military Tournament and, at Christmas, to a pantomime. It was still, as Marion Crawford saw, a fairly narrow upbringing, and she sought to broaden it by taking the Princess for a ride across London on top of a double-decker bus and for a trip on the London underground, with tea to follow in a YWCA canteen. Then a spate of IRA bombs made such informal outings unwise. Summer holidays were spent at Birkhall, a house on the royal Balmoral estate, and Christmas at Sandringham. There was never any problem over what to give Lilibet for Christmas or birthdays. Anything to do with horses was sure to please, books about horses, horse ornaments, more toy horses to add to the growing collection which in due course would move with her to Buckingham Palace and still be there, lined up on the landing outside her bedroom, the night before her wedding.

Her sixth birthday, however, brought her an extra-special present, a gift from the people of Wales, a model of a traditional Welsh cottage. Much more than a doll's house, it stood fifteen feet high, had six rooms and such conveniences as a bathroom with running water and a miniature radio that really worked. Erected in the gardens of Royal Lodge, it provided Margaret as well as Lilibet with endless hours of pleasure before they eventually outgrew it. (Today it equally delights the Queen's grandchildren.) At seven she had her first corgi. It was a Pembroke corgi bought for her by her parents. Its full Kennel Club name was Rosavel Golden Eagle, but this was quickly shortened in the family circle to Dookie. It was inevitable that the younger sister should want one too, and Rosavel Golden Eagle was joined by Rosavel Lady Jane. 'What on earth are they?' people asked one another when the two Princesses were first seen out with their new low-slung pets, but over the next twenty years the corgi would become the fourth most popular breed in a nation of dog-lovers.

Lilibet was nine when the King celebrated his Silver Jubilee in 1935, and he gave her a pearl necklace to commemorate the occasion. With Margaret and their parents, she rode to St Paul's Cathedral in a state landau for a thanksgiving service. For the first time since babyhood, she appeared again on the palace balcony, with sufficient sense of occasion now to wave to the crowds as they cheered. Her grandparents took her with them on tours of a London bedecked with flags and banners. Her grandfather, in his gruff way, pretended to be disturbed by 'all this fuss and expense', but Lilibet was perhaps not too young to sense how deeply touched he really was. She was permitted to stay up late, a rare treat, to hear her grandfather's Jubilee broadcast. Close to him as she was, it must surely have seemed that he was speaking directly to her as he said, over the radio: 'I am speaking to the children above all. Remember, children, the King is speaking to you. As you grow up, be ready and proud to give to your country the service of your work, your mind and your heart.' Can anyone doubt that, listening, the nine-year-old Princess vowed to herself that she would do what Grandpa asked of her?

The strength of character which would serve the future Queen Elizabeth II so well during the years of unforeseen monarchy which lay ahead was fast taking shape. Grandpa, Queen Mary and her father more than her mother were the ones on whom, subconsciously, she modelled herself. She was industrious, meticulous and conscientious. Economic too. Fancy wrapping paper from birthday gifts and ribbons from boxes of chocolates were carefully preserved for future use. Even today she can hardly bring herself to discard such once-used items. Her shilling a week pocket money was carefully saved to be spent during the summer stay at Balmoral (when her governess would take her to the shops in nearby Ballater) or on Christmas gifts for others. While Margaret was busy stuffing herself with the small helping of coffee sugar each girl was given at the end of a meal, Lilibet would sort hers into little piles, according to the size of the crystals, and eat it slowly to make it last. But it was her conscientiousness and meticulousness which showed through most strongly. At bedtime she was meticulous over tidying away her playthings and folding her clothes neatly, hopping madly out of and into bed again to straighten her shoes if they were not perfectly aligned. She was meticulous too over listing the gifts she received on birthdays and at Christmas and writing a thank-you note to each of the donors. She was conscientious – with the exception of the small rebellion in the matter of her French verbs – in the way in which she applied herself to her lessons, even arithmetic, which she considerably disliked. She was similarly conscientious over drying the corgis, hers and her sister's, if ever they were wet, and over washing and drying the miniature tea things in the scaled-down Welsh cottage in the grounds of Royal Lodge. The more harum-scarum younger sister, by contrast, was apt to dodge her share of such childhood tasks if given half a chance.

That the two sisters were very different in character was quickly apparent. Lilibet was the serious one, Margaret the fun-child of the family. Even as a very small girl, the younger sister was inclined to be vain about her appearance, fussy over what she wore. In contrast, the elder sister, according to the recollections of their governess, 'never cared a fig' how she was dressed.

King George V was seventy that year of his Silver Jubilee, and only Queen Mary and other immediate members of the family knew that his health was failing fast. A stay at Eastbourne earlier in the year had rallied him, but there were still critical health problems, and the celebrations of his Silver Jubilee were quickly followed by a fresh onset of his old bronchial trouble. By December, when his family gathered around him at Sandringham as usual, it had become clear that he could not live much longer. Already he was not much more than a shadow of his former dominant self. His voice no longer boomed, he complained constantly of being in pain and lapsed at times into vagueness.

Lilibet and Margaret were at Sandringham with their grandparents over Christmas, but their parents were not. The Duchess was suffering from an attack of influenza which would turn to pneumonia before she was finally well again. Too ill to travel, she spent Christmas at Royal Lodge. The Duke stayed with her, but shortly after Christmas an urgent summons brought him too to Sandringham. The King was dying. Lilibet, but not Margaret, was taken to Grandpa's bedroom to see him for the last time. Then both Princesses were sent to join their mother at Royal Lodge. Margaret, still only a five-year-old at the time, was largely unaware of what was going on. But Lilibet, now nearing ten and always so very close to her royal grandfather, was fully aware and deeply distressed.

The King died on 20 January 1936. Dressed in black, the nine-year-old Lilibet was taken by her parents to see her grandfather's body as it lay in state in Westminster Hall. The solemnity of the occasion made a deep impression on her young mind. The extraordinary silence of those filing past the coffin especially impressed her. It was, she felt, 'as if the King was asleep'.

In fact, of course, George V was King no longer. The reins of monarchy had been taken over by his eldest son, now King Edward VIII. Lilibet's father, the Duke of York, next eldest of the dead King's four sons, was now Heir Presumptive – Presumptive rather than Apparent because there was still a possibility that the new King, forty-one years of age at the time of his accession, would yet marry and have a child of his own to succeed him. The new King's mother, Queen Mary, was one of the very few people, perhaps the only one, who foresaw that things might work out very differently. But, then, she was in the privileged position of being able to see behind the scenes, sensing already that her eldest son was embarking upon a course which, if he did not change direction, could lead only to muddied and troubled waters. As yet she could have no way of knowing for certain which way the pendulum of his conflicting emotions would swing, but she knew her son – knew too that the American woman with whom he had fallen in love would be unacceptable to the nation as Queen Consort. Not because she was American, as many people still seem to think, but because she was a woman already once divorced and who must be divorced yet a second time before she was free to marry the new King. If Queen Mary did not have reason to blame her husband's death on the lifestyle of their eldest son, as Queen Victoria had done three-quarters of a century before, she was conscious that events already in train might result in a situation from which her dead husband's favourite grandchild would one day, years in the future, emerge as Queen.

Lilibet herself, in an age when such things were kept more carefully from children's ears, knew nothing of her Uncle David's infatuation for Wallis Simpson. She knew only that her beloved Grandpa was dead and that her Uncle David was now King. She was not taken to the funeral service. That, her parents felt, might prove too much of an ordeal for her, beyond her childhood understanding. But, again dressed in black, she was taken to Paddington Station to travel by train with others of the family for the interment at Windsor.

A fresh addition to her curriculum, swimming lessons, helped to keep her from brooding too much on the death of her grand-father. She took to the water more readily than her smaller sister, but both ended up later with life-saving certificates after taking a test which involved the two of them jumping into the pool while fully dressed. Alla also taught her to knit. She was never very good at it, though she did manage to fashion a pair of woollen garters for her father to wear with his plus-fours and later, during the war years, knitted a few rather shapeless items to be sent as 'comforts' to relatives and royal servants in the armed forces.

If she knew nothing of the drama which was enacted over the next few months behind the scenes of royal life, with her Uncle David seeking to make Mrs Simpson his Queen, while his mother, brothers and sister sought, individually and collectively, to woo him away from her, she was not alone in that. With the British Press banded together in a loyal conspiracy of silence, the vast majority of the public knew nothing either, though the whole business quickly became a common talking point in America and other countries where newspaper proprietors and editors felt no such loyalty. She met Mrs Simpson only once and, even then, did not know who she was.

It happened that she was with her parents at Royal Lodge the day the new King turned up unexpectedly on the pretext of showing his brother a new American-style station wagon he had acquired. In reality it was another American acquisition he wished to bring to the notice of his brother and sister-in-law, an attractive, smartly dressed, immaculately groomed woman to whom he was clearly attracted and who, in the view of the other adults, adopted a rather possessive attitude towards him. Children, parents and visitors had tea together. 'Who is she?' Lilibet wanted to know when the King and his companions had left again. It would be nearly another thirty years before the two of them, the woman who once hoped to become Queen and the Princess who did, would meet again.

Young as she was, the ten-year-old Princess had some slight, if confused, inkling of what was going on as the abdication crisis neared its climax. For her, the first real revelation came on 3 December, 1936, a Thursday. The British Press had finally decided that it could keep silent no longer and such headlines as 'THE KING AND HIS MINISTERS' and 'GRAVE CONSTI-TUTIONAL CRISIS' could not be concealed from her. With her parents not yet back from a royal visit to Edinburgh, the delicate task of explaining things to her fell upon her governess. Not knowing how much the Duke and Duchess would want their daughter told, Miss Crawford's explanation was perhaps less clear-cut than it might have been.

Over the next few days, as the house at 145 Piccadilly became more and more the focal point of the crisis, the small Princess glimpsed some of the important visitors who came and went, prime minister Stanley Baldwin among them, and heard the shouts of 'Long live King Albert' from the crowd which thronged the street outside. She knew, of course, that the 'King Albert' referred to was her father. She also realized that, with her father as King, she would be Heir Presumptive. Presumptive rather than Heir Apparent because it was still possible that her parents might yet have another child, and a son would rank ahead of her in the line of succession. 'Does it mean that you are going to be Queen?' her six-year-old younger sister asked her. The probability was that one day she would be, and the idea horrified her child's mind. If nursery gossip can be believed, she even prayed at bedtime that God would send her a baby brother with a prior claim.

Her father, though she could not know this at the time, was equally appalled at the thought that his ten-year-old daughter would one day have to shoulder the burden of monarchy. He himself had not the slightest desire to be King, but his integrity was such that he saw it as his duty. So great was the strain on him at this time of crisis that, visiting his mother, Queen Mary, he broke down and wept. To make matters worse, his wife, on whom he relied so much, again succumbed to influenza and was forced to take to her bed.

It was on 10 December, another Thursday, that the elder sister spied a letter on the hall table addressed to Her Majesty the Queen. 'That's Mummy now,' she said in a slightly awestruck voice. Her mother was Queen, her father was King – not King Albert, but King George VI, echoing his father's name – and she was no longer Princess Elizabeth of York but Heir Presumptive. But young as she was, she was still a little confused as to how it had all come about. What had happened, she seemed to think, was all because her Uncle David wanted to marry Mrs Baldwin!

4 HEIR
PRESUMPTIVE

By one of those curious coincidences with which her life has seemed to abound, the future Queen Elizabeth II was doing a history lesson, with its references to lineage and dynasty, at the exact hour on Thursday, 10 December 1936, that her father, along with his two younger brothers, the Duke of Gloucester and the Duke of Kent, was witnessing the Instrument of Abdication which would result in the oldest brother, King Edward VIII, vacating the throne. Along with her small sister, Princess Margaret, she should have gone for another swimming lesson that afternoon, but the outing had to be abandoned, so packed was the street outside 145 Piccadilly with supporters of the new King.

In the week since the abdication crisis was first made public by the newspapers, the nation had divided into three camps. There were those, Winston Churchill among them, who sought to retain King Edward VIII on the throne, come what may. Not that Churchill necessarily favoured the King's own idea that Mrs Simpson, now twice divorced, should become Queen Consort. But Churchill was a man totally loyal to the Crown – and the crown belonged to King Edward VIII, even if he had not actually been crowned. Then there were those – and they were in the majority – who thought that the King should either renounce Mrs Simpson or go and so clear the way for a new King in the person of the next-oldest son of King George V, the Duke of York. And there was yet a third camp, small in number, who thought that, if Edward VIII abdicated, Parliament should amend the Act of Settlement (which sets out the order of succession to the throne)* so as

* The Act of Settlement was passed by Parliament in 1701 mainly to ensure that the Catholic descendants of James II, the son and grandson of his second marriage to Mary of Modena, the 'Old Pretender' and the 'Young Pretender' as they are respectively known, did not inherit the Crown.

to leapfrog over the two sons next in line and bestow the crown on the youngest of King George V's four sons, the Duke of Kent. The thinking of this small third group was based on the belief that the Duke of York and the Duke of Gloucester were both shy, self-conscious men, neither of them likely to make a strong King, which the Duke of Kent would. Moreover, the Duke of Kent already had a son who could one day succeed him, while the Duke of York had only a daughter (the inference, despite the example of Queen Victoria, being that females made less able monarchs than males). The latter is not an argument which would carry much weight today, while the former ignored the fact that the Duke of Kent's character, on today's available evidence, was certainly no stronger than that of the brother who was about to vacate the throne. In the event, the existing line of succession and the established constitutional process were to prevail, with the shy self-consciousness of Lilibet's father concealing a quite remarkable strength of character, as the history of the next fifteen years (which included World War II) would demonstrate.

Queen Mary, at least, was in no doubt as to the future pattern of monarchy. Even before Parliament had ratified the Instrument of Abdication, she visited 145 Piccadilly to pay her respects to the daughter-in-law who, in her eyes, was now the undoubted Queen and stayed on to await the return of the son who saw it as his clear duty to take over the throne. On his arrival, she kissed his hand in token of allegiance just as, on the death of her husband less than a year before, she had kissed the hand of her oldest son. The following day Parliament ratified the Instrument of Abdication and the Duke of York became King. Not the King Albert for whom the crowds in Piccadilly had cheered so enthusiastically, but King George VI (though he continued to be known to his mother, his wife and his brothers as Bertie). The continuation of his father's name, he hoped, would help to obliterate the trauma of his brother's abdication.

As her first lesson in monarchy, Lilibet was taken to Marlborough House to stand at a convenient window with Queen Mary and witness the ceremony of her father's proclamation as King in the neighbouring courtyard of St James's Palace. Margaret watched too, though it was doubtless on the elder sister that Queen Mary concentrated her attention. With their father's return to 145

Piccadilly as the proclaimed King, both Princesses dipped him a curtsy, as they had been told they should by their governess. Curtsying was nothing new to them. They had done it often enough to their grandparents in the days when Grandpa was King George V. But the sight of his small daughters acknowledging him in this fashion came as a small shock to the new King. For a moment he looked taken aback. Then he bent down, took them in his arms and kissed them both. Years later, when the elder daughter became Queen, her children, again on nursery instruction, would greet her in the same formal fashion, Prince Charles bowing to her and Princess Anne bobbing a curtsy. But by then times had changed and the Queen was prompt to issue fresh instructions to her children's nanny. 'I never want them to do that again.'

Though the established order of succession had been maintained with the accession of King George VI, there yet remained a doubt in some minds as to his successor. Was it the elder of his two daughters or did both daughters rank equally as they would if it was land and not a crown which was the inheritance? The doubt was sufficiently strong for a question to be asked in the House of Commons, though it was framed obliquely: Did the Government propose to amend the Act of Settlement? 'There is no need,' replied the Home Secretary of the day, Sir John Simon, and proceeded to elaborate. 'His Majesty's Government is advised that there is no doubt that in present circumstances Her Royal Highness The Princess Elizabeth would succeed to the throne as sole heir.' As though to underline the point, Parliament granted the young Heir Presumptive an allowance of £6,000 a year, rising to £15,000 at twenty-one when she would (at that time) legally come of age.

Early in 1937 the new Royal Family moved into Buckingham Palace.* To the ten-year-old Heir Presumptive, the Palace, with its hundreds of rooms, seemed vast by comparison with 145 Piccadilly. You needed a bicycle to get round, she said, and wished there was a tunnel under Green Park so that she could slip back to her old home and sleep in her old nursery at night. Her mother set quickly about the task of creating a family home within a structure so vast and gloomy that King Edward VII had nicknamed

* Official residence of the reigning monarch since the days of George III, who bought it for £21,000.

A Princess in Piccadilly: Elizabeth at the age of two

(*Below left*) 'What's the time, Margaret Rose?' Outside the Welsh play-house in the grounds of Royal Lodge

(*Below right*) An official engagement: receiving miners' lamps on behalf of the pit pony display at the Royal Show at Windsor in 1939

The Little Princesses at Buckingham Palace after their parents' coronation

Broadcasting to the children of the nation in 1941

The Windsor pantomimes became widely known: the two sisters appeared in *Old Mother Red Riding Boots* in 1945

Wartime:
Training with the ATS and (*below*) with her family and Churchill on VE Day

With General Smuts in Natal's beautiful National Park

The young royals:
Elizabeth married Lieutenant Philip
Mountbatten in November 1947

(*Above*) in the gardens of Clarence
House

And with Anne in Victoria's
treasured christening robe of
Honiton lace

With her husband, mother and sister after the Coronation

Leading in a winner:
Carrozza, ridden by Lester Piggott,
won the Oaks at Epsom in 1957

Her first Christmas Day television speech, 1957

Cheered by Australian children at Northam

it 'The Sepulchre'. She had a small set of rooms redecorated in brighter, more cheerful colours for the two girls. The Princesses had a night nursery each, with Alla sleeping in Margaret's room and Bobo in Elizabeth's, an arrangement which further cemented the growing bond between Princess and assistant nanny. A room overlooking the gardens was turned into a schoolroom. Parents and children had their meals together, something which was unheard of among previous royal generations. But one thing was inclined to sadden the elder daughter. Papa, now that he was King, no longer had the same degree of spare time in which to play with his daughters.

But if he could no longer play with his daughters so freely as hitherto, King George VI found time to begin training the elder daughter towards the role of Queen which she would one day fill. He was a few days short of forty-one when he became King and acutely aware of his own deficiencies. Until now, he had 'never even seen a state paper', he said. Now, all at once and unexpectedly, he found himself required to read, understand and approve them every day, and he found it a formidable task. Resolved that his daughter should be better prepared when her time came, young as she was he began easing her into the manifold aspects of monarchy. He would have her standing beside him on some of the occasions when he was required to receive official visitors. He took her with him when he went to Greenwich to open the National Maritime Museum. He had her at his side yet again for a march-past of international Boy Scouts at Windsor. As shy and self-conscious as her father, such occasions did not come easily to her. 'I wish I was more like Mummy,' she sighed.

As the date of her father's Coronation drew near, she was set to learn a short speech in French with which to welcome President LeBrun of France in his own language. Her father had a special picture book devised for her so that she might better understand the complexity and significance of the coronation ceremony. He went through it with her, explaining the various points, and had her in Westminster Abbey to watch the final rehearsal. Queen Mary too lent a hand with her training. From her vast collection of historical bygones she unearthed a Victorian peepshow in which the coronation procession of George IV was colourfully detailed.

The Coronation took place on 12 May 1937, the date originally

53

decided upon for the Coronation of the new King's brother, now Duke of Windsor and a month later to marry the twice-divorced American for whom he had abandoned the throne. None of the family had much sleep the night before. The new King and Queen were awake by three o'clock in the morning. The Heir Presumptive managed another two hours' sleep. Then she too was awake, hopping excitedly out of bed to peer out of the nursery window to see what was going on.

Her own account of the events of the day, dedicated 'To Mummy and Papa. In Memory of Their Coronation. From Lilibet By Herself', is preserved in the royal archives. Written in a childish hand in one of the cheap exercise books used for lessons in the palace schoolroom, it relates how she was awakened at five o'clock in the morning by the sound of a Royal Marines' band striking up beneath her window. She jumped out of bed, slipped on her dressing-gown and stood at her bedroom window to watch all that was going on. The devoted Bobo, ever mindful of her wellbeing, draped an eiderdown round her for extra warmth.

For the actual Coronation ceremony, both Princesses had new outfits becoming their royal station, shimmering full-length dresses of lace and silver, lightweight coronets, silver sandals and ermine-trimmed robes, though Margaret, now nearing seven, was somewhat put out when she discovered that her sister's robe had a slightly longer train. In fact, this was due to the elder sister's extra height and not to denote superior status as Heir Presumptive. Before taking their seats in the carriage procession, they went along to see their mother in her gold-embroidered silk dress and purple velvet robe, the train of which was even longer. It trailed some ten feet behind her. Lilibet thought her mother looked 'marvellous'.

As the older sister, she was concerned that Margaret might 'disgrace' the family by falling asleep in the middle of the ceremony. Both sisters, after all, had been awake from a very early hour. Far from having to prod Margaret to keep her awake, however, Lilibet had to nudge her to make a little less noise at one stage of the proceedings. Serious and conscientious as she was herself, she was constantly worried that her more high-spirited younger sister would do something wrong; forever checking and correcting her, advising her what and what not to do. Not to point at people, not to laugh at the 'funny hats' at a royal garden party, not to make a dash for the tea table, not to 'wiggle' so much. This last admonition was delivered at the 1934 wedding of the Duke of Kent at which Lilibet was a bridesmaid. Also at the wedding was a thirteen-year-old boy named Philip. As far as can be traced, it was their first time of meeting, though neither of them, while they remember the actual wedding, can remember seeing the other there all these years later.

Lilibet was still at it in 1939, checking that Margaret had a handkerchief about her when they saw their parents off on a visit to the United States, then reminding her that it was to be used for waving goodbye – 'not to cry.' It was the way their relationship would continue down the years to a meeting at Windsor in 1955 when the older sister felt obliged to point out to the younger, now twenty-five, that it would tarnish the Crown if she went ahead with her idea of marrying Peter Townsend.

Over the two years from 1937 to 1939 the future Queen's educational syllabus was broadened to include Latin as well as French and the history of the United States as well as that of Britain and Europe. Her reading included the youthful journal of her great-great-grandmother, Queen Victoria, and one schoolroom task she was set was to learn by heart the stirring speech an earlier Queen Elizabeth had made to her troops at Tilbury in anticipation of a Spanish invasion.

Training for future monarchy continued along with education. From time to time her father would have her with him in his study, going through some state document with her, explaining its significance. Even more than the King, Queen Mary, though now seventy, was indefatigable in training her granddaughter. Once a week she would call for her at the Palace in order to take her somewhere she thought would broaden her knowledge of national affairs. Together they visited the Tower of London and the British Museum, the Bank of England, the big postal sorting office at Mount Pleasant and the Royal Mint. At the Bank of England she was shown, among other things, the bars of gold in the vaults. Jokingly, the Bank's governor said she could have one if she could pick it up and carry it away with her. She tried, but it was too heavy. Visits with Queen Mary to yet more museums and art galleries, along with paintings borrowed from art galleries by the week, helped lay the foundations of today's shrewd queenly knowledge of art and antiques.

With all this, childhood was not entirely forgotten. There was a stay at the seaside, at Eastbourne, where she and Margaret rode on the sands, built sandcastles and paddled in the sea together. There were half-day excursions to a nearby beach when the family stayed at Sandringham. In letters treasured by relatives and friends there are occasional references to bedtime pillow fights and picnics. At Balmoral such picnics were forerunners of today's royal barbecues, with a frying pan taken along in which to fry sausages, onions and those patties of minced beef of which her father was fond and which are today styled 'hamburgers'.

Her passion for horses was as intense as ever and, with her father's accession, she became interested in horse-racing. King George VI, though never the dedicated racehorse owner his daughter was to become, saw it as part of the duties of kingship to maintain and race the small string of thoroughbreds inherited from his father. But it was the daughter rather than the father who awaited the results of races with such impatient eagerness, and she still remembers as one of the big disappointments of her young life the fact that her father's colt Big Game failed to win the 1942 wartime Derby. It was to be an even bigger disappointment, of course, when her own horse Aureole similarly failed to win the Derby of her coronation year.

To give her more exercise at this stage of her young life, tennis lessons were added to swimming. Her father had been a good tennis player in his younger days and in 1926, the year the elder daughter was born, had featured briefly in the men's doubles at Wimbledon. Sadly, his daughter did not take after him. Despite the constant admonitions of her coach – 'You have to run for it' – she seemed to think that the ball should come to her.

Concerned that she had too little contact with other girls of her own age, her parents arranged for her to become a Girl Guide. As Heir Presumptive, however, it could hardly be expected that she should attend ordinary Guide meetings, though she herself would have liked nothing more. Instead, a special company was formed for the purpose which would hold its meetings at the Palace, a fact which gave the mothers of the other Guides quite the wrong idea. Instead of sending their daughters along in Guide uniform, they decked them in party dresses. Later things were organized on a more down-to-earth level, and there were, at Windsor especially during the war years, long healthy hikes and scrumptious camp-fire cook-ups.

The Princess would probably have benefited from, even if she did not enjoy, a spell at boarding school such as her own children would experience a generation later. But the idea of ordinary schooling was foreign to both her parents, and there was no equivalent of Prince Philip in the Royal Family of the time to suggest it. The nearest she came to schooldays was at the age of thirteen when she was driven to and from Eton College for lessons in constitutional history. Eton, of course, is a boys' school, but she did not get to meet any of the boys in their bum-freezer jackets and stiff collars. Her lessons were private, with the Pickwickian vice-provost of the college, Sir Henry Marten, seeking to enliven a dry-as-dust subject by the employment of such novelties as an umbrella which turned in hey-presto fashion into a world globe and a chess-like game in which the kings and queens of her lineage were the counters.

Her training for future monarchy also included what would be termed 'fieldwork' in today's social services jargon. She presented rosettes to the winners of the National Pony Show, a useful exercise in public engagements for a beginner which she would also employ for her own children in the future, and took the salute at a rehearsal for the Aldershot Tattoo. She joined her parents at a luncheon party given for the Polish Foreign Minister. She was taken along to watch the State Opening of Parliament and accompanied her parents on an official visit to Scotland. President Roosevelt suggested that they should take her with them also when they visited the United States in 1939. 'If you can bring either or both of the children with you, they will also be very welcome,' he wrote to her father, 'and I shall try to have one or two Roosevelts of approximately the same age to play with them.' However, the King felt, as he wrote back to the American President, that she was still 'much too young for such a strenuous trip'.

A less strenuous trip, from Weymouth aboard the old, almost unseaworthy royal yacht *Victoria and Albert*,⋆ brought the family,

⋆ Built originally for Queen Victoria in 1899.

parents and daughters, on 22 July to the River Dart in Devon, to Britannia Royal Naval College, Dartmouth – to an encounter which was to have far-reaching effects on the future life of the Princess and a not unimportant, influence on the course of her future monarchy. Three months into her fourteenth year, no longer a nail-biter, she had reached what is an emotionally im-pressionable age in many girls. Finding herself – a girl who hitherto had had almost no contact with contemporaries of the opposite sex – all at once in the close company of an attentive, handsome eighteen-year-old naval cadet out to impress was almost guaranteed to result in the sort of 'schoolgirl crush' other girls have for PE instructors, young curates, footballers and pop stars. The focal point of her 'crush' was, of course, Prince Philip, at that time a cadet at Dartmouth as the King himself had been a generation earlier.

Lord Louis Mountbatten (later Earl Mountbatten of Burma), the uncle who was like a surrogate father to the young Philip, has been credited by some with instigating that 1939 meeting between his nephew and the future Queen in anticipation that it would result in a marital alliance between the royal Windsors and the proud Mountbattens. If so, he was far-sighted indeed. In his dual role of royal aide-de-camp and Prince Philip's uncle, he undoubtedly played an important part in arrangements for the visit, and it may well have been, as has been said, that it was on his suggestion that his nephew was deputed to escort the King's daughters. But if he had a motive other than keeping both Prin-cesses amused and out of adult way, it seems more probable that he was seeking to bring a favoured nephew, and distant royal relative, to the notice of the King himself.

Prince Philip's relationship to the Royal Family stems from Queen Victoria. Like the Queen herself, he is a great-great-grandchild of that redoubtable monarch. Queen Victoria's daughter Alice, who married Louis IV, Grand Duke of Hesse, was his maternal great-grandmother. Her daughter, named Victoria in honour of her grandmother, married Prince Louis of Battenberg (who later changed the family name to Mountbatten and became the first Marquess of Milford Haven). Philip's mother was their daughter and Lord Louis's sister. She married Prince Andrew of Greece, and Philip was the youngest of their children, born several years after his four sisters. Driven out of Greece in 1922, the family lived in Paris in exile long enough for the four girls to marry German princelings. Then the parents separated and Philip was taken care of, educationally at least, by his Mountbatten relatives, initially by his Uncle George, the second Marquess of Milford Haven, and later, when George died, by his Uncle Dickie (Lord Louis). It was on Uncle Dickie's advice that he went to Dartmouth with the intention of making a career for himself in the Royal Navy.

The account of what happened, or is supposed to have happened, at Dartmouth that day in 1939 has been told a score of times since in a variety of ways by a score of different authors, among them the royal governess, Marion Crawford. But the salient facts may bear recounting here as being unfamiliar to readers of a younger generation. There was a twin outbreak of mumps and chickenpox at the college at the time of the royal visit. Because of the outbreak, it was thought unwise for the two young Princesses to attend a service in a chapel crowded with cadets. Instead, they were sent to the house of Admiral Sir Frederick Dalrymple-Hamilton to play with his children, a boy and a girl. Prince Philip, coincidentally, had been appointed 'doggy' – Captain's messenger – for the occasion of the royal visit, and someone, possibly Earl Mountbatten, suggested that he should be sent along to keep an eye on the children.

If Elizabeth does not remember seeing him at the Kent wedding and noticed him no more at her father's Coronation (at which he was also a guest), his effect on her that day at Dartmouth is as undeniable as it was to be indelible. Tall, fair-haired, blue-eyed and youthfully good-looking, the impact he made on the thirteen-year-old Heir Presumptive was such as to cause her to stare at him in a fashion she would have labelled a 'disgrace' had Princess Margaret been guilty of it.

He had lunch aboard the royal yacht with the two Princesses and their governess, and joined them again for both lunch and tea the following day. At tea-time Elizabeth hovered solicitously around him, plying him with shrimps, herself as pink-faced with excitement as the shrimps he devoured so voraciously. Later, when the royal yacht weighed anchor and left, Philip, in a small rowboat, rowed dangerously far out to sea in its wake. A deal of shouting through a loud-hailer from the deck of the yacht was required before he was finally prevailed upon to turn back. 'A young fool,' the King labelled him, according to Marion Crawford. Philip himself would not appear to have seen the exploit as being especially foolhardy. What he did was simply 'out of respect for the King', he said by way of explanation. It is an explanation that carries the ring of sincerity.

5 WARTIME PRINCESS

It was during the grim, austere years of World War II that the future Elizabeth II grew from girlhood to womanhood. She was little more than a child, only four months into her fourteenth year, when Britain declared war on Germany in September 1939, childish enough still to hurl a furious cushion at the wireless set when the voice of Germany's English-speaking propagandist, the Irishman William Joyce, nicknamed 'Lord Haw-Haw', was heard on the air. An early German naval success, the sinking in October of the battleship *Royal Oak* at its Scapa Flow anchorage with the loss of so many lives, distressed her immeasurably. The memory of it was still with her at Christmas. 'I kept thinking of those sailors and what Christmas must have been like in their homes,' she wrote.

The Royal Family was on holiday at Birkhall, on the Balmoral estate in Scotland, when the imminence of war obliged the King and Queen to return posthaste to London. Earlier, with her parents and sister, the Princess had attended a camp-fire sing-song at the last of her father's pre-war boys' camps, singing and acting out the words of 'Under The Spreading Chestnut Tree', as her father had taught her. Now, as those early weeks of war ran their uncertain course, her parents decided that she and Margaret should remain temporarily in Scotland, under the supervision of Sir Basil Brooke, the Queen's Treasurer. The two Princesses spoke with their parents in London on the telephone each evening, handed round tea and cakes at a weekly sewing and knitting bee designed to help Britain's war effort and did lessons as usual with their governess, while the elder sister's lessons with Sir Henry Marten in constitutional history were necessarily conducted by post. Trouble with her teeth resulted in several visits to the dentist and, with the approach of Christmas, she and Margaret went shopping for presents in Aberdeen. The local Woolworth's, with its slogan in those days of 'Nothing over sixpence', enjoyed the bulk of their patronage.

There was less than a week to Christmas when the two Princesses saw their parents again, in the safe, friendly surroundings of Sandringham. Among the Christmas cards the elder sister received was one from the tall, handsome naval cadet who had made such an impression on her during the visit to Dartmouth. However, she was disappointed to discover that Philip's name was not on the list of those destined to receive cards from the Royal Family. She begged her father to send him one – it does not seem to have occurred to her to send him a card herself – and he did so, though rather late in the day. From then on she set about keeping track of Philip's wartime movements. She found out that he had been posted to the battleship *Ramillies*, at that time based on what was then Ceylon, and saw to it that his name was added also to the list of relatives, friends and servants now serving with the armed forces and in need of 'comforts'.

With the return of their parents to London, the two Princesses were transferred from Sandringham to Royal Lodge at Windsor. Then came the fall of France and the probability (as it seemed at the time) of a German invasion of Britain. Royal Lodge, no more than a country house, was no longer a safe place for the girl who represented, as one guest of the Royal Family put it, 'England's future hope'. Canada was quick to offer sanctuary on the far side of the Atlantic, but her mother insisted that the family must remain both united and in Britain as a symbol of confidence in ultimate victory. 'The children can't leave without me,' she said. 'I can't leave without the King. And the King will never leave.' It was a courageous decision, a brave and defiant gesture, at a time when German superiority seemed overwhelming.

Instead of fleeing to Canada, the Princesses were transferred yet again, this time to a hiding-place of which no more was revealed than that it was 'a house somewhere in the country'. In fact, it was less a house than a castle – Windsor Castle. A special detachment of Grenadier Guards was assigned to guard them, and there was a secret emergency plan, code-named Coates Mission, to whisk them away in armoured cars and ship them to Canada in the event that Operation Sealion, the German plan for the invasion of Britain, was launched. So real was the danger at the time that the move to Windsor Castle was seen as a stop-gap arrangement which could last no more than a week or so. However, they were to stay there for five years.

Their parents remained at Buckingham Palace, driving to Windsor to see their daughters at weekends. Later, with German bombs flattening and burning so much of the capital, they drove to Windsor each night to sleep but obstinately insisted upon returning to the Palace each day for 'business as usual'. It is history now that Operation Sealion did not materialize. So it was never necessary to implement the emergency plan. However, there was one night when a warning that German paratroops were landing close to the castle saw the guardian Grenadiers in action. Fortunately, the 'enemy paratroopers' who had been spotted in the darkness proved to be nothing more than a couple of baby foals.

If Windsor Castle was as safe as any structure could hope to be in those days of enemy bombing, it was also gloomy and austere, its windows covered with wire-netting and black-out curtains, dimly lit and under-heated, its massively thick walls further re-inforced with sandbags, its outer perimeter surrounded by trenches, barbed wire and anti-aircraft guns. Its glistening chandeliers had been taken down as a precautionary measure against the possibility of air raids and its valuable collection of old masters stored for safety in the dungeons, which were also the hiding-place of the Crown Jewels.

The dungeons also served as a shelter for the Princesses in the event of an air raid, and there was considerable concern the first time the alert sounded because they were so long getting there. The fault lay with the elder sister. A modest, fastidious child, she refused to go down to the dungeons in her nightwear. 'We must dress properly,' she insisted. Sir Hill Child, the Master of the Household, could hardly argue with a Princess, however young, but he did have something to say to Nanny Knight. 'The Princesses must come down at once in future, whatever they are wearing,' he told her. Alla, in turn, had a word with the elder sister, and thereafter the Princess always kept a small suitcase beside her bed, ready packed. In it were her most treasured possessions, the pearl necklace her grandfather had given her at the time of his Silver Jubilee, such few items of jewellery as she possessed and the diary she always kept so methodically. Plus a few books to read. To enable her and Margaret to dress more quickly, they were also provided with one-piece 'siren suits', similar to the one Winston Churchill made famous in wartime, which they could slip on over their nightdresses. Later, a special bedroom, cased in protective concrete, was constructed for them at the foot of one of the castle towers, and in due course, like many other children in wartime Britain, they became so familiar with aerial warfare that they could tell the difference between 'one of ours' and 'one of theirs' from the drone of the aircraft engines.

The Princess was shown how to handle a stirrup pump in case of an incendiary bomb attack on the castle and was also drilled in the use of a gas mask. She played her small part in aiding the war effort, collecting scrap metal, growing vegetables, picking fruit. She wrote childish letters of encouragement and good cheer to relatives and royal servants serving in the armed forces and even knitted a few 'comforts' for some (though her knitting still left a great deal to be desired).

Part of the castle's security consisted of a system of alarm bells which could be rung in an emergency as a signal for the guard to turn out. The younger and more high-spirited Margaret was forever teasing her sister by pretending that she was going to sound the alarm. Such teasing was calculated to drive the serious-minded Elizabeth almost into a state of frenzy. 'You can't do it. You can't do it,' she would cry, rushing away quickly so that she should not be involved if the younger sister put her threat into execution. All this came to the ears of the officer in charge of the guard who thereupon gave the Princesses permission to sound the alarm for practice purposes. Curiously, now that they were free to do so, not even Margaret had the nerve to sound the alarm, and their governess had to do it for them.

A daytime air raid alert while the Princesses were away from the castle one day saw the two of them take shelter in a cave cut into the chalk of a hillside. And there was a September afternoon during the Battle of Britain when they watched an aerial dogfight in the skies above Windsor. A German aircraft, an ME 109, was shot down in Windsor Great Park. The two Princesses went to view the wreckage, an experience which the Queen has said she still recalls 'vividly'.

Lessons in constitutional history were resumed with Sir Henry Marten. Riding side-saddle was a new lesson added to her already extensive curriculum. The royal troop of Girl Guides was re-formed, with Queen Victoria's old summerhouse serving as Guide headquarters and evacuated Cockney kids among the Guides. It was from them that the future Queen learned the Cockney mimicry which she still delights in using upon occasion. 'Cor lumme, it's rainin' and I ain't got me bloomin' brolly,' she was heard to exclaim on one occasion, years later, when she was leaving the Palace for an official engagement. Unlike the more prim and proper daughters of royal friends who had come along in their party dresses when the troop was originally formed at Buckingham Palace, the Cockney girls who enrolled at Windsor did not see the two Princesses as special people. Copying Princess Margaret, they cheerfully addressed their future Queen as 'Lilibet' and saw no reason why being born royal should prevent either of the two from doing her fair share of the firewood gathering and washing up. Sometimes, to add to the illusion of a real outdoor life, the Guides would spend a night 'under canvas'. While the younger sister thought it great fun to sleep in a tent, wriggling into and out of a sleeping-bag, the elder did not. Shy and modest by nature, she found the business of undressing in front of other girls an embarrassing ordeal.

At Christmas, 1940, she took part in a nativity play, *The Christmas Child*. She was one of the Three Kings while the younger Margaret was the Child. Their parents were among the small invited audience who saw the play when it was staged in St George's Hall at Windsor Castle, and their father was so moved by the sight of his daughters playing their parts that he 'wept through most of it', he confided to his diary. The success of the nativity play led to the famous series of Windsor Castle panto-mimes, scripted and produced by Hubert Tanner, a former Gilbert and Sullivan actor who ran the school created originally by Queen Victoria for the children of people employed on the royal estate. First of the pantomimes was *Cinderella* with Princess Margaret in the title role and the elder sister as Prince Charming. Later came *Sleeping Beauty, Aladdin and His Wonderful Lamp* and the quaintly

65

titled *Old Mother Red Riding Boots*. For her role of the Prince in the very first pantomime the Heir Presumptive was clad in the traditional garb of a tunic and silk tights. Her father, however, was somewhat disconcerted by the brevity of her tunic, which he considered short almost to the point of indecency.

For the future Queen, as for so many other youngsters, the impact of war hastened the process of growing up. At fourteen she was considered old enough to make her first broadcast. She helped to write the script and had several rehearsals. Even so, she was understandably nervous when the time came, despite the reassuring presence of her mother and younger sister. 'All we children at home are full of cheerfulness and courage,' she assured listeners throughout the Empire. 'We are trying to do all we can to help our gallant sailors, soldiers and airmen, and we are trying too to bear our share of the danger and sadness of war. We know in the end all will be well.' Turning to her sister, she said, 'Come on, Margaret – say Goodnight', and the strange rumour which had persisted for years that the younger Princess was deaf and dumb was effectively quashed as she joined Lilibet in saying, 'Goodnight, children, and good luck to you all.' Their grand-mother, Queen Mary, who was spending the war years with the Duke and Duchess of Beaufort in Gloucestershire, was so moved by the broadcast that she wept.

By now, the Princess was writing to Philip. With half a world between them, and a war in progress, letters inevitably took a long time to reach their destination. One from her caught up with Philip in Durban around the time of his twentieth birthday. He wrote back and that October, back in Britain with some leave due to him, was invited to have tea with the Royal Family at Royal Lodge. The King was especially interested in Philip's account of how Britain's Mediterranean Fleet had annihilated the Italian Fleet at the Battle of Cape Matapan. 'It was as near murder as anything could be in wartime,' Philip told him.★

The two young people met again the following month at a party given by the Duke and Duchess of Kent to celebrate their wedding anniversary. The Duke was, after all, the Princess' uncle, while the Duchess was Philip's cousin. It was at that party that the future

★ For his part in this engagement Prince Philip received a Mention in Despatches. His native Greece awarded him its War Cross.

66

Queen and Consort danced together for the first time. She was fifteen.

Despite the gloom and austerity of Windsor, the Princess herself, to a considerable extent, was cushioned from the real horrors of war. Her parents were not, and she must have noticed how, as London and other cities of Britain were devastated by German aerial bombardment, the strain showed more and more in their faces. Courageously, they visited the bombed cities, bolstering the morale of the British people. Dutifully, they insisted on 'keeping the flag flying', the flag being the royal standard, symbol of their daytime residence at Buckingham Palace. And though they made light of things when with their daughters at Windsor, they had more than one narrow escape. Particularly dangerous was the day a stick of German bombs straddled the palace. The King and Queen took refuge under a table in the King's study as bombs exploded in the courtyard and destroyed the royal chapel.

Just ahead of her sixteenth birthday, having reached what the Prayer Book terms 'the age of discretion', Elizabeth underwent the ceremony of confirmation in the private chapel at Windsor Castle. Confirmation was carried out by Dr Cosmo Lang, that same Archbishop who had earlier baptized her and crowned her father. He arrived at Windsor the evening before and had what he described as 'a full talk with the little lady'. She herself was not very talkative, it seems, but the Archbishop thought she displayed 'real intelligence and understanding'. For the ceremony she wore a simple dress of white wool and a small veil of white net. Her grandmother, Queen Mary, had journeyed from Badminton to be present, and Queen Mary's lady-in-waiting, the Countess of Airlie, thought that there was about the future Queen, that day, 'that indescribable something which Queen Victoria had'.

To commemorate her sixteenth birthday she was given her first official appointment as honorary Colonel of the Grenadier Guards. Detachments from all battalions of the regiment took part in a march-past at Windsor. Her parents discussed between themselves whether or not she should wear uniform. With her mother taking the view that she was too young, she took the salute at the march-past wearing a pleated skirt and a woollen jacket. She took this first appointment very seriously. Too seriously, some thought. One inspection of a guard of honour heard her uttering a few criticisms in her ringing girlish voice. A senior officer decided she needed a little advice, though he did not tender it directly. Instead, he asked her governess to point out to her that the first requisite of a good officer was to know how to temper justice with mercy. Because the colonelcy was her first appointment, the Grenadiers have always had a special place in her affections and, years later, she was to react indignantly to a suggestion that two men caught pilfering were from the Grenadier Guards. 'My Grenadiers would never do such a thing,' she protested.

At sixteen she was also required to register for national service. She did so at the employment exchange – 'The Labour', as it was known in less regal circles – in Windsor. The registration form she had to complete asked what type of education she had had. 'Private', she wrote. Was she attending evening classes? 'No'. Did she belong to a youth organization. 'Yes – the Girl Guides'. It was 1942, a time when most other youngsters of her age were being directed into war work pending call-up into the armed forces. But there was no question of her doing either war work or military duties. Her father felt, doubtless rightly, that the role for which she was training in the unforeseen future was more important. Having so reluctantly accepted the position of King when his eldest brother abdicated, he saw more clearly than most the sort of life that lay ahead for the elder daughter to whom he was so attached. 'She will be alone and lonely all her life,' he remarked on one occasion. 'No matter who is by her side, only she can make the final decisions.'

That was perhaps a slightly too pessimistic assessment. Or perhaps it has been that the Princess who is now Queen Elizabeth II was exceptionally fortunate in the husband she would find to stand at her side, a man of sufficiently strong character to be of real support to her while not of such overwhelming ambition that he would ever seek to play King to her Queen. Young though she was, little though she and Prince Philip saw of each other during those wartime years, their relationship, kept alive by the frequent exchange of letters, would shortly plumb another dimension. For Christmas 1942, she sent him a photograph of herself which she endorsed with her pet-name of Lilibet. In return, he sent her a photograph of himself in naval uniform, his hand raised in salute, the insignia of a sub-lieutenant on his sleeve (though he had, in fact, been promoted to the rank of first lieutenant since the photograph was taken). Later he sent her a second photograph of himself, one this time in which he was handsomely bearded. Today those two photographs of her husband as a young naval officer, bearded and clean-shaven, still eye the Queen daily across the cluttered width of the desk at which she does her paperwork. A photograph of her father regards her similarly from a nearby side table. From the moment of that close encounter with her future husband at Dartmouth in the pre-war summer of 1939, they would be the two men who shared her affections. True, the close confinement to which she was subject during the wartime years and the restrictions peculiar to her unique position as Heir Presumptive afforded her very few opportunities for getting to know any other young men. Occasionally her parents would arrange a small party to which two or three carefully vetted young Guards officers were invited as dancing partners for the Princess. But such contacts were too rare and too brief for her to get to know any of them other than on a superficial level. Not that she really desired to know them better. Young as she was, her heart had already been given to Philip.

He was again briefly in Britain over the Christmas of 1943, now second-in-command of the destroyer *Wallace*. Since he had time off because his ship was undergoing a re-fit, the Princess persuaded her parents to invite him to Windsor. If the gulf of years between them had seemed vast at Dartmouth, when he was eighteen and she was thirteen, it seemed less so now that she was rising eighteen and he was twenty-two. At Dartmouth she had been a child still. Now she was an attractive young woman who had graduated from the Girl Guides to the Sea Rangers since their last meeting. Not that she had actually been to sea. Her training was confined to a dummy ship's bridge which had been constructed indoors and, outdoors, to a dinghy on the castle lake.

Philip had dinner with the Royal Family on Christmas Eve. Afterwards he joined enthusiastically in Charades, the Royal Family's favourite game, and there was dancing to the music of gramophone records. During the period of his stay, in company with Lilibet's parents, he also watched a performance of that year's amateur pantomime, *Aladdin*, with the Princess, in the title role, looking especially fetching in a velvet tunic and a pair of silk tights.

The growing rapport between the two young people did not go entirely unnoticed by the King, and later he teased his daughter about it, enjoying making her blush. He liked Philip and very much enjoyed his company, but he did not at this stage take at all seriously the fast-developing relationship between his daughter and the Danish-descended, Greek-born young naval officer. But if the King did not detect which way the romantic wind was blowing, others did and were quick to add their efforts to the prevailing breeze. Philip's cousin King George II of the Hellenes, when the two Kings met at the wedding of a third, that of King Peter of Yugoslavia, took advantage of the opportunity to raise the question of Philip marrying Elizabeth. Her father was momentarily taken aback. Recovering, he protested that his elder daughter was much too young for marriage. Besides, he said, she had not yet had the opportunity of meeting other young men of her own age. Not that he had anything against Philip. Indeed, he very much liked him. But it would be better if he thought no further along those lines for the time being.

While the Princess was not permitted to rush into a hasty marriage such as so many other girls contracted in those traumatic wartime days, war caused her to mature early in the field of royal duty. Each monarch, in turn, appoints members of his or her family as Counsellors of State whose duty it is to deputize if the monarch is absent from the country or too ill to act in person. But under the terms of the then Regency Act, the Heir Presumptive could not be given such an appointment until she attained the age of twenty-one. The King decided to approach Parliament with a view to having this age-limit reduced. He was most anxious, he explained, that his elder daughter should have 'every opportunity of gaining experience in the duties which would fall upon her in the event of her acceding to the throne'. Conscious of the risks the King ran on the hazardous trips he undertook in order to visit British forces in the various theatres of war, Parliament promptly amended the Act so that the Princess could serve as a Counsellor of State from her eighteenth birthday. Those were the days of capital punishment, and one of her first duties, while her father was visiting British troops in Italy, was to sign a reprieve for a man convicted of murder. It was also one of her first encounters with the harsher realities of life and distressed her a great deal.

'What makes people do such terrible things?' she wanted to know, adding, 'I have so much to learn about people.'

Her eighteenth birthday also produced a clamour in certain quarters, and especially among the Welsh, for her to be given the title of Princess of Wales. Winston Churchill favoured the idea. Her father did not and declined to give it his royal approval, pointing out that the title of Princess of Wales is one reserved for the wife of the Prince of Wales, a position and title which Diana enjoys today. But in those days, because King George VI had no son, there could be no Prince of Wales and, accordingly, no Princess of Wales.

Until now, although she and her younger sister each had their own bedroom, they had always shared a sitting-room. But with an increasing build-up of royal duties, a greater degree of concentration was demanded which was not always possible with the higher-spirited Margaret around. So at Windsor, for work purposes, the Heir Presumptive was allotted her own sitting-room. To enable her to undertake a growing list of public engagements her father gave her a car of her own, a Daimler, at that time a marque synonymous with the Royal Family. To accompany her on such engagements she was also provided with her first lady-in-waiting, Lady Mary Strachey, who acted also as her secretary, helping her to cope with a growing volume of official correspondence. That she had graduated completely from royal apprenticeship to Heir Presumptive with her own round of royal duties was signalled when she accepted her first presidency, that of the National Society for the Prevention of Cruelty to Children. She made her first speech in public, addressing a meeting of the governors of the Queen Elizabeth Hospital for Children in Hackney. Young and inexperienced as she was, she was nervous of speech-making and nerves would cause her mouth to dry up to a degree that made her fear she would 'never get a word out'. It was the loyal Bobo who suggested sucking a piece of barley sugar just before making a speech. The Princess tried it, and it worked, psychologically if for no other reason. Though she has less need of it today as Queen, a small cannister of barley sugar still travels with her wherever she goes.

As with her parents, the main thrust of her work in those days as World War II moved towards its final, critical stage, was

71

concerned with bolstering national morale. She visited factories engaged on war work, mines, docks, servicemen's clubs and armed forces' establishments. She helped to host a gathering of Commonwealth prime ministers at Buckingham Palace. She launched a new battleship – *Vanguard* – and, on a visit to one of the numerous American air bases then dotted all over Britain, gave the name *Rose of York* to a Flying Fortress, a massive aircraft by the standards of those wartime days. Champagne being unobtainable since the occupation of France, and with America not yet producing its own vintage, the naming ceremony was carried out with a bottle of cider.

Along with her parents, she went in conditions of stringent secrecy to watch a rehearsal by the paratroopers and glider-borne troops who would be the first to penetrate into Hitler's Europe on D-Day. But D-Day, though it was the beginning of the end for Germany, also brought a new peril to Britain as Hitler struck back with his V1 flying bombs and V2 rockets. These horrifying new weapons spread death and destruction throughout much of southern England. A single rocket, hitting the Guards chapel on a Sunday in 1944, killed 120 of those worshipping there. In all, these weapons killed some sixteen hundred people in London alone in the course of a few months and wounded a further ten thousand. The windows of Buckingham Palace were blown out, and at Windsor there were days when flying bombs droned overhead in seemingly endless succession. The two Princesses were out in the open in Windsor Great Park when one came over. Immediately they threw themselves flat on the ground and waited for that terrible silence which ensued as the engine cut out and the bomb commenced its downward glide with no telling where it might strike. That particular bomb, fortunately, exploded on Ascot Race-course, some considerable distance from where the Princesses were, but still near enough for them to feel the blast of the explosion.

The war had taken its toll of royal relatives, friends, servants. One of the Princess' Bowes-Lyon cousins had been killed during a night action in Libya. Her uncle the Duke of Kent had died when his Sunderland flying boat ploughed into a Scottish hillside while on its way to Iceland. Prince Philip had been in the thick of more than one naval engagement, and her father had several times risked his life on hazardous journeys to visit British troops overseas. It was inevitable that a young woman as sensitive, conscientious and patriotic as the Heir Presumptive should feel that she should be doing more, making a greater sacrifice. 'I ought to do as other girls of my age do,' she said on one occasion. 'Look at Mary.' Lady Mary Cambridge, another cousin, was working as a volunteer nurse in one of the poorest and most bomb-damaged areas of London. The King felt that his daughter's contribution towards bolstering national morale was far more important than anything else she might be doing. But he also knew how she was feeling. He felt the same himself and had been dissuaded only with difficulty from sailing with the D-Day invasion armada. So he made a token gesture in permitting his elder daughter to don the uniform of a second subaltern in the Auxiliary Territorial Service and undergo a four weeks' course in D & M (driving and maintenance).

Frankness compels the admission that even this brief spell of army training was cushioned in a way the Queen has never cushioned her own children. Influenced by her husband, she has permitted her children to take what Prince Philip calls 'calculated risks' – Prince Charles and Prince Andrew as helicopter pilots, Princess Anne on horseback. She herself was allowed to take no such risks in the ATS nor experience even the discomforts she had occasionally known as a Girl Guide. The newspapers of the day might prophesy that she would share the same sleeping-quarters as her sister officers and sleep in a camp-bed as they did, but in fact she did neither. She was chauffeur-driven from Windsor Castle to the training centre at Camberley each day, at least initially – once she had learned to drive, she took the wheel herself – and back to the castle to sleep in her own bed at night. Nor (though she did not know this) were the other girls who shared the course with her 'rookies' like herself, though they pretended to be. They were hand-picked from among the instructors at the centre as non-smokers and non-drinkers, added to which they were given strict instructions not to let rip with the odd colourful adjective in the presence of the Heir Presumptive. Her training as driver and mechanic of a fifteen-hundredweight Bedford truck did not start until eleven in the morning and one day, when she had a cold, she did not go at all. Dutiful in this as in everything else, she very much wanted to go, but her governess, her nanny and even the commanding officer of her unit all joined forces to persuade her otherwise.

Though it was not intended as such, it was perhaps inevitable that the whole business should become something of a publicity exercise. The newspapers tended to exaggerate her achievements, of course, reporting for instance that she had driven her truck from Camberley to Buckingham Palace in the black-out. In fact it was a staff car she drove on that occasion, and the journey was made in daylight. Nevertheless, there were times during the course when she found herself handling heavier vehicles and, brief and cushioned though it was, her spell in the ATS had its benefits. She is possibly the only monarch in the world who, at a push, could change a flat tyre or a set of sparking plugs. She was certainly thorough and enthusiastic. At home her conversation was constantly peppered with references to carburettors and cylinder heads. There was one occasion when, according to her mother, the rest of the family were obliged to listen to a lecture on sparking plugs throughout dinner.

There was also an occasion when the royal parents went to Camberley to see their daughter in training. They watched with straight-faced parental interest as she carried out various adjustments to her vehicle before climbing into the driving cab, but could not restrain their laughter as her continued efforts to start the engine proved in vain. Her father (who was something of a car buff himself in his younger days) had secretly unclipped and removed the distributor cap.

Little more than a child when the war started, she was a young woman of nineteen on VE (Victory in Europe) Day in May 1945. Wearing her ATS uniform, she appeared that evening with her parents and Winston Churchill, more than anyone the architect of victory, on the balcony of Buckingham Palace, brilliantly floodlit after the long years of blackout. Earlier, in the company of her younger sister and two escorts, she was permitted to slip away from the palace and join the celebrating throng in the London streets. It is one of the Queen's more hilarious memories that, in the general state of frenetic jubilation which prevailed, she knocked a policeman's helmet from his head! Three months later, when Japan capitulated also, following the atomic-bomb destruction of Hiroshima and Nagasaki, she was again permitted to join in the public celebrations. Unrecognized, just a young woman in the crowd, she jostled in company with Princess Margaret for a position in front of the palace, joining excitedly in the shouts of 'We want the King' until her parents made their expected appearance on the famous balcony. Those celebrations of VE Day and VJ Day constitute two of the very rare occasions – perhaps the only two – on which she has been free, as the saying goes, to let her hair down in public. For many another young woman, World War II, for all its austerity and discomfort, had afforded a new sort of freedom. For the Heir Presumptive, however, it had been a period (even if she scarcely noticed it herself) when her life was even more constrained than it would have been in any event. If she was not conscious of this, her father was. The King thought of both his daughters, at this stage of their lives, as 'poor darlings' who had 'never had any fun'.

6 PRINCESS IN LOVE

The switch from war to peace did not have the same impact on the Heir Presumptive as it did on the lives of so many other young women of her generation. While other young women were being demobilized, discarding khaki or blue uniforms for 'civvies', looking for jobs or somewhere to live, picking up again the threads of married life, contributing to the baby boom of that postwar era, her own life continued along its fixed course with no more than a slight quickening of tempo. Her public engagements increased until they averaged slightly more than one a week. The volume of her correspondence also mounted. The number of her presidencies increased to include the Life Saving Society, the Student Nurses' Association and the Red Cross. To help her cope, two more ladies-in-waiting were taken on. Because the public had necessarily seen and heard little of her during the war years, she starred in a film titled *Heir To The Throne* about her life and work. She travelled widely, though not yet outside the United Kingdom. She went to Wales to inspect Girl Guides there, to Edinburgh with her parents for a thanksgiving service in St Giles' Cathedral and also toured Northern Ireland. She herself was eager to do more. 'I must do it,' she would say if it was suggested that a public engagement should be cancelled or postponed for whatever reason. 'It's my job.'

A palace servant of the period remembers her as 'a reserved, rather leggy young woman with a loud, carrying voice, dressed always in sensible, fashionless clothes – pleated skirts, woollen twin-sets, boxy jackets, thick stockings and flat, no-nonsense shoes'. Thick stockings, however, soon gave way to something more flattering to her legs, one of the first pairs of nylons to be made in postwar Britain. She was given them on a visit to the

76

factory. To make giving and acceptance legal under the strict clothes rationing regulations which were in force at the time, she promised to send the necessary coupons as soon as she returned to the palace, but one of the factory employees quickly intervened with an offer to surrender some of her own coupons. Queen Mary, who was with the Princess on that occasion, was rather less enthused with these newfangled nylons. 'They look as though they might be rather cold to wear,' she sniffed.

'I wish I was more like Mummy,' the Princess had sighed years before, at the very start of her royal apprenticeship as a girl of ten. There were times when she was. Presented with a set of finely embroidered sheets during her tour of Northern Ireland, for instance, she asked to meet the elderly widow capable of such fine needlework. 'Your poor eyes must ache,' she told her sympathetically. Equally, however, there were times when her conduct was more reminiscent of her imperious grandmother, Queen Mary. Addressed merely as 'Your Highness' on one occasion instead of being given her full and correct style of 'Your Royal Highness', she transfixed the offending party with an icy blue stare. It is a look which others have come to know upon occasions over the years since and which royal aides joke 'can kill at ten paces'. Prince Philip, years later, was regaling guests at a dinner party with an amusing story of an incident at a royal banquet the previous evening when he looked up to find his wife's icy stare focused in his direction. Hastily he changed the subject.

Her brief spell in the ATS, as well as teaching her to drive and service a vehicle, had also had an effect on her outlook, it seemed. It was her mother, not the Princess, who was shocked when one of her daughter's ladies-in-waiting arrived for her spell of duty in those immediate postwar years wearing a headscarf instead of a hat.

But for the most part she was then, is now, every inch her father's daughter. Punctuality was her watchword, as it was his. It still is today. It takes something of real personal importance, like the birth of a grandchild, to make the Queen late for a public engagement. Equally, she does not like to be kept waiting and, on the rare occasion that she is, her impatience shows in the way she taps her foot or fiddles with her engagement ring. But there is one respect in which she has changed with the years. Her desk today

77

is crammed and cluttered, an untidy battlefield on which time is her constant enemy. In those postwar years, when the pressure was less, the desk in her third-floor sitting-room was always as neat and tidy as clothes and shoes had been at bedtime in childhood, the virgin blotting pad flanked by pens and pencils aligned as uniformly as troops on parade.

There was a closer-than-ever relationship between the father and daughter who were also King and Heir Presumptive. The same former royal servant quoted earlier also remembers: 'It was as though sometimes there was a sort of telepathic understanding between them. You would see their eyes flicker in a quick exchange of glances as though they were talking to each other without the need for words.' The King, in some ways, was a possessive father who liked nothing better than to have his elder daughter with him. In some respects he was inclined to treat her like the son he had never had. They would go racing together, to Epsom and Hurst Park as well as to Royal Ascot (which is more of a public engagement), and to the bloodstock sales at Newmarket. At Sandringham he liked her to tag along when he was out bagging pheasants and partridges. She would rise before dawn to accompany him when he went wildfowling. At Balmoral they would go fishing together. It was at Balmoral too that he initiated her into the craft of stalking. Lacking suitable clothes of her own for this more masculine pursuit, and with no clothing coupons to spare for such seldom-used items, she borrowed and donned a pair of her father's plus-fours. The younger, more fashion-conscious Margaret, derided them as 'unfeminine'.

Margaret, at fifteen, was as much the fun-child of the family as she had ever been, always laughing, always singing, always teasing. Her father loved her too, but he was not close to her as he was to the daughter he always called by her childhood pet-name of Lilibet. For Lilibet was the one most like himself, the serious, conscientious one, the daughter who would one day succeed him.

A number of small private dances were held at the Palace around this time, arranged by the King partly out of a desire that his daughters should enjoy some of the 'fun' he felt they had been deprived of during the war years. But there was also another motive. Until now, his elder daughter, as he had told Prince Philip's cousin, King George II of the Hellenes, had had little

78

opportunity to meet young men – other than Philip, that is – of her own age. So the royal guest list for these dances included the names of several eligible bachelors, among them the heirs to two dukedoms and three earldoms. The same eligible young bachelors were also invited to a succession of other royal occasions, to shoot with the King at Balmoral and Sandringham, to join the house party held at Windsor Castle during Royal Ascot week. In those days when the national newspapers paid more attention to hard news and less to royal gossip (a situation which was soon to change), the presence of these potential suitors for the hand of the Heir Presumptive aroused little comment in the domestic Press, though there was plenty of comment in foreign publications in addition to gossip among royal friends and servants. Royal friends, in the main, seemed to regard Lord Porchester★ as a suitable match for the Princess, while foreign publications were divided between the merits of the Duke of Rutland and the Earl of Euston. There was, as yet, no mention of Prince Philip.

But the Princess herself never waivered in her feelings for Philip, even if she did not altogether understand those same feelings. 'I wonder what it is makes a person fall in love,' she said to the loyal Bobo on one occasion. She gave Philip's photograph, the clean-shaven one, the first he ever gave her, a place of honour on the mantelpiece in her sitting-room. When someone suggested that this might lead to gossip, she substituted her other photograph of Philip, the one in which he wore a beard. 'He's incognito in that one,' she said.

In fact, not so incognito as all that. To the few people who knew him, the beard could not hide the fact that it was undeniably Philip, unrecognizable though the photograph might be to the more casual visitor. In common with many other young women of that immediate postwar era, the Princess eagerly awaited the return of the man she loved. Prince Philip had ended his war in the Far East, where, among other things, he witnessed the formal Japanese surrender aboard the USS *Missouri*, flagship of Admiral William Halsey. He was still sporting his blond beard when he and the Princess met again on his return to Britain, but shortly after, to please her, he shaved it off.

★ Now Earl of Carnarvon.

79

Over the next few months, during spells of leave or whenever he had a weekend off duty, Prince Philip was so frequently at Buckingham Palace or Royal Lodge, the young couple were so often and so happily in each other's company that even the King could no longer be under any illusion as to their feelings for each other or be deceived into thinking that his elder daughter looked upon Philip simply as a distant relative. Despite his earlier doubts, he was more and more forced to the conclusion that Lilibet really had fallen in love with 'the first young man she ever met' and that what he was witnessing was a form of courtship.

Patterning itself on the ambience of the period, courtship was romantic rather than passionate, leisurely more than whirlwind. It consisted of walking the corgis in the grounds of Royal Lodge, riding in Windsor Great Park, occasional games of croquet on the velvety lawn and, when the weather was warm enough, swimming in the green-tiled pool. Seldom were the young couple completely alone. Either the royal parents were around or there were servants coming or going or there was 'Maggie', as Philip called Princess Margaret, tagging along. 'Maggie' was there too on Sunday evenings when, back from a weekend at Windsor, the couple had supper together in Lilibet's room at the Palace. With the Princess now twenty and Philip coming up to twenty-five, their physical feelings for each other were sublimated into boisterous games played in the red-carpeted corridors, with Margaret joining in, and in rather childish practical jokes. Between Philip and Bobo, the Princess' old nanny and long-time confidante, there was a small degree of antagonism, as though they saw each other as rivals for the girl's affection, as perhaps they were.

Evenings out were similarly in the company of others, a party usually of six if they went to the theatre followed by dinner at the Savoy or dancing at the Bagatelle Club. Such theatre outings included Ivor Novello's *Perchance To Dream*, the barnstorming American musical *Oklahoma!* which had recently opened in London, and plays such as *The Hasty Heart* and *The First Gentleman* (a peculiarly appropriate title in light of Philip's future status). Princess Margaret, then fifteen, was in the party which went to see *The First Gentleman*. To make up the number, so was a World War II fighter ace who had been recently seconded from the Royal Air Force to serve the King as an equerry, Group Captain Peter

Townsend, a name which would figure large in royal history in the years to come.

Only on the dance floor, on such evenings, could Princess and Prince be briefly alone. To them, one of the hit songs from *Oklahoma!* – 'People will say we're in love' – quickly became 'our tune'. The Princess would request the band to play it for them. Philip bought her a recording of it which, in the privacy of her own room, she played over and over again until it was all but worn out. From time to time Philip also managed to contrive other occasions for them to be alone for an hour or so, taking the Princess for outings in his nippy little sports car, an MG. Accustomed to the greater spaciousness of her own Daimler, the Princess thought it was 'like sitting on the floor' the first time she squeezed into it. Such outings sometimes took them in the direction of Coppins in Buckinghamshire, home of the widowed Duchess of Kent, Princess Marina. A cousin of Prince Philip and keen to promote his suit, she was more understanding than most of their need to be alone together. So too, on her own admission was the royal governess, Marion Crawford, who would occasionally devise pretexts to get the teasing, chattering Margaret out of their way.

If occasional excursions to Coppins could be kept secret, theatre outings and such, with Prince Philip always forming one of the party, could not hope to go unnoticed. With the newspapers beginning to emerge from the pre-war awe with which they had always regarded the Royal Family, though not yet indulging in the far more blatant royal gossip of today, it was inevitable that they should speculate on the growing relationship. Four times between the tail-end of 1945 and the early months of 1947, one newspaper or another reported that betrothal was imminent – and four times the King caused an official denial to be issued. If such denials were perfectly truthful inasmuch as the King himself had yet to sanction a formal betrothal, those issued later were also misleading. Not that they were completely believed in all quarters. After the drab austerity of the war years, the nation was ready and eager for a royal wedding to brighten things up. Some tried to hurry it along. Teasing shouts of 'Where's Philip?' greeted the Princess on one of her public engagements, a factory visit. Many young women would have been delighted. She was not. It distressed her to realize that her romance, still a fragile thing at that stage, had become a subject of public gossip, and she returned to the Palace almost in tears. 'Poor Lilibet,' Princess Margaret sympathized. 'Nothing of your own – not even your love affairs.' If the Princess was upset by the turn matters were taking, so were others, though for different reasons. As one royal aide put it, 'There is too much talk and speculation. If there is not to be an engagement, the boy ought not to be around so much.'

The problem was that the King was torn, personally and politically. Personally, possessive as he was inclined to be of his elder daughter's affection, he had no great desire to surrender her to another man. But he was also sensible enough to realize that, sooner or later, surrender was inevitable, sensitive enough to be aware of her feelings for Philip, and a fair-minded man. More and more, as he came to know Philip, he came to realize that he was, as the King put it on one occasion, 'the right man for the job' – the job being that of husband to the Heir Presumptive and her Consort in the future when she became Queen. Having reconciled his feelings, the King faced up to the political issues, one of which was posed, even if she did not fully understand it, by Princess Margaret in conversation with her sister. 'He's not English,' it suddenly occurred to her. 'Does it make a difference?'

Indeed, it did. His years at boarding-school, at Dartmouth and in the Royal Navy had made Philip completely English in thought, word and deed. But by birth he was technically Greek, and a Prince of Greece at that. The one or two members of the Cabinet whom King George VI took into his confidence concerning his elder daughter's desire to marry Prince Philip expressed the view that the prospective bridegroom should become a naturalized British citizen before there was any betrothal announcement. The King agreed. So did Philip himself. In fact, with a view to obtaining a permanent, as distinct from a temporary wartime, commission in the Royal Navy, Philip had taken up the question of British citizenship some time before, only to discover that normal naturalization procedures had been suspended for the duration of the war.

What none of them realized – neither the King nor the Cabinet members in whom he confided nor Prince Philip – was that Philip, legally, was already a British citizen. The 1701 Act of Settlement, passed by Parliament in a hasty attempt to keep the Catholic heirs of James II from inheriting the throne, had ordained that the future line of succession should be through James I's granddaughter Sophia, Electress of Hanover, and 'the heirs of her body', all of whom would automatically enjoy British nationality. Philip, nearly two and a half centuries later, was one of those heirs, though it would be a further quarter-century before another of Sophia's many European descendants would finally establish their legal right to British nationality.

Unaware that he was already British by virtue of the Act of Settlement, Philip accepted the view that he should become a naturalized British citizen. With the war over and normal naturaliz-ation procedures again operative, it should have been no problem. For Philip there was problem after problem. Both the British government and the King of Greece, it seemed, were extremely anxious that he should remain Greek, at least for the time being. With civil war raging in Greece, the British government felt that granting citizenship to Philip might be seen as implying support for the royalists in Greece. The Greek King, conversely, thought that for his cousin to become British might be interpreted as abandoning the royalist cause in Greece.

Only with his cousin's consent could Philip forgo his title as a Prince of Greece. Only when he was no longer a Greek prince could he apply for British citizenship. And even then, with the British government opposed to such a step, the omens were not favourable. In vain he went to see his cousin, King George II, who was staying at Claridge's in London until the question of his return to Greece could be resolved. In vain the uncle who was like a surrogate father to him, now Earl Mountbatten of Burma, wrote to King George VI on his nephew's behalf. In vain Elizabeth herself appealed to her father. Philip's naturalization must wait. Any question of betrothal must wait.

The delay was keenly disappointing to two young people in love. Fair-minded as he was, the King sought to soften their disappointment by inviting Prince Philip to join the Royal Family at Balmoral that summer. Marion Crawford, in her memoirs, writes that Philip was invited to Balmoral simply as 'a young man they all liked who would make an amusing addition to the party'. Other writers since have interpreted that visit to Balmoral as being a test of suitability similar to that which Queen Victoria once imposed on those she thought might serve as royal sons-in-law or daughters-in-law. Neither assessment strikes quite the right note. Prince Philip, at that time, was already a great deal more than 'a young man they all liked'. The Princess was in love with him and he with her. The King already accepted him as a potential son-in-law, however far distant in the future. So the question of assessing his suitability did not arise. He went there as a suitor who would be unofficially engaged to the Princess, at least as far as she was concerned, before he left again.

At Balmoral, Prince Philip went stalking with the Princess and on the grouse moors with his prospective father-in-law. Also in the royal shooting party – yet another curious coincidence – was twenty-three-year-old Viscount Althorp, who would later become one of the King's equerries and, later still, would father a daughter named Diana who would grow up to become Princess of Wales. Like Princess Elizabeth, Prince Philip possessed no special clothes for such shooting and stalking excursions. Unlike her, he did not borrow from the King but made do with such few clothes as he had with him, flannel trousers, a sweater and his Navy walking-out shoes. The shoes, unfortunately, proved inadequate for the heathery Balmoral terrain, and there was a day when Philip had to content himself indoors while his shoes were taken to a cobbler to be repaired. The etiquette of the grouse moors, he found, was very different from what little rough shooting he had done previously, as witness the instance when he decided to change his position just as the King was about to let fly. The Queen's father was not the sort of man to mince his words in such circumstances because the offender was his potential son-in-law. For his part, Prince Philip, then and later, was always a little in awe of the King, never in his presence the sometimes arrogant young extrovert some others thought him at the time.

Philip stayed at Balmoral for a month. Again, there were few opportunities for him and the Princess to be alone together, though very occasionally they would manage an unchaperoned stroll in the gardens in the interval between afternoon tea and changing for dinner. But at some time in that month, in Balmoral Castle or the area around, they became unofficially 'engaged'. Or perhaps it would be more accurate to say that they reached an understanding of their future which included marriage. The exact when and where of their 'engagement', if that is what it was – no ring was given or accepted; that came much later – remains their secret. Some other writers have essayed a guess at the circumstances, saying that they became engaged beside 'some well-loved loch' or even purporting to know that it was Philip who did the proposing and that the Princess 'accepted him then and there'. It is quite possible that Prince Philip did propose formally. A young man accustomed to giving orders at sea, he is unlikely to have waited for Elizabeth to do so, Queen-to-be though she was, as Prince Albert of Saxe-Coburg-Gotha waited upon Queen Victoria. And it is probable that the Princess did accept immediately. As they both knew, Philip would have proposed – officially – and she would have accepted weeks before but for the stumbling blocks represented by the British government and the Greek King.

But stumbling blocks there still were in the way of turning their Balmoral tryst into formal betrothal. That the King was not one of them (though he may have been secretly pleased that his elder daughter would remain part of the family for a little longer) was shown when he invited Philip to join the family gathering at Sandringham that Christmas. The power struggle in Greece was temporarily over, and King George II had returned there following a plebiscite which came out in favour of the monarchy. But his position there was precarious, and he was still opposed to Philip surrendering his Greek title and becoming a British citizen in case such action might contribute towards plunging Greece back into civil war. In Britain, at the request of King George VI, Clement Attlee, who had succeeded Churchill as prime minister following the 1945 General Election, raised the question of the Heir Presumptive being betrothed to Prince Philip formally in Cabinet. There was no outright objection, but a deal of huffing and puffing. Ernest Bevin, the Foreign Secretary, thought it would be better if the formal announcement of betrothal was delayed until the British troops remaining in Greece had finally been withdrawn. There were also vague mutterings about Philip's three surviving sisters all being married to Germans, Britain's wartime enemies.

The Princess was naturally disappointed, and Philip doubtless frustrated, by the need for further delay. But delay fitted in well with the King's plans. He was eager to have his elder daughter with him, for the family unit to be still complete, when he made his forthcoming tour of South Africa. That the young couple's hopes and plans were moving, however slowly, towards fruition was seen when, two days before leaving for South Africa, the King and Queen along with their elder daughter dined with Earl and Countess Mountbatten and their nephew Philip at the Mountbatten home in Chester Street. The young couple, at least, saw the occasion as an unofficial engagement party. Indeed, the Princess seemed to think it would be followed by an immediate announcement of her betrothal. But her father, when she spoke to him about it the next day, shook his head. Betrothal could not be formally announced, would not become official, until their return from South Africa. Nor did he yield to her plea that Philip should be permitted to come to Portsmouth and see them off. For Philip to do that, the King pointed out, would inevitably attract the sort of attention it was most desirous to avoid.

In an endeavour to keep everything as low-key as possible, to avoid further speculation in the newspapers, it was arranged that Philip would shed his Greek title and take out British citizenship while the Princess and her family were absent from the country. The King offered him a British title to replace the Greek one, but Philip declined. He had had, for the moment, quite enough of being a prince. However, he would obviously need a surname. As a British citizen he could hardly go around signing himself simply 'Philip'. Initially he thought of calling himself Oldcastle, which the College of Heralds informed him was the anglicized version of Oldenburg, the German family back to which his ancestry could be traced. But Chuter Ede, the Home Secretary, had a better idea, and it was on his suggestion that Prince Philip decided to take the name of Mountbatten, his uncle's name and the anglicized version of his mother's maiden name of Battenberg.

On 1 February 1947, along with her parents and sister, Princess Elizabeth boarded the battleship she had named *Vanguard* on her earlier visit to Northern Ireland, for the voyage to South Africa. It was, with the aid of hindsight, a tour the King should never have undertaken, involving as it did some ten thousand miles of overland travel, public engagements in forty-one cities and towns and visits to three British protectorates as well as a week spent in what was then still Southern Rhodesia. It was hardly the sort of trip to benefit a man of always uncertain health whose constitution had been further undermined by the stress and strain of the war

86

years. But dutiful as always, the King insisted upon going, hoping that his personal presence might help to resolve the acute political differences that had arisen in South Africa. The result of such an arduous tour on such a frail physique was almost predictable. His health worsened as the tour progressed and, by the time it was over, he had lost seventeen pounds in weight. With his wife constantly worried about him, with their elder daughter pining for the absent Philip, the younger daughter was often at a loose end. The same royal equerry who had accompanied the two Princesses to *The First Gentleman* was assigned to keep her amused, Peter Townsend.

That the royal tour of South Africa would have such far-reaching consequences in two very different directions, on the King's health and the emotions of Princess Margaret, was by no means apparent at the time. Behind them they left the hardest winter Britain had known for nearly seventy years, a winter during which the severity of the weather was compounded by a shortage of coal and the continued rationing of food, both the aftermath of World War II. Far from feeling themselves well out of it, both the King and his elder daughter experienced a sense of guilt at being 'right away from it all and enjoying ourselves so much'. The words are those of the daughter. In fact, initially, she did not enjoy herself. Philip's photograph on the dressing-table in her cabin was little consolation for his absence. Missing him, she too lost weight. She wrote to him constantly. However, she brightened considerably when word came through that Mountbatten, Philip, Greek by birth, a serving officer in His Majesty's Forces currently residing at 16 Chester Street, London SW1 (the Mountbatten residence), being possessed of an adequate knowledge of the English language and being financially solvent, had been granted British nationality. Another hurdle in the way of betrothal had been finally and successfully overcome.

From then on, and the more so as the tour progressed and reunion with Philip loomed ever nearer, she did enjoy herself to a large extent. Sometimes flying – she made her first ever flight in South Africa – and sometimes travelling by the luxurious 'White Train', specially built for the royal visit, she saw for the first time the grandeur and rugged beauty of southern Africa, from Table Mountain to the Victoria Falls. Though she accompanied her parents for the most part, she also had her own smaller quota of public engagements. In East London she opened a new graving dock. At a parade of Basuto Girl Guides she noticed a small contingent kept apart from the rest. She asked about them, found out that they were lepers and insisted on going over to talk to them.

There was all the excitement too of her twenty-first birthday. Gifts poured in. Since she was in diamond-mining country, it was only to be expected that many of the gifts would be in diamond form, two superb blue-white stones from De Beers, a casket of diamonds in East London, yet another casket of them in Cape Town. Those gifts formed the basis of the huge and highly valuable collection of jewels she possesses today. She was in Cape Town on her twenty-first birthday. It was celebrated in style, with a military parade in the morning, a youth rally in the afternoon and a radio broadcast from Government House in the evening. It was in that broadcast that she dedicated her life to the service of monarchy. 'I declare before you all,' she said, 'that my whole life, whether it be long or short, shall be devoted to your service and the service of the great Imperial Commonwealth to which we all belong. But I shall not have the strength to carry out this resolution unless you join in it with me, as I now invite you to do. I know that your support will be unfailingly given. God bless all of you who are willing to share it.'

The words were not actually her own. They were written for her by her father's Private Secretary, Alan Lascelles. But they came so close to expressing what she felt that, reading them through beforehand, she was so moved that she could not hold back her tears. Thirty years later, celebrating her Silver Jubilee in 1977, she was to recall that day of her twenty-first birthday and those words of dedication. 'Although that vow was made in my salad days, when I was green in judgement,' she said, 'I do not regret or retract one word of it.'

It was 11 May 1947 when *Vanguard* docked back in Britain. So delighted was the Princess to be home again, so overjoyed at the prospect of seeing Philip again, that she performed a jigging little dance on deck for all to see. Philip was not there to greet her – her father was still anxious to avoid headlines in the newspapers – but they had dinner together later. And still their betrothal could not be officially announced. There were formalities to be gone through first, the countries of the Commonwealth to be 'consulted'.

During this period of further delay, Philip was in and out of the Palace all the time, parking his MG in the inner courtyard, sometimes tinkering with the engine, slipping into the Palace itself by a little-used door and taking the flights of red-carpeted stairs two and three at a time. Young and athletic as he was, he scorned to use the lift. He took the Princess to meet his mother, who was now in London and staying with her mother, the Dowager Marchioness of Milford Haven, at an apartment in Kensington Palace. When his parents separated, Philip's mother had gone first to live with one of her daughters in Germany while his father headed for the warmer climes of the south of France, where he died in 1944. The war years found Philip's mother back in Greece where she undertook relief work and established a small hostel for war orphans. Later still, she moved to one of the Greek islands where she founded the religious order known as the Sisterhood of Martha and Mary, and she was wearing the grey robes of the order when the Princess met her for the first time that day at Kensington Palace.

To mark the Heir Presumptive's return from South Africa, along with her coming-of-age, she was presented with the Freedom of the City of London. And that year, for the first time, she had a part to play in the annual ceremony of Trooping the Colour. Those earlier lessons in riding side-saddle came into their own as, instead of looking on from the comfort of a carriage, she rode proudly at her father's side in a feminine version of the uniform of the Grenadier Guards.

On 8 July it was plainly obvious to the few who glimpsed the Princess as she darted about the Palace that something very unusual was in the offing. 'She was as excited as I ever knew her to be,' recalls one who saw her that day. The reason for her excitement did not become clear until evening, when Philip arrived yet again at the Palace. But this time his visit was different from those that had gone before. He had a suitcase with him. He was staying the night. The Buhl Suite at the front of the palace had been prepared for him, a choice of accommodation with which he was not altogether happy once he realized that the Victoria Memorial, just beyond the palace gates, afforded an excellent vantage point for an enterprising photographer. 'I think we had better keep the curtains drawn,' he said to the footman who had been assigned to act as his valet. If it was framed as a suggestion, it was tantamount to an order and was duly carried out. In curtained privacy Philip lit his last cigarette. He had promised the Princess he would give up smoking.

The following day, while Philip was being measured for new suits, new shoes and a new topper, the Princess, in the company of her parents, went to the International Horse Show. That evening there was a family dinner party to celebrate betrothal, though the world outside the palace gates was not yet aware that the Princess was formally betrothed. She looked flushed and excited, proudly displaying her engagement ring. The gems of the engagement ring, a square-cut solitaire diamond set amidst a cluster of smaller diamonds, had come from a ring Philip's mother had been given by his father a generation before. Philip had had them furnished with a new platinum setting which proved to be not quite the right size, as the Princess demonstrated by spinning the ring round and round on her finger. It was later returned to the jeweller to be altered.

At half-past midnight came the official announcement, which had been issued to the BBC, the newspapers and overseas news agencies five hours earlier but embargoed until then. It was brief and straightforward. 'It is with the greatest pleasure that the King and Queen announce the betrothal of their dearly-beloved daughter The Princess Elizabeth to Lieutenant Philip Mountbatten RN, son of the late Prince Andrew of Greece and Princess Andrew (Princess Alice of Battenberg), to which union the King has gladly given his consent.' The long wait was finally at an end.

The following day was a crowded one for the betrothed couple. They posed for photographers in the morning, went to Marlborough House to see Queen Mary in the afternoon and appeared together on the Palace's famous balcony in the evening after hearing the announcement of their betrothal read on the nine o'clock news. Next day brought a royal garden party at which they made their first public appearance (apart from appearing on the palace balcony) as an engaged couple. It was Philip's first experience as the 'star' of a public function, and he was tense with nerves as he escorted the Princess through the ranks of assembled guests. A friend of the King commented that they made a very handsome couple and that Philip was indeed a fortunate young man.

'I hope he realizes what he's taking on,' replied the King. 'One day Lilibet will be Queen and he will be Consort. And that's a much harder job than being King.'

7 THE YOUNG BRIDE

For the Princess, the next few months passed quickly in a whirl of wedding preparations. Of these, the most important was her wedding dress, the design and manufacture of which was entrusted to Norman Hartnell, who had also made the bridesmaid's dress she wore at the wedding of her uncle, the Duke of Gloucester, twelve years before. To ensure that no cut-price mass-produced copies were on sale in the shops ahead of the wedding, work on the ivory satin creation with its embroidered garlands of York roses worked in raised pearls was carried out behind whitewashed windows. At the end of each day Hartnell's design was carefully locked away in his office safe and, as yet an additional precaution, a camp-bed was installed so that his workroom manager could sleep on the premises. Odd as it may seem all these years later, there was considerable concern in that fervently patriotic postwar era that the silk used for the dress should not be spun by 'enemy' silkworms bred in Italy or Japan. Certainly not, Hartnell hastily assured the nation. They were 'friendly' silkworms from Nationalist China.

Although World War II had been over for two years, clothes rationing was still in force. However, the Princess – 'in common with other brides', as Buckingham Palace was at pains to point out – was allotted some extra clothing coupons to enable her to shop for her trousseau. In the event, the extra coupons were hardly needed as gifts of material and clothing, including scores of pairs of those new nylon stockings which Queen Mary thought 'rather cold to wear', poured in from all over the world, and some of the rooms at the Palace looked like nothing so much as the clothing section of a big departmental store. Such was the affection in which the Princess was held that loyal subjects were willing to sacrifice even their own clothing coupons to ensure that she lacked nothing. But these were scrupulously returned to the senders.

Wedding gifts of all sorts similarly arrived in an endless stream, among them a lump of Welsh gold to be fashioned into the wedding ring. More than enough for a single ring. 'We can save a piece for Margaret,' the elder sister said, delightedly. And not only for Margaret. That gift of gold would be stretched down the years to provide wedding rings also for Princess Anne and the Princess of Wales. Previously it had always been an unwritten rule that gifts on the occasion of royal weddings were accepted only from donors actually known to the Royal Family. But there had never before been such an avalanche, and the task of returning all those that did not come within this category would have been formidable, if not impossible. So it was decided to accept them all, with the result that a final total of 2,660 gifts went on display at St James's Palace, with the money paid in admission fees going to charity. They ranged from a diamond and sapphire necklace with matching ear-rings given to the bride by her father to a wastepaper basket from the devoted Bobo, from a picnic set from Princess Margaret to a piece of linen woven by Mahatma Gandhi, from a mink coat to a sewing machine. There was a thirteen-piece set of Sheraton furniture from the City of London and a thirty-piece dressing-table set in silver gilt from the Diplomatic Corps. Nor was Philip forgotten. For him there were, among other things, a pair of Purdey guns (from the King), two sailing dinghies and a walking-stick. The Princess hoped to wear or use 'everything', she said, enthusiastically. Though it was a commitment she could not hope to fulfil in its entirety, many of those wedding gifts have continued in use down the years. The silver gilt dressing-table set, for instance, still travels with her wherever she goes.

Philip had not yet taken up polo. So there was no risk, as there would be years later with Prince Charles, that he might turn up for the wedding ceremony in bandages following a mishap on the polo field. But he was a fast and impetuous driver, a fact which found him telephoning the Princess one night to say that he had had an accident on his way back to Corsham, the naval base where he was an instructor. He had, in fact, overturned his car and ended up in a ditch, fortunately unhurt. Shortly after he was in collision with a taxi at Hyde Park Corner. The Princess was with him on that occasion, and there was concern for her future safety if Philip's driving record did not improve. 'It really wasn't his fault,' she assured her parents. Royal chauffeurs were also worried at the possibility of damage to their Daimlers if Philip continued his practice, revealed for the first time when he toured the Isle of Arran with his bride-to-be and her parents, of ordering the chauffeur into the back seat and doing the driving himself.

The Archbishop of Canterbury, who would officiate at the wedding ceremony, had a small worry of his own. In his view, the bridegroom, for all that he was now a British citizen, was still a member of the Greek Orthodox Church. The news came as a surprise to Philip. From schooldays he had always thought of himself as being Church of England. The matter was resolved in a private ceremony at Lambeth Palace which saw Philip's religion 'nationalized' as effectively as his citizenship had been. Philip himself was inclined to look upon the whole business as something of a joke. 'It isn't everyone who gets married within a couple of months of being baptized,' he quipped.

For his part, the King, with his fastidious attitude towards such things as titles, order of precedence and uniforms – after the wedding he would complain about an admiral who had attended the ceremony minus his dress sword – was concerned that his elder daughter would be marrying a mere junior naval officer, now that Philip was no longer a Prince of Greece. She would, of course, retain her own royal title, but Princess Elizabeth, Mrs Philip Mountbatten, though the equivalent would later seem acceptable enough to her daughter, did not in those more title-conscious days of the 1940s seem appropriate to a Princess who was also Heir Presumptive. Philip had earlier, at the time of taking British citizenship, declined the King's offer of a British title. Now, with the wedding day fast approaching, the King renewed his offer and, this time, Philip accepted. Accordingly, Lieutenant Philip Mountbatten became His Royal Highness The Duke of Edinburgh, Earl of Merioneth and Baron Greenwich, a triple title which shared him out neatly between Scotland, Wales and England. He also created Philip a Royal Knight of the Most Noble Order of the Garter, Britain's highest order of chivalry, while being careful to date this new honour four days after the award of a similar honour to his elder daughter, thus making it clear that in this, as in many other things, the wife, as Heir Presumptive, ranked ahead of the husband.

As it happened, the new titles bestowed on the bridegroom came too late for inclusion in the wedding programme, which was already at the printers, so that Philip would be described in that merely as Lieutenant Philip Mountbatten RN. And for all his concern over the niceties of title and precedence, the King would seem to have been guilty of a small lapse in that he did not make Philip a Prince. It may have been that he thought that the style of His Royal Highness was synonymous with the title of Prince (which, with everyone continuing to refer to him as 'Prince Philip', the public certainly seemed to think). Or, yet again, it may have been another royal device to ensure that the husband ranked, however fractionally, below the wife; that while she would continue to be a Princess, he would not be a Prince. However it happened, whatever was or was not in the King's mind, it would be left to the wife, several years after she became Queen, finally to make her husband a Prince of the United Kingdom.

As on the occasion of her father's coronation, the Princess was awake early on 20 November 1947, her wedding morning, jumping out of bed and donning a dressing-gown to peer out of a window at the crowds already massing beyond the palace railings. She was as excited as any other young bride on her wedding day. 'I can't believe it's really happening,' she said. 'I have to keep pinching myself.' She was also nervous, so pale that Bobo and others, at one point, became momentarily 'alarmed' for her. Three of Hartnell's assistants helped her into her wedding dress.

If the bride was understandably nervous, the Duke of Edinburgh (as Philip now was) was equally edgy, even touchy, as he donned naval uniform and buckled on his dead grandfather's dress sword in his grandmother's apartment at Kensington Palace. A stag party the night before had caused him to oversleep and his best man, David Milford Haven, suggested that 'a hair of the dog that bit him' might help. Philip agreed to the extent of sipping a small sherry. Despite oversleeping, he was ready with time to spare. He and Milford Haven were on their way out to the waiting car when a cautionary headshake from the duty police officer warned them that they were too early and they retreated inside again.

At Buckingham Palace, a series of unfortunate mishaps served to increase the bride's highly nervous state as time ticked away towards her long-awaited appointment at Westminster Abbey. She wanted very much to wear the pearls her parents had given her as one of their wedding gifts and was disappointed to learn that they were on display with other gifts at St James's Palace. John Colville, her Private Secretary, went to fetch them for her, but inevitably this meant delay. There was further delay when the tiara she had borrowed from her mother specially for the occasion broke as it was being fixed into place and a jeweller had to be contacted to repair it. It came as almost the last straw when, only minutes before she was to leave for the Abbey, her bridal spray was nowhere to be found. By the time it came to light (a servant had placed it in a refrigerator to keep the orchids fresh) she was in such a state of nerves that her father, like the bridegroom's best man, suggested a quick drink. 'Oh, I couldn't,' she said.

The Archbishop of York, in his address at the wedding ceremony, looked upon it as 'exactly the same as it would be for any cottager who might be married this afternoon in some small country church'. In spirit, doubtless it was, but the actuality was very different. The setting was not 'a small country church' but Westminster Abbey. The ceremony was witnessed by a greater gathering of royalty (even if many of them were royalties in exile) than had gathered for the King's coronation. Present were the Kings and Queens of Denmark and Yugoslavia, the Kings of Norway, Romania and Iraq, the Queen of the Hellenes, Queen Helen of Romania, Queen Victoria Eugénie of Spain, the Prince Regent of Belgium, the Princess Regent and Prince Bernhardt of the Netherlands, the Crown Prince and Princess of Sweden, Prince Jean and Princess Elisabeth of Luxembourg, the Count and Countess of Barcelona, and the Duchess of Aosta. Notably absent were Prince and Princess Gottfried of Hohenlohe-Langenburg, the Margrave and Margravine of Baden, and Prince and Princess Georg of Hanover. As citizens of Germany, the old enemy, they had not been invited despite the fact that they were the bridegroom's sisters and brothers-in-law. However, to ease hurt feelings, Philip's cousin, the widowed Duchess of Kent, flew to Germany shortly afterwards with an album of wedding photographs.

Unlike her unborn son, who a generation later would elect to be married in the princely style of 'Charles P.', the Heir Presumptive of 1947 was married in her full maiden name of Elizabeth Alexandra Mary Windsor. Unlike her future daughter-in-law, Diana, her marriage vows included a promise to love, honour *and obey* her husband.

There were more small mishaps during the actual ceremony. A six-year-old page, Prince William of Gloucester (who would die so tragically at the age of thirty*), tripped and would have fallen if Princess Margaret, in her role of chief bridesmaid, had not caught him. The bride's train snagged on the steps of the altar, and it took the combined efforts of the King and the best man, David Milford Haven, to free it.

Leaving the vestry on the arm of her new husband, the Princess paused briefly and curtsied to her parents. It was her own small, unexpected, unrehearsed addition to the proceedings, and the King, in particular, was deeply moved. Back at the Palace after the ceremony, there was the traditional appearance on the balcony for the benefit of the excited, cheering crowd beyond the palace railings. But there was no display of affection, no kissing, as there would be with Charles and Diana a generation later. Such public display of private emotions was unthinkable to the Royal Family of 1947.

In keeping with the austerity of the times, the wedding feast was limited to fillet of sole followed by casseroled partridge, with ice cream to conclude. Hardly a banquet, even if it was served on gold plates.

The family flocked into the courtyard to watch the bride and groom climb into the landau which would take them to Waterloo Station, where their honeymoon train awaited them. No one dreamed of fixing a 'Just Married' notice to the rear of the landau. That too was unthinkable in 1947. The scattering of a few rose petals was high jinks enough. The bride's latest corgi, Susan, travelled with them. Also hidden in the landau against the rawness of that November day was a hot water bottle. Their luggage had already been loaded aboard the royal train, a collection of fifteen suitcases holding the bride's trousseau while the Duke of Edinburgh, as Philip now was, made do with two. The crowd lining

* Elder brother of the present Duke of Gloucester, he was killed when his plane crashed on take-off during an air race in 1972.

97

the route roared its enthusiasm as the landau clip-clopped along the Mall and turned into Whitehall. If some members of the Labour government of the day were concerned that the costly spectacle of a royal wedding was hardly in keeping with the austerity of the postwar era, others saw it differently. The general public, grudging not a penny of the cost, saw it as Winston Churchill did: 'A joyous event; a flash of colour on the hard road we have to travel.' So busy was the Duke acknowledging the tumultuous reception the newlyweds were accorded that he failed to notice that the landau was approaching the Cenotaph, that sad reminder to the British dead of two world wars. But the long training of the Heir Presumptive saw her give him a timely nudge and, in the nick of time, he raised his hand in salute.

The newlyweds passed their first night together in the spacious privacy of Broadlands, the Mountbatten residence in Hampshire, which was placed at their disposal by Philip's uncle and aunt. A generation later their eldest son and his bride would similarly spend their first night there. Profiting perhaps from the experience of his parents, the Prince of Wales, in 1981, did not remain at Broadlands with his bride over the period of a weekend. The newlyweds of 1947 did, a fact which imposed upon them an obligation to attend Sunday morning service in nearby Romsey Abbey. The result was near-chaos. So eager were people to catch a glimpse of the newlyweds that chairs, step-ladders and even a sideboard were manhandled into position to serve as viewing platforms. The more curious even pressed their faces against the abbey windows in an endeavour to see inside while the service was in progress. A switch to Birkhall, on the royal estate in Scotland, enabled the couple to pass the second half of their honeymoon in greater privacy, though bad weather marred their stay there and the bride found herself playing nurse to a husband who had developed a heavy head-cold.

Delighted though she was to be married to Philip at long last, the bride did not forget the parents to whom she was so close. Indeed, in a letter to her mother she wrote that the long period she and Philip had had to wait had probably been for the best. The letter brought a reply from her father saying how glad he was that she did not think he had been 'hard-hearted' about things. The King's letter was tender-hearted in the extreme, the letter of a devoted husband and doting father, a family man who wrote of 'the great blank in our lives' which had resulted from their daughter leaving home.

For the newlyweds, there was the problem of finding a home of their own. If they had less difficulty than many ordinary newlyweds were experiencing in an era of housing shortage, things were by no means straightforward. The King had earlier offered them the tenancy of Sunninghill Park, a house in his gift near Ascot. The place was in a sorry state of repair following occupation by the military during the war and disuse since, with a bunch of squatters having moved into the old Nissen huts in the grounds, and the Duke was not over-enthused by the prospect of living there. Nevertheless, work of repair and renovation was put in hand to make the place habitable, but the project came to an abrupt halt when the building was mysteriously gutted by fire.

As a stop-gap measure, the couple moved into an apartment at Kensington Palace, loaned to them by Princess Alice and the Earl of Athlone while they were away in South Africa. As a naval officer, the Duke was transferred to a desk job at the Admiralty, going back and forth much like any other young husband except that there was necessarily a deal of time off for the public engagements which now came his way as the King's son-in-law. Like any other young bride, the Princess delighted in 'playing house' and was never happier than when the servants had a day off. On those days she would do the cooking herself and husband and wife would share the chore of washing up. Years later, as Queen, she would surprise at least one of her prime ministers, Harold Wilson, by personally grilling him a steak when he stayed with her at Balmoral.

By the time the Athlones returned to Britain, the Princess already knew that she was pregnant, though the public was not to be let into the secret for some time to come. It was the King's wish that his first grandchild should be born under his own roof. To please him, the couple moved to Buckingham Palace, with Princess Margaret obligingly vacating the old nursery so that it could be turned into a private apartment for her sister and brother-in-law. Weekends were spent at Windlesham Moor, a mansion at Ascot which they rented part-furnished from the widow of the financier Philip Hill. The upkeep of this establishment quickly emphasized the difference in status between wife and husband. Parliament had voted the Princess an allowance of £40,000 a year on marriage but granted the Duke only £10,000 a year. Nevertheless, he insisted that it was for him, as the husband, to meet the cost of running Windlesham Moor. Even in 1948, when things were considerably cheaper, it quickly proved impossible for him to meet the outgoings of a mansion so large that the drawing-room alone extended to fifty feet, and to upkeep grounds of around fifty acres, and the Princess quietly met some of the bills with her own cheques. There was also some small embarrassment on the occasion of a house-warming party. They had engaged a butler, but no footmen – 'We don't need them,' the Duke insisted – and, in consequence, the detective inspector assigned to protect them found himself pressed into service as washer-up. After that, the Princess insisted on engaging two footmen, paying their salaries herself.

For her, this was to be one of the most idyllic periods of her life, comparable to those childhood days at 145 Piccadilly when 'the sun always seemed to be shining' and those carefree days as a naval wife in Malta which were still to come. She was married to the man she loved, back home living with the parents she also loved, and pregnancy, as yet, was causing no inconvenience. The only small ripple to disturb the otherwise tranquil surface of married life stemmed from the fact that her new husband and her old nanny, now fulfilling the role of her personal maid, still did not quite take to each other, and it was at times as though they were in competition for her attention and affection.

Under Philip's influence, the Princess emerged from her hitherto serious shell. Squeals of delight would escape her at his rather schoolboyish practical jokes, and there are servants' tales of her dashing from their bedroom in nightgown and négligé, with Philip, in pyjamas and bathrobe, whooping in pursuit. She, in turn, teased him over the way he worried about his weight and jogged methodically round the grounds in an endeavour to sweat off a few pounds. Like all young brides, she was eager to please her husband, even to the extent of bowling to him so that he could practise his batting. She was eager too to make amends to his sisters for the way they had been slighted over the wedding and had two of them, at different times, to stay at Windlesham Moor.

With Michael Parker, an old naval comrade of the Duke's who was now serving as his equerry, to make a trio, husband and wife

(*right*) Like any mother, Elizabeth keeps a tight grip on Andrew near water

(*below*) Waiting for the Balmoral train at Euston: Andrew handles the corgis while young Edward tugs at his mother's hand

Growing informality:
Meeting the Mounties at Prince Edward Island in 1964, and (*above right*)
New Zealand walkabout at the West Coast Industries Fair at Greymouth
in 1970

The Investiture of her eldest son as Prince
of Wales, 1969

A Silver Wedding portrait

Family Reunions:
The Queen and Prince Philip had tea with the Duke and Duchess of
Windsor in Paris in 1972
(*Below*) Anne married Captain Mark Phillips the following year

25 years a Queen:
Walkabout in London and laying
a wreath at the Cenotaph on
Remembrance Sunday

Formal occasions:
Lord Mountbatten's funeral and (*below*) the Queen as Head of the Commonwealth with her High Commissioners, 1984

(*Opposite*) The Queen wore long coverall dresses—this one is of sapphire silk—on her tour of the Gulf in 1979. Here she meets King Khalid of Saudi Arabia

went along to a fancy dress ball given by the US ambassador as 'the waiter and the porter and the upstairs maid'. For another fancy dress occasion, at the home of Philip's cousin, Princess Marina, the Princess wore the black lace, mantilla and hair-comb of a Spanish *señora* while the Duke pranced around as a policeman with jangling handcuffs. There was also a visit to Paris which, in that far less permissive era, aroused criticism back home because they went horse-racing and night-clubbing on the sabbath.

It was not until after the Paris visit, during which the Princess felt faint while laying a wreath at the Arc de Triomphe and the Duke had to go to her aid, that the public was let in on the secret of pregnancy. Even then, after the royal custom of the time, the announcement was made only obliquely. It did not actually say that she was expecting a baby, as more recent announcements concerning the Princess of Wales have done; merely that she would 'undertake no public engagements after the end of June'. However, a delighted public had no difficulty in interpreting what that meant.

So it was a happily expectant Princess who, along with her husband, accompanied her parents to Balmoral that year for the customary long summer vacation. But unknown to her, fate was already casting a long and ominous shadow. During that stay at Balmoral, in the course of grouse shooting, the King more than once complained of pain in his legs. He put it down to cramp. In fact, as later X-rays and blood tests would reveal, it was arteriosclerosis (hardening of the arteries) so severe that at one point amputation of one leg was under consideration by royal physicians. The Duke was told of his father-in-law's condition, but not the Princess. Devoted father that he was, the King insisted that his elder daughter must go into childbirth with an untroubled mind, that she must know nothing until after her baby had been born.

There was no question in those days, as there would be with Princess Anne and the Princess of Wales a generation later, of the father witnessing the baby's birth, holding his wife's hand as she went into labour. Instead, as his first child was being born in an outsize bathroom at the palace which had been converted for use

Opposite: Marcus Sarjeant fired blanks at the Queen in 1981 as she rode to the Trooping of the Colour.

as a labour ward, the Duke was engaged in an energetic game of squash with Michael Parker, followed by a cooling dip in the palace pool. Shirt-sleeved, he joined his royal in-laws in their private sitting-room to await news of his wife and child. But one big step forward in royal childbirth had already been taken. There was no Home Secretary hovering around to authenticate the birth. The King had had quite enough of that anachronistic nonsense and had brought it to an end.

Told that his wife had given birth to a son, the Duke was as elated as anyone has ever seen him. He dashed along to the delivery room to see mother and baby, dashed away again, came hurrying back with a big bunch of roses and carnations for the Princess, ordered bottles of champagne to be opened in celebration and insisted on everyone in the vicinity, even down to a footman who chanced to be passing at the time, having a drink to 'wet the baby's head'.

The Princess followed her mother's example by breast-feeding her baby. She was particularly fascinated by the infant's fine hands and long fingers, quite unlike either her own or her husband's. 'It will be interesting to see what will become of them,' she commented. As we now know, they would become musical enough to play the cello and artistic enough to paint in water-colours, though neither talent would be developed to its full potential. Queen Mary, when she first saw her great-grandson, detected a resemblance to Queen Victoria's husband, the Prince Consort. The Duke, a few months later, joked that the baby looked like nothing so much as 'a plum pudding'.

It was the Duke who suggested that the boy should be called Charles in place of one of the more traditional royal names. The King bestowed on him the title of Prince . . . in the nick of time. It was only five days before the baby's birth (as things turned out) when it occurred to the King that royal titles could not be transmitted through the female line. As things stood, that meant that his first grandchild would not be a Prince or Princess unless he did something about it. What he did was issue a royal edict decreeing that children born to his elder daughter (though not the younger) should have the same titles they would have had if it had been their father instead of their mother who was in the line of succession.

Queen Victoria's christening robe was again brought out of storage and the Prince Consort's gold lily font again fetched from Windsor for the christening ceremony at Buckingham Palace. The high-bodied perambulator in which the Princess herself was wheeled around in babyhood was refurbished for walks in the palace gardens. Her baby's crib, hairbrush and silver rattle were similarly souvenirs of her own babyhood.

Her schedule of breast-feeding ended abruptly during the customary visit to Sandringham that Christmas. The Princess succumbed to what proved to be measles, and it was deemed wise for mother and baby to be kept apart until she was well again and the danger of infection past. When and to what extent she was told of her father's far more serious ill-health is uncertain. A plan for the King and Queen to tour Australia and New Zealand had had to be postponed – and would now never take place – and in February 1949 a lumbar sympathectomy was performed in the same room at the palace in which, three months before, his daughter had given birth to her first child. The operation was a success, but the strain of it undermined the King's fragile health still further and left him with only four years to live.

The Princess and her husband had realized earlier that the start of a family necessitated a home of their own. The Princess wanted to remain as close as possible to her parents, and the nearest available property was Clarence House (today the home of the Queen Mother). Like Sunninghill Park, it had precious little to commend it when the couple carried out their first inspection. Occupied by the Red Cross until it was bomb-damaged in wartime and unused since, it was in a sorry state of neglect, much of its roof gone and its rooms heaped with rubble. But it was only just down the road from the Palace. So they decided on it and the work of renovation was put in hand. With the baby's birth adding urgency to their desire for an establishment of their own, though perhaps more on the part of the Duke than the Princess, they were soon visiting Clarence House every day, and sometimes twice a day, to see how the work of repair and renovation was coming along. One such visit even saw the Princess mixing some paint to show the decorators the exact shade of green she wanted in the Adam-style dining-room.

The baby was nearly eight months old before the work of

restoring Clarence House was completed at a cost of £55,000. So eager was the Duke to move in that moving day found him divesting himself of his jacket and lending the removal men a hand. For the first time in the nearly two years they had been married they were able to see many of their wedding gifts in a proper setting, the two settees and eight matching armchairs from the City of London, the eighteenth-century mahogany dining-table and its twenty ladder-backed chairs from the Royal Warrant Holders' Association, the mahogany sideboard and side tables given to them by Queen Mary, the Hepplewhite cabinet which no fewer than forty-seven members of the Royal Family had clubbed together to buy them. But into the baby's nursery went some old favourite items, the fruitwood table the Princess had had in her own nursery as far back as 145 Piccadilly, the glass-fronted cabinet holding the glass and porcelain miniatures she had collected since she grew too old to collect toy horses, and, most important, her old rocking horse.

Having been brought up by a nanny herself, the Princess was quite happy to leave her baby in the care of another, Helen Lightbody, who had been previously with the Duke and Duchess of Gloucester. But while well content to leave nursery routine in such capable hands, the Princess was new enough to motherhood to be constantly in and out of the nursery herself, playing with baby, helping to feed him at meal-times, donning a waterproof apron to give him his bath. The Duke too was happy and eager to share the fun of baby's bath-time.

Just as her own mother had been obliged to leave her when she was small, the Princess was often parted from her baby by the necessity to fulfil public commitments (though never for so long as those months in 1927 when her parents were away in Australia and New Zealand). Before and after the move into Clarence House, she and her husband carried out a succession of visits to Scotland, Wales, Northern Ireland and the Channel Islands. The crossing to the Channel Islands was so rough that the Princess was seasick. Even so, she refused to entertain a suggestion that she should cancel her intended visit to Sark because of the bad weather and went there on a day when the sea was so turbulent that she had difficulty in getting ashore. Indeed, but for the Duke's sea-going experience she might never have made it. Three times she tried to jump ashore from the heaving deck of the torpedo boat in which she made the crossing, and three times she failed. Then the Duke, judging his moment with experienced precision, gave her a push which landed her safely in the arms of a royal aide already on the quayside. Having a husband at her side proved helpful in other ways too. When her shyness caused her to dry up in conversation, a not infrequent occurrence in those early days, the Duke was quickly at her side, his effervescent nature and chatty manner quickly bridging what could have been an embarrassing silence.

'Independence Day', the Duke had joked when they moved into Clarence House on 4 July, a date celebrated by Americans if not by the British. Independence was something of which he was more and more beginning to feel the need. Experience of life so far, including wartime sea-going in the Royal Navy, had hardly conditioned him for the sort of role, a mixture of royal engagements and desk-work at the Admiralty, he was now required to play. He did what was required of him conscientiously and dutifully enough, while all the time longing for something more active, even more adventurous. Finally he sought the King's permission to resume an active naval career. Permission was granted, and in the autumn of 1949 the Duke flew out to Malta to join the Mediterranean Fleet as second-in-command of the destroyer *Chequers*.

While she understood her husband's desire, even *need*, to lead a more active life, to return to the sea, the Princess was unsettled at being separated from him. She was torn between a desire to be with her husband and an equal desire to remain with her baby, not yet a year old. The idea that all three of them could be together in Malta does not seem to have occurred to her. Or if it did, perhaps she was counselled that the experience would be too unsettling or the Maltese climate too unhealthy for so young a child. She solved the problem, as young mothers have always done and still do, by getting her parents to take temporary charge of the baby while she flew out to join her husband in time to celebrate their second wedding anniversary together. Assured that the baby was getting along fine in her absence, she decided to stay on in Malta over Christmas.

She returned home to find the baby well and thriving, too young still to have really missed her. Satisfied with the success of the experiment, she flew out again to Malta to spend her twenty-fourth

105

birthday with her husband. There was an extra cause for celebration too that birthday, the knowledge that on her earlier visit to the island she had again become pregnant. Those spells in Malta would remain in her memory as the nearest she ever came, or ever would come, to living an ordinary life. For the first time she was free to do almost as she liked without the inhibitions of royal protocol, free to come and go as she wished without the clock-watching requirements of public engagements. She drove round the island in her own car, shopped at market stalls, sat beside other naval wives in a local salon to have her hair done. When the Duke was free from naval duties, they swam and sun-tanned together, picnicked in isolated coves, dined by candlelight at a local hotel. She watched the Duke play his first, and rather inexpert, games of polo, springing to her feet, her face draining of colour, when he was thrown by the polo pony she had bought him as a Christmas gift.

She returned to Britain in good time for the birth of her second baby. The Duke, with some leave due to him, flew home to be on hand if not actually with her when the baby was born at Clarence House on 15 August 1950. It was a girl, and they decided to name her Anne, with no objections from King George VI as his father had objected when the same name (minus the final *e*) was originally proposed for Princess Margaret. His duty as a father temporarily complete, the Duke returned to Malta and naval duty, this time as lieutenant-commander of his own ship, the frigate *Magpie*. Later in the year, leaving both her children in the care of her parents, the Princess again flew out to join him in Malta and spend Christmas with him.

On her first visit to Malta the Princess had stayed with the Duke's uncle, Earl Mountbatten (at that time commanding the first cruiser squadron in the Mediterranean) and Countess Mountbatten at their home, the Villa Guardamangia, near Pieta. Later, when the Mountbattens left Malta, she and the Duke rented the villa for themselves, shipping out their own china, glassware, cutlery and linen from Clarence House. They looked forward to a long stay, with the Villa Guardamangia serving them in the nature of a second home. But they had reckoned without the King's failing health.

8 HER FATHER'S DEPUTY

King George VI's life was a constant battle against ill-health. He was never a completely well person. In boyhood he suffered from knock knees to a degree which necessitated wearing corrective splints. Fear of his father compounded by being forced to use his right hand when he was naturally left-handed caused him to stammer. As a Dartmouth cadet and World War I naval officer he suffered successively from influenza, pneumonia, appendicitis and gastritis, and in 1917 he was invalided out of the Navy with duodenal ulcers. A man of indomitable character, he immediately joined the Royal Naval Air Service instead and transferred to the Royal Air Force when it came into being in 1918. His strength of character again showed itself when his brother abdicated. Though he knew that his health was not up to the stress and strain of monarchy, he saw it as his clear duty to become King in his brother's stead. World War II inevitably added to the strain to which he was constantly subject, and he was only in his early fifties when he entered upon a period of quickening decline. But there was never any decline in his strength of character. Increasingly fragile though his health was after the lumbar sympathectomy he underwent early in 1949, he remained a man who enjoyed life; a King who liked his little joke. 'You used a knife on me. Now I'll use one on you,' he quipped to James Learmouth on one occasion when the surgeon called at the Palace to check on the progress of his royal patient. The 'knife' turned out to be a sword which the King had hidden behind a cushion. Knighthoods have been bestowed in many unusual circumstances, but surely never before by a Monarch clad in dressing gown and slippers.

The King never completely recovered from the effect of that operation and would never know again even the fragile strength of earlier days. By June he was still too weak to play his part in the annual ceremony of Trooping the Colour. A highly nervous Heir Presumptive was obliged to deputize for her father, riding side-saddle to take the salute on Horse Guards' Parade with the King as a spectator in an open carriage. His seeming recovery later, enabling his son-in-law to resume an active naval career and his elder daughter to join her husband in Malta, was an illusion, a triumph of royal spirit over the fragility of the flesh. Struggling against the weakness of his body, he resumed his customary ten-hour working day. He insisted upon again performing the more important of royal public engagements, such as the State Opening of Parliament. But more and more, however reluctantly, he was compelled to transfer the burdens of monarchy to the slender shoulders of his daughter. The result, for the Princess, was the busiest period of her life to date as she became more and more her father's deputy, deftly dovetailing her personal life as a young wife and mother with her official role as Heir Presumptive. Commuting back and forth between Britain and Malta, she helped to host President Auriol of France, the King and Queen of Denmark, Queen Juliana and Prince Bernhardt of the Netherlands, and the King of Norway on their visits to London. Young and healthy as she was, keen and conscientious as she was, she took it all in her stride. Indeed, she found time even for such extracurricular activities as a visit to the royal stud at Hampton Court to admire a newborn colt named Aureole. Her increasing knowledge of bloodlines and the keen eye she had developed for thoroughbreds had her hoping that the week-old colt might one day rival her great-grandfather's Derby winners, Persimmon and Diamond Jubilee.

Hindsight suggests that it might have been better, might have prolonged the King's life a little longer, if he had surrendered the reins of monarchy entirely to his daughter, as Queen Wilhelmina of the Netherlands had done to hers. But with his indomitable spirit, his strong sense of duty, his concern that his elder daughter should enjoy a few more years of freedom from total royal responsibility, that was something he did not even contemplate. The spring of 1951 found him again struggling against ill-health as he opened the Festival of Britain, intended as a symbol of Britain's emergence from the gloom of the postwar years. By the following month his health had deteriorated to such an extent that the Princess again had to deputize for him at the annual ceremony of Trooping the Colour. And this time he could not even look on from the comfort of an open carriage but had to be content with the black and white images flickering on the television set in his bedroom at the palace.

The initial medical bulletin stated that the King was suffering from 'an attack of influenza', and indeed this was the original medical diagnosis, later to be changed to 'a small area of catarrhal infection'. In fact, the King, a heavy cigarette-smoker, was suffering from lung cancer. He himself would never be told that he had cancer. The necessity for further – and urgent – surgery was explained to him in other ways.

His intended tour of Australia and New Zealand, postponed earlier, had been re-scheduled for the following year. Clearly there was now no question of going, but he took heart from the fact that the Princess was willing to go in his place even though it would follow closely on the heels of her own tour of Canada and the United States. So that he could accompany her, the Navy granted her husband a spell of 'indefinite leave' which would last to the present day. For the Duke, it was the end of his naval career.

Conscientiously dutiful though she is, the Princess doggedly refused to leave for Canada and the United States until she knew that her father's operation had been successful and he was out of danger. This meant a two-week delay in her departure from Britain. Such delay would mean the elaborate itinerary for the tour being completely re-scheduled with all the complications that that would cause in the two countries she was to visit. It was the Duke who pointed out that, if they flew the Atlantic instead of going by sea, as royal tours had previously always been undertaken, the schedule could remain unchanged. It was, in 1951, a revolutionary proposal. Clement Attlee, prime minister of the day, was horrified at the risk the Heir Presumptive would be running. Flying back and forth to Malta was one thing, crossing the Atlantic by air quite another. But finally he agreed. The flight, in that pre-jet era, took seventeen hours.

The fact that the Princess included an outfit of mourning clothes in her luggage should not be interpreted as anticipating her father's death. It is a normal part of luggage on a royal tour against the possibility of any death obliging the Royal Family to go into mourning. But the possibility of the King dying in her absence could not be ignored. So she was also obliged to take with her a bulky sealed package containing the state papers she would have to deal with and sign in the event of her sudden accession to the throne. Few daughters can have undertaken such responsibility as that Canadian–US tour represented with their hearts so burdened.

As a result, the tour did not get off to a very good start. Worried about her father, nervous on top of that, the Princess, initially at least, struck many Canadians as being stiff and starchy. If the Princess was worried about her father, the Duke was worried for her, and worry made him sometimes abrupt and tetchy. Despite her personal worries, the Princess more than once displayed those human touches which are more the hallmark of her mother than they were of her shy and serious father. A crippled boy in hospital had been hoping to take a photograph of her when she stopped by his bed, but found at the last moment that his flash equipment would not work. She told him to get it seen to and she would be back. She kept her word, and the youngster got his picture.

Every day she telephoned London to find out how her father was. Good news of his improving condition – or so it seemed to be at the time – coincided with a square dance which popped up unexpectedly in her schedule. In more buoyant spirits as a result of the news from home, but lacking the sort of casual clothes which go with a square dance, she sent the indispensable Bobo to a nearby departmental store to buy her a suitable skirt and blouse. Her husband similarly invested in his first pair of jeans, donning them so hurriedly that he took part in the square dance with a tag still on display revealing the price paid for them.

Even by royal standards, the tour was a crowded one, though not so hectic as others which would follow in the years ahead. Over the course of five weeks the Princess and the Duke travelled a total of sixteen thousand miles, shook perhaps twice that number of hands – three thousand handshakes in two hours were logged at a reception in Toronto – and visited every Canadian province, with functions at more than seventy different places. In Ottawa alone, in the course of one day, they attended fifteen different functions, not counting an official luncheon and a state banquet at both of which the Princess made speeches. Bad weather impaired part of the tour, and it was the Duke's inventive brain which conceived the idea of a transparent plastic cover to the royal car so that the Princess would be protected from the elements while remaining clearly visible to the crowds who flocked to see her. Once thought of, the Duke's idea was produced and fitted in double-quick time by the workers at a Toronto aircraft factory. In the course of those five weeks in Canada the Princess met the Dionne quintuplets, watched her first game of ice hockey and attended the Calgary Stampede warmly wrapped in an electric blanket, in addition to many more prosaic visits to hospitals, factories and paper-mills. On her visit to McGill University, cheer-leaders led seven thousand exuberant students in a raucous greeting of 'Yea, Yea, Betty Windsor . . . Rah, Rah, Rah!' By contrast with Canada, her two-day side trip to Washington, where she and the Duke were the guests of President Truman, must have seemed almost a rest-cure. The President took his royal guests to visit his ageing mother. Just as the Princess at the time of the abdication had somehow confused Mrs Simpson with Mrs Baldwin, wife of the prime minister, so the President's mother now confused the Princess's father with Winston Churchill, who had just been returned to power as prime minister in the British General Election. 'I am so glad your father has been re-elected,' she told the Princess. 'A fairytale princess', the President labelled her. 'As one father to another,' he wrote to King George VI, 'we can be very proud of our daughters.'

The King was indeed proud of the manner in which his elder daughter had fulfilled her first solo Commonwealth assignment and pleased with the support which had been forthcoming from her husband. He showed his pleasure by appointing both as members of the Privy Council. Lilibet had proved her worth in Canada and, the King felt sure, would acquit herself equally admirably as his deputy for the coming tour of Australia and New Zealand.

That Christmas of 1951 found the family re-united at Sandringham, though not quite as usual. Happy as he always was in the company of those he loved, the King tried hard not to let his daughters and grandchildren see how desperately ill he still was. But some things it was impossible for him to disguise. The operation for the removal of his left lung had left him too weak to climb stairs, and a room on the ground floor had to be turned into a bedroom for him. When local carol-singers paid their traditional call and were invited inside as usual, his voice was not strong enough to join in the singing of his favourite carols. He was compelled to remain seated, instead of standing, when he distributed gifts to members of his staff, as he did each Christmas. And the fact that royal physicians had not objected when he asked if he could still smoke cigarettes was an additional clue to the fact that his life now hung by a thread. But if his wife, the Queen, had no illusions, though always cheerful in his presence, the nation at large thought that their King was on the road to recovery. His radio broadcast on Christmas Day fostered this hope. Only a few knew how painstakingly it had been pre-recorded, a few words at a time.

In the weeks which followed Christmas, as his elder daughter and son-in-law prepared for the royal tour of Australia and New Zealand, the King talked of taking the convalescent cruise to South Africa which royal physicians had suggested would be beneficial. Determined not to give in, he continued to tackle the contents of his Boxes regularly each day. He resumed his favourite sport of shooting, though no longer able to walk from beat to beat, gun in hand. Instead, his valet carried his gun for him while the King travelled in a Land Rover which had been specially equipped with electrically heated gloves to boost the circulation in his thin blue hands. Shooting done for the day, he was too exhausted to join others of the family for the cheerful chit-chat of the afternoon tea ceremony, but would retire to his ground-floor room to lie down and rest until it was time to dress for dinner.

Despite all this, he insisted upon travelling from Sandringham to London to see his daughter and son-in-law off on their trip to Australia. The night before they left he took the family to see the American musical *South Pacific*, which he enjoyed immensely. The following day was cold, with a biting wind. Despite the weather, he had himself driven to London Airport, standing bare-headed in the open as he wished his daughter God-speed. Photographs taken at the time showed him for the desperately sick man he was. He himself, as he said goodbye to the Princess, perhaps knew that he was dying. 'There was a look in his eyes as though he knew he was seeing her for the last time,' recalls someone who was there. And perhaps he was thinking of more than his daughter's tour of

Australia and New Zealand when he said quietly to the loyal Bobo: 'Look after Lilibet for me.'

With her on her departure from London the Princess again took that bulky sealed package which would be opened in the event of her accession to the throne. And this time it would be opened. Though she left Britain by air, it was not the intention to fly all the way to Australia. Royal travel had not yet moved that far into the future. Instead, she would fly to Africa, where she would board the liner *Gothic* at Mombasa for the rest of her long journey. Or such was the plan. But first there would be a brief stop-over in Kenya, mainly to give her a brief holiday at the Sagana Royal Lodge, a wedding present which she had not yet seen. Some public engagements were inevitable, of course, among them a civic reception, a state banquet, the official opening of the Kenya Regiment's new headquarters and a visit to a maternity hospital before the Princess and Duke were free to drive some seventy miles up-country to the Royal Lodge, a stone and cedar-built hunting lodge on the slopes of Mount Kenya. During the few days they spent there before fate called an abrupt halt, they went riding together in brilliant sunshine and fished for trout in the curiously cold waters of the Sagana River. The Princess was also busy with her camera, making a film of the wild life which abounds in the area. Her parents had visited Kenya in 1924, not long after they were first married and before she was born, and she hoped her home movie would bring back happy memories. She thought it would be a good idea too if her father had another holiday in Kenya. 'I'm sure the climate here and these peaceful surroundings would do him the world of good,' she said.

On 5 February, along with the Duke, Michael Parker and the Duke's cousin Lady Pamela Mountbatten (later Mrs David Hicks), who was accompanying her as lady-in-waiting, she drove to Treetops, a rest-house overlooking a clearing and water-hole in the Aberdare Forest. Not the Treetops of today. That is very different, as she saw for herself when she paid a nostalgic return visit in 1984. The Treetops in which she spent the night of 5–6 February 1952 was later destroyed by fire, and a tourist hotel today stands in its place. But in 1952 it was no more than an overgrown tree-house, a three-bedroomed structure built some thirty feet above ground level in the branches of a giant fig tree. Access was by way of a steep wooden ladder which the Princess climbed under the quizzical gaze of a nearby herd of wild elephant. She was wearing a yellow shirt and, in the interests of modesty, a pair of tan-coloured slacks.

Once safe in the tree-house, she brought out her camera and added some shots of the elephant herd to the home movie she was making. Baboons eyed her curiously from the branches of an adjoining tree. She filmed them too, even managing to tempt one within close-up range with an offering of sweet potato. She slept for a few hours in one of the three small bedrooms of the tree-house, but was up in good time to film some rhino when they came down to drink from the water-hole at dawn. By which time, because Sagana is three hours ahead of Greenwich in time and because in Britain the new monarch succeeds the old at the moment of death, she was probably no longer her father's deputy but Queen in her own right.

'Probably' because her father died in his sleep (from thrombosis, following another day spent out shooting) and so the exact time of death is unknown. But it is possible to narrow things down. It was midnight at Sandringham (three o'clock in the morning in Kenya) when a policeman patrolling the grounds heard someone, and it could only have been the King, fiddling with the casement of his ground-floor bedroom window. It was half-past seven in the morning at Sandringham (half-past ten in Kenya) when the King's valet, entering his bedroom to rouse him, discovered him dead in bed. Unless the King had died only within the last thirty minutes prior to his valet's arrival, the Princess, by the time she returned to Sagana at ten o'clock that morning (Kenya time) was already Queen Elizabeth II.

She was still unaware of both her father's death and her own accession to the throne as, later that day, she sat at her desk in the cream-walled sitting-room of the Lodge, catching up with some arrears of correspondence. She had no knowledge of the fact that, for several hours now, senior officials of the dead King's Household in London had been making frantic efforts to establish contact with her, a task rendered more difficult because the only means of communication with the isolated Lodge was a single telephone line strung out across the bush.

The sad news of her father's death, the historic news of her own accession, would not reach her until mid-afternoon, and then only in curiously roundabout fashion. It reached her via a Reuter news-flash received at the offices of the *East Africa Standard* in Nairobi. This was passed on to Granville Roberts, the paper's correspondent covering the royal visit who was staying at an hotel in Nyeri, some eighteen miles from Sagana. He, in turn, told Lieutenant Colonel the Hon. Martin (later Lord) Charteris, Private Secretary to the Princess, who chanced that day to be lunching at the same hotel. It was then a little before two o'clock in the afternoon (Kenya time). At Charteris' request, Roberts telephoned the Royal Lodge and informed Michael Parker of the situation. Parker, wisely, decided at first to keep the news to himself until official confirmation was received. However, when official confirmation had still not been received by the time the King's death was being announced in a radio news bulletin, he sought out the Duke of Edinburgh and told him.

In some fashion which is unclear, Bobo and John Dean, the Duke's valet, also came to know of the King's death. They were sitting together outside the lodge, Dean cleaning the Duke's shoes, when they saw the Queen – as she now was, though she still did not know it – coming towards them. She paused where they were sitting. 'We shall have to go riding earlier than usual tomorrow,' she said. In normal circumstances 'tomorrow' would have been the last day of her stay at the Lodge, and she would have been leaving later in the day to board the *Gothic* at Mombasa. Bobo and Dean knew that there would be no riding for her on the morrow, that she would not now be going to Mombasa, but it was not for them to break the news of which she was still unaware.

Emotionally overwrought as those in the royal party were, memory plays tricks, and there are different versions of what happened during the next few minutes. The Duke may have appeared suddenly on the scene, as one person recalls, taking his wife by the arm and leading her towards the solitude afforded by the Sagana River. The new Queen, as someone else remembers, may have gone back into the Lodge in search of her husband. Either way, it was the Duke who broke the news of her father's death to her, and there is no dispute that she then went into her bedroom to be alone with her grief.

But the grief-stricken daughter was also a young woman who

had been trained from the age of ten in the iron discipline of monarchy. So though her eyes were red with weeping when she emerged from her bedroom an hour later, her voice was calm and composed as she gave her first orders as Queen. There could be no question now of continuing her journey to Australia and New Zealand. Clearly she would have to return to London. So she issued instructions for apologetic cables to be sent off to the governments of those countries and herself dictated other, more personal, cables to be sent to her mother and her father's mother, the ageing Queen Mary. London finally succeeded in establishing contact. There was much to be discussed over the solitary telephone located in a small back room of the Lodge, not least the name by which the new Queen wished to be known. Monarchs have the privilege of selecting their own royal names, and the Queen's father had elected to mount the throne as King George VI though his first name was actually Albert. Even so, the question would seem to have taken the new Queen by surprise. 'My own, of course – what else?' she replied when Martin Charteris, having hurried back from Nyeri, relayed London's inquiry to her.

It fell to Michael Parker, as soon as the telephone was free, to make arrangements for getting the new Queen back to her capital. Fortunately the Argonaut in which she had flown out as Princess was still at Entebbe, standing by in anticipation that there would be surplus baggage to be conveyed back to Britain. The problem was how to get the Queen from Sagana to Entebbe as expeditiously as possible. East Africa Airlines were asked if they could help. The only aircraft immediately available, they said, was an unpressurized Dakota. It was better than nothing and was quickly airborne for Nanyuki, the nearest airstrip to the Lodge.

Before leaving, the new monarch carried out her first duties as Queen. She presented the Provincial Commissioner with a set of cufflinks. She signed photographs of herself for the staff of Royal Lodge. Bobo and John Dean hastened to complete the royal packing. In the rush it was inevitable that a few items should be overlooked and left behind, among them the Duke's field-glasses. It was around six o'clock (Kenya time) when the party set out on the short drive to Nanyuki. The unpressurized Dakota which awaited them there was hardly the most comfortable of royal transports, but the flight to Entebbe was without incident. They transferred to the waiting Argonaut, only to be delayed for three hours as the violence of a tropical storm prevented the aircraft taking off. It was nearly midnight before the new Queen was finally airborne and on her way back to London.

9 THE 62ND MONARCH

When news of her father's death reached her, the mourning outfit the new Queen had taken with her was already aboard the liner *Gothic* at Mombasa in readiness for the onward journey to Australia which would not now take place. With no way of retrieving it, she had left Sagana for the flight back to London wearing one of the light, colourful dresses which were all that had been required for the brief holiday in Kenya. She could hardly arrive back home on the occasion of her father's death dressed so informally and a brief touchdown at El Adem, a desert staging post, enabled radio contact to be made with London. As a result, a second mourning outfit awaited her arrival at London Airport. Landing at a distance from where royal relatives and parliamentary dignitaries were waiting to greet the new Queen, the royal Argonaut paused briefly while the new mourning clothes were carried aboard. With Bobo's help, the Queen changed from her light dress into conventional black by the time the aircraft had come to a final stop.

Waiting to greet the Queen were her uncle, the Duke of Gloucester, Philip's uncle, Earl Mountbatten, prime minister Winston Churchill, foreign secretary Anthony Eden, Clement Attlee, leader of the Opposition, Lord Woolton, leader of the House of Lords, and Harry Crookshank, leader of the Commons. While the others waited on the tarmac, Gloucester and Mountbatten, as relatives, boarded the aircraft to pay their condolences. 'Do I go down alone?' the Queen asked. Heads nodded in assent.

Clearly the Queen needed all her iron self-control to keep her emotions in check as she descended the aircraft steps to be greeted by the waiting dignitaries. Initially, she dared not trust herself to speak, and it was not until she had already been silently welcomed back by several of those present that she murmured her first words as Queen on British soil: 'This is a very tragic homecoming.' She was not alone in being filled with emotion. Like her, Churchill dared not trust himself to speak, and tears trickled openly down his cheeks. They were perhaps less tears of grief for a dead king than an expression of loyal devotion to the twenty-five-year-old wife and mother who was the new young Queen – the sixty-second monarch to reign over Britain, latest in a line which dates back over eleven hundred years to those ninth-century days of the Saxon warrior king, Ecgbert the Great.*

The royal standard flew from her car as she drove from the airport, and a larger version was run up at Clarence House on her arrival. Elsewhere flags flew at half-mast in mourning for her father. Instead of cheering, crowds along the royal route stood in sympathetic silence. Shops and factories, theatres and cinemas were closed, and the lights of Piccadilly Circus, though her journey home did not take her in that direction, were temporarily extinguished. Awaiting her at Clarence House was a personal letter from her mother, who was still at Sandringham. Also awaiting her attention were the contents of one of the famous Boxes which reach the Monarch with the regularity of a factory production line. She had seen such Boxes before, of course, had their contents explained to her by her father, but this was the first of the thousands with which she would have to deal in her own right during the years of monarchy which lay ahead, though the leather-covered lid was still addressed in gold lettering to 'The King'. There had not yet been time to effect a change.

Her first action, however, was not that of a new monarch but as a grieving daughter. Having read her mother's letter, she put a call through to Sandringham and talked to her on the telephone. Her first visitor was announced, Queen Mary, less a grandmother at that moment than a loyal subject of the granddaughter who was now Queen. 'Your old Granny and subject must be the first to kiss your hand,' she said. Later came the sixteenth Duke of Nor-

---

* While there has always been a degree of disagreement among historians as to who was England's first real King (from the Anglo-Saxon *cyning*, meaning chief), Ecgbert has surely the best claim. As King of Wessex, between 815 and 829, he conquered Devon, Cornwall and Mercia, forced Kent, Sussex and Essex to submit to his rule, absorbed Mercia into his growing kingdom and compelled Northumbria to acknowledge him as 'overlord'. He died in 839.

folk, Earl Marshal of England, and the Earl of Clarendon, who held the high office of Lord Chamberlain. The anachronisms of monarchy would sometimes seem to impose unnecessary burdens, and it was the new Queen's duty to 'command' that arrangements be made for the dead King's funeral, though these had already been put in hand.

Next morning came her Declaration of Accession, a ceremony which her grandfather, King George V, confided to his diary was 'the most trying ordeal I ever had to go through'. He was an ex-naval man in his mid-forties at the time of his accession. How much more of an ordeal must it have been for a young woman of twenty-five who had just lost the father to whom she was so devoted. It was, moreover, an ordeal she was required to endure alone. Her husband might escort her from Clarence House to nearby St James's Palace, but once there he was required to leave her side and take his place with the other members of the Council of Accession. Looking pale despite her recent exposure to Kenyan sunshine, her eyes misting at the passages referring to her dead father, she read the Declaration in a composed voice.

> On the sudden death of my dear father I am called to fulfil
> the duties and responsibilities of Sovereignty . . . My heart is
> too full for me to say more to you today than that I shall
> always work, as my father did throughout his reign, to uphold
> the constitutional Government and to advance the happiness
> and prosperity of my peoples, spread as they are the world
> over. I know that in my resolve to follow his shining example
> of service and devotion, I shall be inspired by the loyalty
> and affection of those whose Queen I have been called upon
> to be and by the counsel of their Parliaments. I pray that God
> will help me to discharge worthily this heavy task that has
> been laid upon me so early in my life.

Having made her Declaration and signed the Oath, the Queen withdrew to an ante-room where she was quickly joined by her husband and her uncle, the late Duke of Gloucester. Shortly afterwards the Earl Marshal emerged on to the balcony of St James's Palace to a fanfare of trumpets to read the proclamation:

> The Lords Spiritual and Temporal of this Realm, being here
> assisted with those of His late Majesty's Privy Council, with

representatives of other Members of the Commonwealth, with other Principal Gentlemen of Quality, with the Lord Mayor, Aldermen and Citizens of London, do now hereby with one voice and consent of tongue and heart proclaim that the High and Mighty Princess Elizabeth Alexandra Mary is now, by the death of our late Sovereign of happy memory, become Queen Elizabeth the Second, by the Grace of God Queen of this Realm and of Her other Realms and Territories, Head of the Commonwealth, Defender of the Faith.

The proclamation was a worthy attempt to combine historic tradition with the changes which had taken place in the postwar period. The title it accorded the new Queen was not in fact her correct one. Her full statutory title at that time should have been: Elizabeth the Second, by the Grace of God of Great Britain, Ireland and the British Dominions beyond the Seas Queen, Defender of the Faith. But this title was clearly out of date in several respects. The reference in it to Ireland was ambiguous inasmuch as she was Queen only of Northern Ireland, while there was no reference at all to her special position as Head of the Commonwealth. Moreover, some Commonwealth countries found it objectionable to be lumped together as 'British Dominions' with its implication of subservience to Britain.

The title employed for proclamation purposes, though it skated round these pitfalls, had no statutory weight behind it. Over the next sixteen months, with a view to setting this right, consultations took place with the Commonwealth governments of the day – the monarchies of Canada, Australia, New Zealand and South Africa (though South Africa would cease to be one when it quit the Commonwealth in 1961) and with India, which was now an independent republic. Pakistan too had been granted independence but was not yet a republic though intent on becoming one.* As a result of these consultations, a royal proclamation issued simultaneously in Commonwealth countries four days ahead of the Coronation gave the Queen a new title, slightly different in each country but with a substantial element common to those which

* Pakistan became a republic in 1956 and withdrew from the Commonwealth twelve years later.

121

remained monarchies.* Commonwealth countries which have remained monarchies on becoming independent since then have adopted broadly similar titles while those with their own monarchies or preferring to become republics recognize her, as do those of which she remains Queen, as Head of the Commonwealth.

At St James's Palace, in 1952, the Queen watched the ceremony of her own proclamation from behind the lace curtains of an upstairs window. But the full impact of it all, she has said, did not dawn upon her until later and then in curiously prosaic fashion. It was a day not long after when she was at Windsor Castle and saw a milk bottle there bearing her royal cypher – EIIR.

Duty done, ceremony executed, tradition satisfied, the Queen could yield to her grief as a daughter. Later that day she motored to Sandringham. She left London chauffeur-driven. But once clear of the capital, the car stopped by the roadside. The chauffeur moved into the rear seat, the Duke took the wheel and the Queen sat beside him. Arriving at Sandringham, she and her mother did their best to comfort each other. The King's coffin was not yet sealed, and she was asked if she would like to see the body. She shook her head, preferring to remember her father as he was in life. That evening, after sunset, the coffin was lifted onto a bier and wheeled from the house to the parish church of St Mary Magdalene where the Royal Family worship when at Sandringham. The royal piper preceded the cortège, playing 'The Flowers of the Forest'. Behind the coffin came the Queen, her mother, the Duke, Princess Margaret and a handful of royal servants who had been with the King so long as to qualify almost as personal friends. Inside the church, gamekeepers in green tweed and estate workers in their Sunday-best blue serge took it in turns, four at a time, to watch over the coffin throughout the night. Atop the coffin lay a single wreath. It was from the Queen, but the inscription on it had been written by a grieving daughter: 'To darling Papa from your sorrowing Lilibet'.

From Sandringham the King's body was transported to London where it lay in state for three days while one-third of a million people filed past in homage. On the last of those three nights the Queen herself went to Westminster Hall, watching the scene inside

* The Queen's new title in the United Kingdom is included in the summary of her life and reign given at the beginning of this book.

from the shadows of a side entrance. Throughout the funeral service and the subsequent interment at Windsor, where she scattered earth on the coffin from a silver bowl and where the Lord Chamberlain, as his last gesture of service to the dead King, snapped his staff of office in two and cast the pieces into the grave, that sense of royal discipline drilled into her from childhood enabled her to hold back her tears. But afterwards, in the privacy of the car taking her back to Clarence House, she broke down and wept as she had not done since the news of her father's death was first broken to her in Sagana.

If the two years leading up to her father's death, during which she had been obliged to take over or help out with many of his functions, had been exceptionally busy ones, the months following her accession were to prove busier still as she contended with the triple roles of Queen, wife and mother. But crowded days also had their compensations, affording her little time to grieve for her dead father. A day soon after her accession found her receiving in audience the Sheriff of the City of London, the Lord Provost of Edinburgh, the Chairman of the London County Council, the Governor of the Bank of England, the Presidents of the Royal Society and the Royal Academy. Within weeks she was holding her first investiture, awarding new knighthoods with the same sword her father had used on Sir James Learmouth. On the Thursday of Holy Week she distributed the Royal Maundy for the first time, giving specially minted coins of sterling silver to as many old men and old women as the years of her age, in continuance of a custom begun nine hundred years before by Edward the Confessor. Wearing a purple robe and a diadem handed down from Queen Victoria, she opened her first Parliament. Each evening there arrived for her a summary of proceedings in Parliament to be read and digested. Her days brought similar summaries of Commonwealth affairs along with that endless succession of despatch boxes covered in red, green and black leather, addressed now to 'The Queen' and each containing its quota of state papers to be read and remembered or approved and signed with the flourishing 'Elizabeth R', quite unlike her normal writing, which was now her official royal signature. With all this, she still found time to telephone her mother each morning, to visit Queen Mary each day and to have her two children with her for a few minutes after breakfast. She would even find time, later, to give each child in turn lessons in reading, writing and telling the time. A further ninety minutes in late afternoon and early evening were equally reserved as the children's playtime. At her request, the custom of receiving the prime minister in audience each Tuesday evening had its timing altered – it was put back half-an-hour – so as not to clash with the children's playtime.

With the best will in the world, however, not everything could be squeezed in. The artist Edward Halliday had earlier been commissioned to paint a family group of husband and wife and their two children which the Duke intended as a birthday gift for her. Such were the new-found pressures of monarchy that she could no longer spare time to pose, and the painting had to be finished with Bobo acting as the Queen's stand-in.

That she was not ascending the throne as a new broom eager to sweep clean was quickly apparent. 'I want everything to continue exactly as it did with my father,' she said. Indeed, it would have been difficult to have done otherwise. Despite her years of royal apprenticeship and all her father had taught her, in those early days she still had much to learn. To ease her into the complexities of monarchy, she continued to surround herself with those courtiers of the old guard who had served her father before her, Sir Alan Lascelles, Sir Piers Legh and Lord Tryon among them. She appointed one of her father's former pages, Maurice Watts, to be her personal page. As a servant, Watts was not on the same level as those courtiers who form what is known as the Queen's Household, but it was he as much as anyone who set the formal tone for the new reign, insisting, for example, that other members of her staff who wished to see her should be properly announced instead of merely tapping on her door and walking straight in, as had been customary in the days when she was still a Princess.

The new Queen had been on the throne only a little over two months when she effected the change which came as a bitter blow to her husband and infuriated his uncle, Earl Mountbatten. It was on 9 April 1952 that she declared it her 'Will and Pleasure that I and my children shall be styled and known as the House and Family of Windsor and that my descendants, other than female descendants who marry and their descendants, shall bear the name of Windsor'. She did so on the combined advice of the prime minister, Winston Churchill, and Alan Lascelles, the Private Secretary she had inherited from her father.

There are those who argue that the Queen's name was never other than Windsor, that as a royal Princess she did not take her husband's name on marriage, as other brides do. If that were so, then her Order in Council with its reference to 'I and my children' would seem to have been most curiously worded. Nor is it a view which was shared at the time by Philip's Mountbatten uncle. He held the opinion that she had taken the name Mountbatten when she married his nephew and protested indignantly at what he considered was a decision to abandon it in favour of her father's name of Windsor.* 'There was no legal provision for any female, not even an heir presumptive to the throne, to retain her maiden name on marriage', he wrote in his privately published work *The Mountbatten Lineage*. But neither the uncle's indignation nor the nephew's hurt feelings had any effect. 'So the House of Mountbatten only reigned for two months,' *The Mountbatten Lineage* ruefully concludes.

If it was a blow to the Duke of Edinburgh's feelings as a husband and father that his wife and children were not to bear his name, there was much else to make him feel insecure in those early days of his wife's monarchy. He was not permitted to see the contents of the Boxes with which the Queen had to deal each day and could not be present when she received the prime minister in audience on Tuesday evenings. The great-great-grandfather Queen and Consort shared, Prince Albert, may have played King to Victoria's Queen, but the Duke of Edinburgh, a century later, was clearly going to be given no opportunity to do the same, a fact which was underlined when he found himself relegated to a seat below his wife's throne at the state opening of the first Parliament of the new reign. However, there was some consolation for him in being assigned 'Place, Pre-eminence and Precedence next to Her Majesty'. Though he himself could never succeed to the throne, he now ranked in order of precedence above the young son who

---

* In fact, Windsor and Mountbatten are alike names assumed in the middle of the 1914–18 war as a counter to both families' German antecedents. Upset by gossip that he was pro-German, the Queen's grandfather, King George V, took the name of Windsor and ordered royal relatives to take similar stoutly British names. So the Battenbergs became Mountbattens.

would one day be King. There was further consolation the following year when the Queen appointed him to act as Regent (in place of Princess Margaret) in the unlikely event that their son should become King Charles III while still a minor. And later still, just before the birth of Prince Andrew, would come another Order in Council which, ambiguously worded though it was, would have the effect of turning at least Princess Anne's name from Windsor to Mountbatten-Windsor (until, of course, she became Mrs Mark Phillips).

The continuance of the name of Windsor for the Royal Family was not the only matter in which the Queen acted upon the advice of Winston Churchill. But for him she might not have taken up residence at Buckingham Palace. Successive monarchs have had little love for that imposing edifice at the end of the Mall, variously criticizing it as too big, too small, too gloomy or too 'musty', this last by the Duke of Windsor in the days of his brief reign as King Edward VIII. The Queen's father, when he took over from his brother as King, described the Palace as 'an icebox', though this state of affairs has since been remedied by the introduction of central heating. The Queen, when she first went to live there as a ten-year-old Princess, found it a bewildering labyrinth of a place, and the prospect, fifteen years later, of going back to live there again did not exactly enthuse her. Both she and the Duke would have preferred to remain at Clarence House, a smaller residence of more homely atmosphere, using the Palace only for administrative purposes and state occasions. It was Churchill who persuaded her otherwise. The Monarch must live at Buckingham Palace, he insisted, though doubtless more eloquently. To inconvenience the Queen as little as possible, the transfer was carried out while she was at Windsor Castle over Easter. Her principal concern, as she told the children's nanny, Helen Lightbody, was that they should be unsettled as little as possible. This was accomplished by making the rooms at the Palace which would serve as a nursery as much like their old nursery at Clarence House as was possible.

Because it held such sad memories for her, the Queen decided against using the room which had been her father's study. Instead, she chose to work in what had been her mother's sitting-room, using it as both sitting-room and study. The Duke was allotted the King's old room, though not his Chippendale desk. The Queen had that moved into her room and positioned in the bay window recess so that she could see out as she worked. In other ways too she kept her father's memory alive, setting a photograph of him on a side table close to her desk, using his sword for investitures. The door from the inner quadrangle which gives access to the elevator serving the royal apartment had long been known as the King's Door. Palace staff now started referring to it as the Queen's Door. The Queen, when she heard of this, said that she would prefer them to continue using the old name. Similarly, later, she decided that the King's Troop of Royal Horse Artillery should continue under that name instead of being re-titled the Queen's Troop.

She quickly showed that she was far from being the 'mere child' Churchill originally thought her. Indeed, the Prime Minister was slightly embarrassed during an early audience with the new Monarch when she referred to 'the situation in Baghdad', a topic on which it seemed she was rather better informed that he was. Far from being a 'mere child', she was every inch her father's daughter, down to the occasional flash of temper, as was evident the day a senior courtier emerged from her room pale-faced and shaking. 'While she's alive, the King will never be dead,' he mumbled as he walked away.

As Monarch, she worried that she was not doing things perfectly or not doing enough. She wanted − or so it seemed − to do everything herself, sometimes working herself into a state of nerves in the process. She was especially nervous at the first state opening of Parliament, and having her husband seated below her instead of supportively beside her did nothing to help. She was conscientious in the extreme. Seized with an attack of abdominal cramp on the occasion of an investiture, she forced herself to complete it down to the last knighthood and medal before retiring to her room to rest. In a period of twenty weeks she fulfilled 140 public engagements. That learned medical journal *The Lancet* queried whether she was trying to do too much and might undermine her health in the process. Churchill would later voice the same doubt, and even that indefatigable worker Queen Mary expressed the hope that the 'poor little girl' was not being overworked. But to her aides, who saw her daily, it seemed that she thrived on hard work. If she was sometimes inclined to do too much, her husband, by contrast, was sometimes hard put to it to know how to fill his time. Such jobs as did come his way, like helping to select designs for new postage stamps, can hardly have been meaningful to a man who not long before had been skipper of his own ship. With no real part to play in the royal scheme of things, it was understandable that he should have found his new role of Consort boring and, at times, even depressing.

The Queen's work followed her, as it had followed her father before her and his father before him, even on holiday; in summer to Balmoral, where she now took over her father's place at the head of the family dining-table; to Sandringham at Christmas. From Sandringham that Christmas she made her first broadcast as Queen to the countries of the Commonwealth. Between making Christmas stockings for the children and distributing gifts to her staff, she continued to deal with the contents of her Boxes. One visitor to Sandringham that Christmas was fashion designer Norman Hartnell. He had designed her wedding dress and now they discussed what form her coronation gown should take. Queen Victoria had been crowned in white, Hartnell said. 'But she was not married at the time,' the Queen pointed out. Philip joined in the discussion, and it was partly his idea that the gown should be embroidered with the national symbols of all the countries of which Elizabeth was Queen – England's rose, Scotland's thistle, the Irish shamrock and the Welsh leek, the Australian wattle and the New Zealand fern, Canada's maple leaf and others besides. No one seemed to realize that so much embroidery in pearl, crystal and diamanté would result in the finished gown weighing a staggering thirty pounds.

If she did not ascend the throne as a new broom determined to sweep clean, the Queen was new enough and enthusiastic enough to want a say in every aspect of monarchy. In the run-up to her coronation, it was not only her coronation gown which concerned her. Nor simply the special cosmetics being devised for her, though she had her say in that too. 'Remember that I am not a film star,' she cautioned the beauty expert responsible. The result was a combination of peach-tinted foundation, red-blue rouge, light brown mascara and a red lipstick with a blue undertone. It was her personal choice that two of the architects of victory in World

War II, Viscount Montgomery of Alamein and Earl Alexander of Tunis, should respectively bear the Royal Standard and carry the Orb at the coronation ceremony. It was her decision too that Britain's infant television service should be permitted to transmit from inside Westminster Abbey. She was opposed in this by the Private Secretary she had inherited from her father, Sir Alan Lascelles. He held, with Walter Bagehot, the eminent Victorian historian, that to let the world in on the mysteries of monarchy would be to lose some of its magic. But the Queen was insistent that her people should share the majesty and joy of the occasion with her. So the comparatively few families who possessed television sets in 1953, along with as many relatives and neighbours as could crowd into their sitting-rooms, were privileged to witness everything save those few minutes of sacred ritual when the Queen's hands, breast and head were anointed with holy oil.

Nor would she entertain well-meaning suggestions from various quarters designed to lessen the strain on her on Coronation Day. 'Did my father do it?' she asked when it was suggested that part of the 4½-hour coronation ritual should be omitted. Told that he had, she responded, 'Then I will too.' Similarly she vetoed a suggestion for shortening the processional route and firmly turned down the idea that she should be crowned with the lighter Imperial State Crown, as Queen Victoria was, rather than the massively historic St Edward's Crown.* She was equally determined that no mistake on her part should mar the sacred solemnity of her coronation. She had the crown taken from its resting-place in the Tower of London to the Palace so that she could accustom herself to its weight and balance, wearing it as she worked at her desk, as she partook of afternoon tea with the children and even as she mixed and ladled dog food into the corgis' feeding bowls. With chairs to represent the state coach and a sheet pinned to her shoulders in place of the velvet robe she would be wearing on Coronation Day, she rehearsed the tricky task of entering and leaving the coach with dignity. She approached everything about the ceremony with the utmost seriousness and sincerity. An at-

---

* The present St Edward's Crown weighs five pounds and was made for the coronation of Charles II after Oliver Cromwell had had the original crown melted down.

tempt by the Duke of Edinburgh to introduce a slightly lighter note at one rehearsal was firmly discouraged. 'Please come back and do it again,' the Queen said to him as he moved away. 'Properly this time.'

Queen Mary, who had contributed so much to the training of her granddaughter towards her era of monarchy, was still fit enough when preparations for the coronation were first put in hand to accompany her on an outing to Kensington Palace to inspect the coronation gown worn by Queen Victoria. But her health was fading fast, and with the approach of her eighty-sixth birthday it became increasingly apparent that she was unlikely to live to see her granddaughter crowned, as she had seen her father-in-law, husband and second son each crowned in turn. Her dearest wish, she told the new young Queen, was to see her with the crown on her head. Royal legend has it that she did, that the Queen took the crown to Marlborough House secretly one night and, in the bedroom where the old Queen lay dying, donned it for her benefit.

Legend, in this case, has the ring of probability. And it is a fact that, royal to the last, Queen Mary, as her life ebbed away, insisted that her death must not be permitted to postpone her granddaughter's coronation. She died ten weeks before Coronation Day.

No one who witnessed the spectacle of the Queen's coronation is likely ever to forget it. Despite the rain, it was an occasion of pageantry and grandeur such as lives in the memory. All the adjectives the newspapers have ever used to describe the Queen's majesty – 'radiant', 'serene', 'poised' – were true on that day. 'I have never seen the Queen look more beautiful,' recalls a former royal servant who was among the first to glimpse her as she descended the Grand Staircase of Buckingham Palace in her glittering gown and crimson robe, Queen Victoria's diamond diadem circling her brow. 'Emotion brought a lump to my throat.'

He was not the only one to be overtaken by emotion that day. The Queen herself, as she drove to Westminster Abbey in the massive four-ton state coach, was so moved by the enthusiastic cheers of those who crowded London's streets that her eyes filled momentarily with tears. It was an era, and one which would extend for several years to come, when the sixty-second Monarch exuded that same aura of youth and freshness that her daughter-in-law, the Princess of Wales, exudes today, a charisma which was felt far beyond the shores of Britain. In America the news-magazine *Time* featured her on its cover. The film *A Queen Is Crowned* broke box-office records in several American cities. Americans and Australians, along with visitors from Sweden and Sarawak, Swaziland and the Sudan, flocked to London in their thousands merely to glimpse her for a few seconds as she passed by to or from her coronation. To reinforce the capital's available accommodation, seven liners were moored in the Thames to serve as floating hotels.

Unlike the coronation of her father, when there was difficulty buckling on the royal sword, the crown was almost put on back to front and the King stumbled and nearly fell when someone stood on his robe, the Queen's coronation went off without a hitch. Throughout the long ceremony her concentration waivered only once, her eyes straying momentarily to where her small son, Prince Charles, knelt on a stool between his grandmother and aunt, Princess Margaret, witnessing the historic rites in which he will one day play the leading part.

As the Queen rode through London after the ceremony, on her way back to the Palace by a roundabout processional route, Princess Margaret lingered in the entrance to Westminster Abbey awaiting her own carriage. With her was Group Captain Peter Townsend, the World War II fighter ace who had been seconded to Buckingham Palace as a temporary equerry on a three-month basis and who, because King George VI had taken a liking to him, was still in royal service nine years later. He had been with the Royal Family on their South African tour, had accompanied Princess Margaret when she went to Holland for the inauguration of Queen Juliana, her first solo engagement overseas, and, with the death of the King and the accession of the new Queen, had moved from Buckingham Palace to Clarence House as Comptroller to the Queen Mother. Shortly, as royal plans stood, he would be accompanying her and Princess Margaret on their planned tour of what was then Southern Rhodesia. But while his career in royal service had undoubtedly prospered, his perhaps hasty wartime marriage had failed, and some six months previous he had divorced his wife on the grounds of infidelity. Now, on Coronation Day, at the entrance to the Abbey, as the Queen's twenty-two-year-old sister brushed her hand possessively along his medals, laughing up into his eyes, came the first public indication that the two of them were in love.

That affectionate gesture on the part of her younger sister was to precipitate the first crisis of the Queen's reign. She herself already knew that the couple wished to marry. Princess Margaret had told both her sister and her mother that she was in love with Townsend. Townsend himself had raised the matter with the Queen's Private Secretary, Sir Alan Lascelles. A courtier of the old school, Lascelles was horrified and told Townsend bluntly that he must be either 'mad or bad' to dream of marrying the Queen's sister. Townsend should leave royal service forthwith, Lascelles had advised the Queen. Knowing how much Townsend's departure would distress her sister, the Queen did not immediately act upon that advice. Now the very thing that Lascelles feared had happened. What had been an intimate family matter was suddenly world news.

The problem was still with the Queen when she went to Epsom the following week to witness the running of the Coronation Derby. For her it was a very special Derby, with hopes of a royal victory if only nothing happened to unsettle Aureole, the temperamental chestnut she had first seen as a week-old foal in her father's stud. All racing thoroughbreds are high-strung, but Aureole, as she knew from personal experience, was sensitive in the extreme. She had narrowly escaped a nipped finger while trying to coax him with an apple during a visit to the Boyd Rochfort training establishment at Newmarket. Only a timely shout on another occasion had enabled her to sidestep in time as Aureole kicked out at her. Now, in the paddock at Epsom, it happened again. A good-luck pat from a loyal racegoer unsettled the royal horse to such extent that it was quietened only with difficulty and failed to run as the Queen knew it could. 'If I had to be beaten, I'm glad it was by you,' she said graciously to Gordon Richards, whose mount Pinza beat Aureole to the winning post by a comfortable four lengths.

The newspapers continued to trumpet the love story of Princess Margaret and Peter Townsend. 'It is unthinkable that a royal princess, third in line of succession to the throne, should even contemplate marriage to a man who has been through the divorce courts,' pontificated one editorial. A generation later that reads like nonsense. Townsend, after all, had been the innocent party, the wronged husband. Princess Margaret, for all that she was third in line, stood little chance of actually succeeding to the throne. Today she is no more than eleventh in line and could retreat still further in the event that Prince Edward marries and has children in the future. But in the 1950s attitudes were very different. Divorce was still frowned upon, and even innocent parties were viewed with suspicion. As Margaret's sister, the Queen desired only her happiness, but as Monarch and Supreme Governor of the Church of England, so strongly opposed to divorce, she hesitated over giving consent to her sister's proposed marriage, as she was required to do under the Royal Marriage Act passed at the behest of George III. A more pragmatic prime minister might have devised a way out, as Harold Wilson would do years later when her divorced cousin, the Earl of Harewood, sought royal consent to his proposed marriage to the former secretary who had borne him a son. But Winston Churchill, prime minister again since 1951, was not Harold Wilson. While he personally saw no objection to Margaret's marrying Townsend, a majority of his Cabinet colleagues did, and he felt it his duty to reflect the majority view in the advice he gave the Queen: she should not consent to the marriage and Townsend should go. Instead of accompanying the Queen Mother and Princess Margaret on their trip to Southern Rhodesia, Townsend was detailed to go with the Queen and Duke of Edinburgh to Northern Ireland. By the time Princess Margaret returned from Africa he had left both royal service and Britain, having been despatched abroad as British Air Attaché in Brussels. But if the Queen hoped that that would be the end of the story, she was to be disappointed. In a little more than two years the crisis would surface again.

Her coronation behind her, it was time for the new Queen to be seen by the countries of the Commonwealth, or at least as many as could be sandwiched into half a year's nonstop travel, a round-the-world itinerary which still ranks as the longest royal tour ever. The statistics are staggering – 18,850 miles of sea travel, 19,650 by air, 9,900 by road and 1,600 by rail. In the course of it all she opened seven parliaments, attended 223 balls, banquets, receptions, garden parties, exhibitions and sports meetings, sat through 276 speeches, made 157 speeches on her own account and shook hands an estimated 13,000 times. She took her coronation gown with her to wear on special occasions, but not her crown. That is not allowed to leave the shores of Britain. With the new royal yacht *Britannia* not yet completed and the old unseaworthy *Victoria & Albert* already gone to the breaker's yard, most of the sea-going section of the itinerary was aboard the liner *Gothic*, its holds simultaneously, and oddly, conveying a miscellaneous cargo of cars, pianos, wallpaper and brandy. In New Zealand over a period of forty-five days the Queen saw, and was seen in, thirty-nine different cities and towns. In Australia it was sixty-eight different places in an even more crowded schedule of fifty-seven days, during which time she unveiled three memorials, made four broadcasts, planted six trees and was heaped with 468 gifts ranging from a diamond necklace to a nylon nightdress. A young and glamorous figure, the Queen attracted even vaster crowds in those days than her daughter-in-law would do a generation later, a staggering half a million people in Adelaide alone. Inevitably, and despite the meticulousness of the arrangements, there were alarms and excursions along the way. In New Zealand her personal jewel collection, a shimmering mass of tiaras, necklaces, brooches, bracelets, rings and ear-rings, some items family heirlooms, others gifts marking her wedding or coronation, the whole lot estimated to be worth close to £1 million even in those days, was lost for a few hours. The Queen herself did not get to hear of the incident until after the jewels had been safely located again. In Australia it was the Queen's favourite cream cheese which vanished in the course of a royal picnic. And this was never recovered. The Australian driver of the vehicle containing the picnic things had mistaken it for his 'tucker' and eaten it.

The last leg of the long journey was made aboard *Britannia*, which had sailed from Britain to meet the Queen at Tobruk. Before leaving the *Gothic*, however, in a gesture worthy of her Tudor namesake, she summoned the liner's captain, David Aitchison, commanded him to kneel on the deck and knighted him. Awaiting her aboard *Britannia* were the children, Charles and Anne, five and three years old respectively. The Queen had missed them during her long weeks away – 'More than they miss us,' she confided at one stage – and was delighted to see them again. She was delighted too with her new royal yacht. 'It's beautiful,' she exclaimed, enthusiastically. Her homecoming was like Coronation Day all over again, but on a vaster scale. The whole of Britain's south coast became a giant grandstand from which to view the progress of the royal yacht with its blue-bottle hull and snow-white superstructure. From ports and jetties an armada of small boats set out to escort the Queen for the last few miles. As the first fishing smack dipped its flag in salute, the Queen gave an order, and the ensign of the royal yacht dipped in return. Winston Churchill, never a man to miss the heart-warmth of the great occasion, had himself conveyed to the mouth of the Thames to join the Queen aboard *Britannia* for a triumphal homecoming with crowds cheering, ship's sirens hooting and church bells pealing.

There was to be a further triumph for the Queen later that year, on the racetrack. It was the year in which Aureole, in racing parlance, finally 'came good'. There were a few horse laughs in various quarters when it was whispered that the Queen had called in a Harley Street physiotherapist to treat the unpredictable animal, but she had the last laugh when Aureole, following treatment, won the Hardwicke Stakes, the Coronation Cup and the year's most valuable race, the King George VI and Queen Elizabeth Stakes. Not that Aureole was completely cured. He still managed to unseat his jockey before the start of the King George VI and Queen Elizabeth Stakes, while the crowd's shout of 'They're off' at the start caused him to swerve across the course. Last in the field at that point, Aureole was fourth with a mile to go and led for the last furlong to win the race. The Queen could hardly contain her excitement as she led her horse into the unsaddling enclosure.

It was largely thanks to Aureole that the Queen headed the list of winning owners that year. King Edward VII had commemorated the turf victories of Persimmon by having a larger-than-lifesize statue of the horse erected at Sandringham. His great-granddaughter, more modestly, had a small statuette of Aureole fashioned to grace her new sitting-room at Windsor.

Just as, on her accession to the throne, she had not been particularly enthused about moving into Buckingham Palace, so the Queen found Windsor Castle hardly the most relaxing place to which to retreat at weekends. She longed for something smaller and cosier, like her mother's weekend home, Royal Lodge, where she had spent such happy times as a Princess. With Prince Philip's help, she had already set about turning what is known as the Queen's Tower at Windsor into something similar. If the two of them did not actually pick up paint-brushes and tackle the work themselves, they did at least pore over colour cards and leaf through pattern books to decide upon colour schemes, wallpaper, curtains and furnishing fabrics. A gloomy old dining-room with walls of time-blackened oak was re-done in white and gold to serve as a sitting-room furnished with an array of comfortable sofas and armchairs. Two antique cabinets were converted to become respectively a drinks cabinet and what today's teenagers would call 'a music centre'. In fact, it held a record-player and a collection of gramophone records. Similarly, what had once been a drawing-room was lightened and brightened as a new dining-room. Bedroom and bathroom were also modernized and redecorated, with the bathroom given a false ceiling, similar to that which Prince Philip had introduced into the Buckingham Palace study which had been the King's and was now his, to reduce its massive height. Later that year Prince Philip made a trip to the Yukon. He returned with an idea picked up from a hotel in Whitehorse at which he had stayed. As a result, renovation was extended to the guest rooms at Windsor. Out went the heavy old Victorian furniture to be replaced with divan beds which could serve as sofas in daytime, and dressing-tables which doubled as writing desks.

Any hope the Queen may have entertained that Peter Townsend's banishment to Brussels would end the romantic attachment between him and Princess Margaret was heading for disappointment. With letters and telephone calls bridging the gap between them, absence served only to make the couple's hearts grow fonder. She still wanted to marry Peter, Margaret told her sister, and the dilemma which had confronted the Queen earlier was now more agonizing than ever. As Margaret's sister, naturally she desired her happiness. As Queen, she was bound to disapprove of the idea of her sister marrying a divorced man with two sons as strongly as her mother, more personally, had once disapproved of the Duke of Windsor's desire to marry Mrs Simpson. She sought advice from Anthony Eden, who had succeeded Churchill as her prime minister. Though himself divorced and remarried, Eden's advice was the same as Churchill's had been: the Queen should withhold consent.

On 21 August 1955 Princess Margaret celebrated her twenty-fifth birthday, an important anniversary under the Royal Marriage Act. At twenty-five, in theory at least, she could marry Townsend without her sister's royal consent by giving the Privy Council a year's notice of her intention to do so. The Queen still hoped her younger sister would 'see sense', she said. For Princess Margaret there remained the problem of Parliament's reaction if she went ahead. That summer, when Eden visited the Queen during the Royal Family's annual holiday at Balmoral, the younger sister sounded him out. While Parliament might not actually oppose marriage to Townsend, he told her, it would expect her to retire from public life, and would certainly cancel her official allowance, at that time £15,000 a year. His view, as prime minister, was that the proposed marriage would serve to damage the Crown.

On 12 October Townsend returned to London, and the following day the ill-starred lovers were reunited at Clarence House. They spent the weekend together at the Berkshire home of royal relatives, Mr and Mrs John Lycett Wills. The Queen, still seeking a way out for her sister, again raised the matter with Anthony Eden during his customary call at the Palace the following Tuesday. His advice was still the same: if Margaret wished to marry Townsend, she must do so of her own volition and take the consequences. He did not put it quite so bluntly, but that was the gist of it. With the story making bold headlines for the newspapers, the country was as divided as it had been over the dilemma of King Edward VIII and Mrs Simpson.

That weekend, before leaving London for Windsor Castle, the Queen unveiled a memorial to her dead father. Time had assuaged her grief, but her undiminished love for him showed in a speech which was intensely personal in content. She was clearly feeling the emotion of the occasion as she recalled his courage in the face of illness and the degree of personal sacrifice he had been called upon to make during his years of kingship, shirking no task, however difficult, and never faltering in 'his duties to his peoples'.

Throughout all the strains of his public life (the Queen said) he remained a man of warm and friendly sympathies – a

137

man who by the simple qualities of loyalty, resolution and service won for himself such a place in the affection of us all that when he died millions mourned for him as for a true and trusted friend.

At Windsor, that weekend, the Queen and Duke were joined by Princess Margaret. Marriage to Townsend was again the principle subject of conversation. Margaret went to her bedroom that night still tearfully defiant. So it was perhaps Townsend himself, when they met again at Clarence House the following Wednesday, who finally prevailed upon her to 'see sense'. Older and more worldly wise than the Princess, he may have seen more clearly than she did how much sacrifice marriage to him would entail for her. Certainly it was Townsend who was mainly responsible for the touching words of the public statement in which the Princess announced that she had decided not to marry him.

For the Queen, as she moved from her twenties into her thirties, it was a time of life when crisis must have seemed to crowd quickly on the heels of crisis. With her absorbed ever more deeply in her role as Monarch and the Duke ever more restless within the restrictions of his own ill-defined role of Consort, there was an occasional sense of strain in her own marriage. Even so, there was nothing to justify the headlines of a 'Royal Rift' which erupted around the world in 1957. As an outlet for his restlessness, the Duke had taken advantage of an invitation to open the 1956 Olympic Games in Melbourne to tack on what surely still ranks as the most adventurous royal tour ever. His idea of using the royal yacht to visit a number of lonely Commonwealth islands and isolated outposts took him deep into the Antarctic and away from home for four months. In his absence, gossip overheard and misheard at a dinner party would lead to newspaper stories hinting that royal husband and wife were on the verge of divorce. The marriage that actually was on the verge of divorce was that of Michael Parker, the Duke's Private Secretary, and his wife, Eileen. The Queen, in more recent years, has endeavoured to ease the strain royal service imposes on the marriages of those who undertake it. Duties and tours are more shared out these days to minimize the absences from home of royal aides and servants. But earlier such absences were a contributing factor in the break-up of more than one marriage, and Eileen and Michael Parker, at the time Parker accompanied the Duke on his Antarctic expedition, had already separated. In the babble of dinner party conversation, however, the 'he' and 'she' concerned were somehow confused with the Queen and her husband. The result was a spate of newspaper stories around the world which considerably upset the Queen. 'Why must they print such terrible things about us?' she sighed at one point.

Until then, it had always been Royal Family policy to ignore newspaper gossip about their personal lives. But gossip about her marriage was something the Queen was not prepared to tolerate. She ordered an official denial to be issued: 'It is quite untrue that there is any rift between the Queen and the Duke of Edinburgh.' However, it brought little, if any, respite, and the newspaper stories continued until the couple were finally and publicly seen to be happily re-united on a subsequent state visit to Portugal. On their return to London, the Queen further showed her love for her husband by elevating him to 'the style and titular dignity of a Prince', an action on her part which simultaneously rectified her dead father's apparent oversight at the time of their marriage.

Yet another crisis, very different in content, had confronted the Queen during the period of her husband's absence. She had spent Christmas at Sandringham as usual with the children, all three of them talking to the Duke via the royal yacht's radio-telephone on Christmas Day. Early in January her stay there was interrupted by the necessity to return to London when Anthony Eden resigned his post of prime minister from ill-health following the débâcle of the combined British-French-Israeli attempt to invade Egypt and take over the Suez Canal. As Monarch, it was – and is – her prerogative to appoint each new prime minister. Today, her choice is clear-cut. It would clearly be pointless to nominate other than the elected leader of the political party commanding a majority in the House of Commons. But in 1957, with the Conservatives in power, they did not yet have a system for electing a leader, as the Labour party did. So Eden's resignation left a vacuum which could be filled by several possible contenders, notably Eden's deputy, R. A. Butler (later Baron Butler of Saffron Walden), and the perhaps less fancied Harold Macmillan (later Earl of Stockton). So the Queen found herself with the highly responsible, and perhaps slightly embarrassing, task of having to choose between the two. She sought advice from the elder statesmen of the Conservative party, the ageing Churchill and the fifth Marquess of Salisbury, whose family had been whispering into the ears of the nation's monarchs since the days of the first Elizabeth. Both men – Salisbury after sounding out members of the Cabinet – advised her to plump for Macmillan. She did so. Indeed, she could hardly have done otherwise. But her choice provoked an outcry of dissent and accusations that, as Monarch, she was inclined to favour 'people of the tweedy sort'.

If her Coronation, as had been said, was a form of marriage between her and the nation, it seemed as if the honeymoon was over, at least for a time, as she became subject to a spate of criticism. Among the more notable of her critics was Lord Altrincham (who later renounced his title to become plain John Grigg). It was he who accused her, in his *National & English Review*, of surrounding herself with people of the tweedy sort. The Court, he wrote, 'emphasizes social lopsidedness' and had 'lamentably failed to move with the times'. Some of his comments were not perhaps without justification, or so it seemed at the time, with the Queen seemingly content, even anxious, that things should continue exactly as they were in her father's day, more concerned to uphold the old order than to initiate a new Elizabethan age. True, there had been a few changes, and others were in the pipeline. The Queen had already decided that the next series of presentation Courts, with their lines of curtseying, ostrich-plumed debutantes, should be the last. She had already instituted a spatter of informal luncheon parties at which she and the Prince (as Philip now indubitably was) could meet and talk with a cross-section of politicians and trade unionists, businessmen, educationalists and scientists, even the odd painter, actor, writer, pop star and sporting celebrity. It was also in her mind, as the old guard of royal aides retired one by one, to replace them with advisers selected more for their professional abilities and less for their social connections.

Most important of all, taking a long-term view of the future of monarchy, was her decision to send Prince Charles to school, though this owed more perhaps to Prince Philip than to the Queen herself. Schooldays were something entirely foreign to her

With her eldest grandchild Peter Phillips outside the miniature Welsh Cottage where she and her sister once played

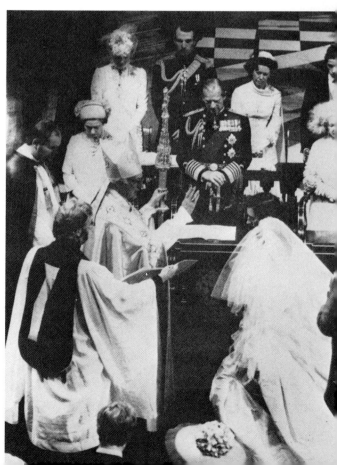

The family gathered at Charles and Diana's wedding

A talk with King Hassan of Morocco over lunch, 1980

Meeting members of HMS *Invincible*, the ship on which Prince Andrew served, on its return from the Falklands in 1982

With Indira Gandhi on her tour of India in 1983

Heads of state gathered at the D-Day celebrations in Normandy in 1984.
Right to left: President Reagan, the Grand Duke of Luxembourg, the
Queen, President Mitterand, King Baudouin of Belgium and King Olaf
of Norway

Overleaf: The Queen has always loved horses.
Royal Windsor Horse Show, 1984

experience. Prince Philip, on the other hand, had not only been to school but thoroughly enjoyed it. It was his idea that the Heir Apparent 'should go to school with other boys and learn to live with other children and absorb from childhood the discipline imposed by education with others'. In consequence, Charles would start at Cheam, his father's old school, that autumn and later again follow in his father's footsteps to Gordonstoun.

Lord Altrincham, of course, could not know what was in the Queen's mind at the time he penned his article for the *National & English Review*. In any event, he was inclined to overstep the mark with a number of personal allusions to the Queen. Her personality, he wrote, was that of 'a priggish schoolgirl', and her style of speaking was 'a pain in the neck'.

If Altrincham's outburst was hurtful enough in these respects, worse was to follow. That autumn the Queen visited the United States for the first time since she was a Princess. Arriving there, she was immediately confronted with copies of the *Saturday Evening Post*, at that time one of the country's most prestigious and influential publications, containing a highly critical article headlined 'Does Britain Really Need a Queen?'

Written by Malcolm Muggeridge, TV pundit and former editor of *Punch*, the article had in fact been previously published in Britain, appearing in the small circulation *New Statesman* under a different, less provocative title and had gone virtually unnoticed. Certainly the American version came fresh to the Queen, and she was not a little put out to find the monarchy of which she was so proud being compared to 'a royal soap opera . . . a substitute or ersatz religion' and further castigated as 'pure show' and 'a generator of snobbishness and a focus of sycophancy'. If she was upset, Philip, ever a loyal consort and protective husband, was furious. 'If they must print such things about us, does it have to be while we are actually here?' he demanded, indignantly. But his on-the-spot anger was as nothing compared to the fury of diehard loyalists back home when Britain's newspapers picked up and reprinted some of Muggeridge's more trenchant views. Altrincham had earlier suffered the indignity of having his face slapped in public. Reaction to the *Saturday Evening Post* article was even stronger. Muggeridge was spat upon as he walked in the street, a contract he had to write a series of articles for a London newspaper was abruptly terminated and he was banned, for a time at least, by the BBC.

In one other respect which the critics of the day would seem to have overlooked, the Queen had already taken a clear-cut step towards moving monarchy more firmly into the second half of the twentieth century. More and more she was turning to air travel to speed her about the world. In the course of her 1953–4 Commonwealth tour she had flown more miles than she had travelled by sea. That 1957 visit to the United States was made by air. Over the years since, she has relied more and more upon air travel, visiting Commonwealth countries and foreign capitals with an ease and frequency undreamed of in previous reigns, far and away the most travelled monarch in Britain's history. If monarchs were still identified by their habits and practices as in the days of Edmund Ironside and Richard the Lionheart, the Queen would surely be Elizabeth the Airborne.

Her 1957 visit to the United States had been preceded by a visit to Canada – in fact it was as Queen of Canada, not Queen of the United Kingdom, that she crossed the border into the United States – where she took yet another step towards moving monarchy into the twentieth century by appearing on television. Nervous of this new medium, she had previously turned down a suggestion by the BBC that her Christmas Day message to the Commonwealth should be televised instead of merely broadcast by radio. Approached again by the Canadians, and encouraged by the fact that Prince Philip had earlier made a successful television appearance, she agreed, however hesitantly. The result was an outstanding success, though those who saw her can have had no idea how nearly it was a disaster. Despite two rehearsals, the Queen was visibly tense and nervous as the minutes ticked away to transmission time. It was Prince Philip, watching her on a monitor screen, who saved the situation. Not being in the same studio, he could not encourage her personally as, earlier in her reign, he had sometimes done when she dried up in conversation on public occasions. But he could send a message. 'Tell the Queen to remember the wailing and gnashing of teeth,' he said, a joking reminder that he himself had gone wrong while reading the lesson at an earlier church service. The relayed message brought a big smile to the Queen's face – at the exact moment the programme went on the air. So delighted was the Queen that, returning to London, she was now happy to accede to the BBC's request that her Christmas message should move into the age of television.

Despite the earlier gloomy prophecy in *The Lancet*, the Queen's health had so far stood up well to the rigours of monarchy. Indeed, she seemed to thrive on hard work and the occasional crisis. But now came a recurrence of the feverish head colds to which she had been subject in childhood. Part of her Christmas break at Sandringham saw her confined to her room with a chill. In April 1958 she was again so unwell that several engagements had to be cancelled. In June, though still not well, she insisted obstinately on playing her full part in the traditional Trooping the Colour ceremony on a day of pelting rain. The following month she was obliged to cut short a tour of Scotland and the North East because of soaring temperature, inflamed eyes and loss of voice. An operation to irrigate the sinuses was carried out under local anaesthetic. Before and after her operation the Queen continued to tackle the contents of her Boxes as assiduously as ever, sometimes working at her desk, sometimes sitting up in bed. But outside engagements had to be cancelled, among them a tour of Wales and a visit to the Commonwealth Games being held that year in Cardiff. To make up for her non-appearance, the Queen recorded a speech to be broadcast at the closing ceremony of the Games. 'The British Empire and Commonwealth Games in the capital, together with all the activities of the Festival of Wales, have made this a memorable year for the Principality. I have therefore decided to mark it further by an act which will, I hope, give as much pleasure to all Welshmen as it does to me. I intend to create my son, Charles, Prince of Wales today. When he is grown up, I will present him to you at Caernarvon.' Prince Charles was nine at the time, and his investiture in Caernarvon would not be for another eleven years.

10 MOTHER AGAIN

The year 1959 brought another lengthy separation between the Queen and Prince Philip, though hardly by their own wish. It was at the request of the Government that the Prince undertook a further royal tour of islands and outposts similar to that in 1956–7 which had led to rumours of a rift between the couple. He was gone this time for three months. So eager was the Queen to see him again that, on the day of his return, she could not wait contentedly at the palace but drove to the airport to welcome him back. He returned in exuberant mood, playing some dashing polo at Windsor and having an accusing finger pointed in his direction when a brace of photographers found themselves sprinkled with water at the Chelsea Flower Show. It was around this time that Prince Andrew was conceived.

The Queen, earlier, had wanted more children: a family of four, two boys and two girls, she once confided in governess Marion Crawford. But a vastly increased work-load occasioned by her father's illness and subsequent death, leading to her own accession as Monarch, had hardly been conducive to increasing the family. Now thirty-three and with the younger of her two existing children almost nine, her third pregnancy, as her husband seemed to hint in a subsequent speech, was perhaps more a 'happy accident' than the result of family planning. The Queen was nevertheless delighted, though pregnancy could hardly have come at a more inopportune time. Immediately ahead of her lay the longest tour of Canada she had ever undertaken, with a visit to Ghana to follow. The Ghana visit was quietly postponed, but, because it was so imminent, the Queen firmly declined to have the Canadian tour either postponed or abridged; she refused even to let anyone on an official level be informed of her condition. Her sole concession to pregnancy before leaving for Canada was to engage an extra seamstress so that royal dresses could be let out if necessary to conceal her condition as the tour progressed.

The result, as she toured Canada from coast to coast over a period of nearly seven weeks, was an up-and-down mixture of days when she seemed to glow with the bloom of approaching motherhood and others on which she looked pale and strained almost to the point of exhaustion. A variety of medical excuses was produced to account for her less good days, but more experienced journalists accompanying the royal party were not slow to suspect pregnancy. Mamie Eisenhower, wife of the American President, became the first outsider to know, as distinct from merely suspect, the truth. 'My, you look beautiful,' she exclaimed, impulsively, as the presidential party joined the Queen and Prince Philip aboard the royal yacht for the official opening ceremony of the St Lawrence Seaway. Smiling, the Queen confided the reason for the extra bloom of beauty she wore that day. Later, with the Queen plagued by the pangs of morning sickness, it was necessary also to inform the Canadian prime minister, John Diefenbaker. He immediately suggested cancelling the remainder of the tour, but the Queen would still not entertain any such suggestion. In consequence, she was so exhausted by the time the tour finally ended that the idea of a leisurely cruise home aboard *Britannia* had to be abandoned, as did planned visits to the Shetland and Orkney Isles. Instead, the Queen flew straight back to London to be examined by royal physicians. Fortunately, examination found nothing wrong that a restful stay at Balmoral could not cure.

It was during her third pregnancy, on one of the occasions when she received the prime minister in audience, that the Queen brought up the question of the royal name. Even if she did not actually say so to Harold Macmillan, she was clearly feeling that, in adopting the name of Windsor on her accession to the throne, she had been less than fair to her husband and was seeking to adjust the balance. Less concerned than Churchill had been with the importance of a dynastic name, Macmillan raised no objection. The outcome was an Order in Council declaring it the Queen's 'will and pleasure' that, while she would still retain her maiden name of Windsor, some at least of her descendants would now be Mountbatten-Windsors. Exactly which descendants would be affected by this

145

new Order in Council has never been clarified. Initially, it was thought that it would not apply until that distant date when the expected third child, Prince Andrew, was not only himself a father but a grandfather. That this is not the case was revealed when Princess Anne married Captain Mark Phillips in the name of Anne Mountbatten-Windsor. The Prince of Wales, on the other hand, when he married Lady Diana Spencer, chose to do so under his royal title of 'Charles P'.

Eleven days after the Queen's still unclear declaration, on 19 February 1960, came the birth of Prince Andrew. Obedient as always to the dictates of royal duty, the Queen continued to plug away at the contents of her Boxes up to the day before the baby was born. The day following the birth, she had her Boxes sent to her bedroom so that she could catch up on her paperwork, a bedside telephone linking her with her Private Secretaries. Nursing and feeding her new baby necessarily also took up much of her time. Conscious of the age-gap which separated the newcomer from his brother and sister – Charles was already eleven and Anne rising ten – she revealed some concern lest he should be brought up as virtually an only child. 'We'll have to think about a little playmate for Andrew,' she said at one point. It was said lightly enough, but, as later events would show, she was not altogether joking. She was concerned too that the new baby should not suffer the same degree of public exposure that her two older children had experienced throughout childhood. In the months that followed, in her desire to protect Andrew from public exposure, she was inclined to go to the other extreme, declining to release photographs for publication, permitting journalists only the minimum details of the baby's wellbeing and upbringing. The result was a crop of rumours culminating in blunt enquiries by probing European journalists as to whether there was 'something wrong' with the baby. The strapping Prince Andrew of today affords a more than adequate answer.

The Queen had further cause for happiness that year of her thirty-fourth birthday. Her sister, Princess Margaret, seemed finally to have found a new love, and a week after the birth of Prince Andrew came the announcement of her betrothal to photographer Antony Armstrong-Jones (later to become Earl of Snowdon just ahead of the birth of the couple's first child). They were married that November. Sadly, it was to prove a marriage not destined to stand the test of time.

The Queen's travels during eight years of monarchy – her six-months Commonwealth tour, six weeks in Canada, a visit to Nigeria, state visits to the United States and six European countries – had been more than sufficient to justify the sabbatical she permitted herself to enjoy during the first few months of renewed motherhood. But Andrew's first birthday found her back on her travels, engaged on a fifteen-thousand-mile tour embracing India, Pakistan and Nepal as well as Iran and Turkey. A tour of Ghana, unavoidably postponed in 1959 because of pregnancy, was reconstituted soon after. It came at a time when Ghana was in a state of considerable unrest with threats against the life of President Nkrumah, who would be hosting the Queen, and Harold Macmillan, the prime minister, saw it as his duty, on the occasion of his weekly audience at Buckingham Palace, to point out the risks involved. If he did not go so far as actually to advise against going, it was perhaps because he could not. She would be visiting Ghana not as Queen of the United Kingdom but as Head of the Commonwealth, a nice distinction which the Queen is always at pains to observe. Even so, the prime minister made his point. But the Queen shrugged off the idea that she might be in danger. 'The Queen has been absolutely determined all through,' the prime minister noted later. 'She is impatient of the attitude towards her to treat her as a woman and a film star or mascot.' He added, almost echoing the words of the speech which the first Elizabeth made to her soldiers at Tilbury and which the second Elizabeth learned by heart in the days of her childhood, 'She has indeed "the heart and stomach of a man".'

Little more than two years later Macmillan was obliged to resign his post of prime minister because of ill-health. The Conservative party had still no clear-cut system for electing a leader, and again the Queen found herself with the responsibility of appointing a new prime minister. And again the result was controversy. Before making up her mind, the Queen went to see Macmillan in hospital but, unlike the previous occasion, took no further soundings. The retiring prime minister produced a list of six names for her consideration. His own choice as the man most likely to find general support, he said, was the fourteenth Earl of Home (later

147

Sir Douglas Alec-Home). So it was Home the Queen summoned to the Palace to be her new prime minister. The controversy which ensued, and which resulted in both Iain Macleod and Enoch Powell declining to serve in the Home administration, was based on the argument that the Queen had, in effect, permitted Macmillan to name his successor. It was the second time in six years that the Queen had discovered that the use of her royal prerogative was not without drawbacks, and it must have been with a sigh of relief that she greeted the proposal, eighteen months later, that the Conservatives, like the Labour party, should elect their future leaders by ballot.

Her eldest child was already a schoolboy at Gordonstoun, her daughter at Benenden, and she herself was in her thirty-seventh year when the Queen discovered that she was again pregnant. If her idea of 'a little playmate' for Andrew was about to be realized, her dream of a family of two boys and two girls was not. Her fourth child, born on 10 March 1964, proved to be yet another son, Prince Edward. Once again the Queen found it necessary to dovetail the sometimes conflicting demands of monarchy and motherhood. But twelve years' experience had matured her to a degree which enabled her to digest the contents of a state document in half the time it had once taken and equipped her to take her own decisions instead of waiting upon the advice of others. So she could afford to devote more time to the new baby; to Andrew too, whom she was teaching to read and write as she had once taught Charles and Anne. Just as she had been obliged to leave Andrew in his first year to tour India and Pakistan so, later in 1964, she kissed her new baby goodbye for yet another transatlantic crossing as Queen of Canada.

That visit to Canada was to prove very different from any previous royal tour. The Queen's visit to Ghana, despite Harold Macmillan's head-shaking, had gone off peacefully enough. The Canadian visit did not. Hindsight suggests that it was unwise of the Canadian government to include Quebec in the Queen's itinerary at a time when extremists were seeking to force the secession of the province from the rest of Canada. Following upon the assassination of the American president, John Kennedy, only the previous November, there were threats that the Queen's visit would see Quebec turned into 'a second Dallas'. Despite such threats, there was no thought of changing the planned itinerary. The result was such a level of violence on the streets of Quebec, with truncheon-wielding riot police battling it out with jeering French-Canadian extremists, that at least one member of the royal entourage questioned whether it was safe for the Queen to fulfil her public engagements. The Queen brushed the idea aside with the same indifference she had displayed earlier to Harold Macmillan's mention of the risk she would be running if she went to Ghana. 'Nobody's going to hurt me,' she said. It was less a display of courage than an expression of her inherent belief that nobody could want to harm her. The Canadian authorities were not quite so sure and sensibly ensured that she travelled around Quebec in a bullet-proof Cadillac while police sharpshooters kept watch from rooftops against the possibility of an assassination attempt.

It was now nearly thirteen years since the Queen had succeeded to the throne. Throughout that time she had dealt only with Conservative prime ministers. Now for the first time, following the 1964 General Election, she had a Labour prime minister to deal with, Harold Wilson. Apart from a rather sticky start, Monarch and prime minister got along surprisingly well. Wilson was the fifth prime minister with whom she had found herself dealing, and Churchill, her first, was to die the following year. The Queen rarely attends funerals other than those of royal relatives. The time factor involved would be too much of an additional burden. But Churchill's funeral was different. He was a world statesman, more than anyone else the main architect of victory in World War II. So his funeral became a state occasion with the Queen heading the twelve monarchs and heads of state who, along with sixteen prime ministers, were present to pay their last respects.

The ex-King whose cause Churchill had sought to champion in the weeks leading up to the Abdication was also in London that year. For the Duke of Windsor eye surgery had become necessary, and he entered the London Clinic. The Duchess travelled to London with him from their home in Paris. The Queen, probably because she was no more than a child at the time of the Abdication, not fully understanding and thus one stage removed from the strong emotions it aroused in older members of the Royal Family, was never so bitter about the Windsors as her mother was. The Queen Mother, throughout the years of her husband's monarchy,

149

would never meet the Duke of Windsor, though earlier he had been her favourite brother-in-law. But the Queen, in the year of her accession, invited him to lunch at Buckingham Palace when he was in London visiting his ageing mother, Queen Mary. The following year she invited both Windsors to her Coronation. Because the invitation was worded in the names of 'His Royal Highness the Duke of Windsor and Her Grace the Duchess of Windsor', the Duke declined the invitation, as he later refused one to the wedding of Princess Margaret. It was a sore point with him right up to his death that his wife was denied the 'Royal Highness' designation accorded to her sisters-in-law in Britain.

In an attempt to heal the breach which had for so long divided the Royal Family, the Queen visited her uncle while he was in the London Clinic. Though she had seen him from time to time over the years since his Abdication – at her father's funeral, at that Palace lunch, at the funeral of Queen Mary – it was her first meeting with the Duchess since that long-ago encounter at Royal Lodge when she was a child of ten and the Windsors not yet married. There was no mention of her visit (nor of a second one a few days later) in the *Court Circular*, an omission explained on the grounds that it was 'a personal and family matter'. But the fact that the Queen was accompanied on her visit by her Private Secretary suggests that the 'personal and family' matters discussed were not confined to the ordinary chit-chat common between relatives. However, there was to be no subsequent change in the status of the Duchess. In this, as in other ways, the Queen would remain her father's daughter.

An opportunity further to heal the family breach presented itself in 1967 when the Queen unveiled a memorial to her grandmother and the Duke's mother, Queen Mary, at Marlborough House. The Duke and Duchess were again invited to London for the occasion, with the Queen deftly side-stepping the question of the couple's different status by defining the ceremony as 'private' (though it was witnessed by more than a thousand people) and extending them a personal rather than formal invitation. The overture was successful, and the Windsors accepted the invitation. Queen Mary died without once meeting the daughter-in-law for whom her eldest son deserted the throne. Nor did the Queen Mother meet her during the fifteen years she was Queen. But in 1967, at her daughter's instigation, finally she did, though her acknowledgement of the fact was restricted to a formal handshake.

Before then, in 1965, the opportunity had also presented itself for the Queen to make further amends to Prince Philip's sisters for the manner in which they had been slighted at the time of their brother's wedding. She had already gone a long way towards doing so, inviting them to her Coronation, having them and their children to stay with her at Balmoral and elsewhere. But because she was Queen, she had hitherto been obliged to turn down reciprocal invitations to visit them in Germany. Prince Philip had visited his sisters many times, sometimes taking one or more of the two elder children with him. But the Queen, because even her private visits must not run counter to Britain's foreign policy, had been obliged to stay behind. By 1965, however, the old enemy was forgiven, and a state visit to West Germany was arranged. Indeed, it would have taken place a year earlier but for the birth of Prince Edward. A free weekend in the course of that state visit afforded the Queen the opportunity to go to Salem, where all three of her sisters-in-law, with their families, were waiting to welcome her. While there she also visited the school where Prince Philip had been briefly educated in the 1930s before transferring to Gordonstoun and was amused to see the desk he had occupied still displaying the capital P he had carved on it in boyhood.

Simmering at this time was the Rhodesian question. Where the dignity of the Crown is concerned, the Queen is as firmly regal as any monarch before her. Years later she would see the American-led invasion of Grenada, the small Caribbean island of which she is also Queen, as a violation of her sovereignty. So, in the 1960s, she saw Ian Smith's unilateral declaration of independence in the same light. When her then prime minister, the pragmatic Harold Wilson, flew to Salisbury in a last attempt to persuade Smith not to take the independence route, he took with him a letter for Smith written in the Queen's own handwriting. Her letter made it clear that she viewed what Smith proposed as an abnegation of his duty to the Crown. And when the Rhodesian leader replaced her Governor with one of his own, she riposted by making her man, Humphrey Gibbs, a Knight Grand Cross of the Victorian Order, one of the highest honours in her personal gift. But she would not countenance a direct appeal to her Rhodesian subjects over Smith's head in case it provoked violence, and agreed with Harold Wilson that there should be no attempt to bring Rhodesia back to the constitutional path by the use of armed force.

From the moment the Queen succeeded to the Crown, the relationship between her and Prince Philip inevitably became an ambivalent one, and not without its problems at times. If she, on marriage, had promised to love, honour *and obey* her husband, Prince Philip, at the time of the Coronation, had equally sworn an oath to serve her as her 'liege man of life and limb and of earthly worship'. For the most part they have managed to strike a successful balance, with the Prince playing a supportive role to the Queen in public while the wife treats the husband as head of the family in private. Yet it was perhaps as more than merely head of the family that Prince Philip, in their eldest son's eighteenth year, chaired a small but high-level conference at Buckingham Palace to decide how Prince Charles could best be trained for his future public role of Prince of Wales and sometime King. Earlier, it had been largely Prince Philip's decision that Charles should be sent to his father's old schools, Cheam and Gordonstoun. Charles was unhappy at Gordonstoun but, once there, could hardly be transferred to another school in Britain without its being interpreted as a slur on the Scottish establishment. So he was made to stick it out, though he was given a break – with no reflection on Gordonstoun – by sending him for a time to school in Australia. The experiment worked so well that his younger brothers, Prince Andrew and Prince Edward, would later have part of their education in Canada and New Zealand respectively, a sequence of events which the Queen saw also as helping to maintain the increasingly fragile links between Monarchy and the Commonwealth.

The Queen herself also attended that Buckingham Palace conference to decide the final polishing of the Heir to the Throne, but took no part in the actual discussion. The young man most concerned was not present, though his desire to go on from Gordonstoun to university went through on the nod. Prince Philip's view was that, after university, a cadetship at the Royal Naval College, Dartmouth, and a spell in the Royal Navy would constitute the best possible training for a future King, an opinion shared by Earl Mountbatten, who was also present. And so it was decided. Harold Wilson, the Labour prime minister of the day, murmured something about one of the new 'redbrick' universities, but the final choice was left to the Queen and Prince Philip. They plumped for Cambridge.

Prince Philip has said himself that, constitutionally, he does not exist. Yet the training of the next King is surely as much a constitutional as a family matter. Does the Queen, in private, seek her husband's opinion, even take his advice, in other constitutional directions also? The everyday relationship between wife and husband would suggest that there are times when she does. And why not? Prince Philip is, after all, not only her husband but the pre-eminent member of her Privy Council. Indeed, the idea has been mooted more than once that she should bestow upon him the title of Prince Consort, as Queen Victoria did Prince Albert. That she has not done so would seem to be due, as far as these things can be gauged, to the fact that it is a title Prince Philip himself is not anxious to possess. He has no wish to be compared with Prince Albert, to appear in any way desirous of playing King to his wife's Queen, as Albert did. But that he is Consort in fact if not in title was underlined by the Queen in 1967 when she had the old Consort's throne brought out of storage and installed on a level with her own throne in the House of Lords for the state opening of Parliament.

For both the Queen and her husband this was a period of their lives when they were worried over the health of their respective mothers. Except for cracking a bone in her foot when she slipped on some steps at Windsor in 1961 and a brief spell in hospital for an appendectomy in 1964, the Queen Mother, until now, had enjoyed vigorous good health throughout her sixty-six years. But in 1966, just before Christmas, a hospital check-up following an attack of laryngitis revealed a partial obstruction of the abdomen. An operation to relieve the obstruction was deemed urgently necessary, and she spent Christmas in hospital. The Queen, visiting her there, was delighted to learn that tests for malignity had fortunately proved negative. By the end of the month the Queen Mother was back home at Clarence House and by mid-January sufficiently recovered to join her elder daughter at Sandringham, with many more years ahead in which to enjoy each other's company.

Prince Philip's mother, Princess Alice, some fifteen years older than the Queen Mother, was not destined to live as long. When news came soon after that she had been taken ill in Germany, Philip flew there to bring her back to London for treatment. The Queen, meantime, had an apartment prepared at the palace for her to move into when she left hospital. That this was more than simply the action of a dutiful daughter-in-law was shown by the frequency with which she was to be found in her mother-in-law's palace apartment, chatting with her, during the months the ageing Princess lived there. Christmas the following year found the old lady too ill to accompany the rest of the family to Windsor. So, on Christmas Day, the Queen, with Prince Philip, drove back to the Palace to have Christmas tea with her. Princess Alice did not quite live to see another Christmas.

It was the combined influence of Prince Philip and his uncle, Earl Mountbatten, which persuaded the Queen, in 1968–9, to embark upon that exercise in royal publicity which resulted in the television documentary *Royal Family*. Her natural distaste for projecting herself in whatever form made her extremely hesitant at first, but as filming progressed she entered ever more enthusiastically into her 'starring' role. Prince Philip, by contrast, though the more enthusiastic of the two originally, became ever more impatient over the time it took to set up lights and cameras and more and more irritated by the frequency with which the same scenes were shot again and again. The forty-three hours of film shot actually took up time on seventy-five different days over the course of nearly a year and were then whittled down to one hour and fifty minutes of eventual transmission. Scenes ranged from the feeding of the royal corgis to a diplomatic reception at which the Queen seemed perturbed that she could not spot the US Ambassador, from a barbecue picnic in the hills around Balmoral and the decking of the royal Christmas tree to a buffet supper for Olympic athletes at Buckingham Palace at which Princess Anne was seen chatting to the young army officer she later married.

The finished documentary, seen by 23 million viewers the first time it was shown in Britain and later by television audiences in 130 countries, was transmitted just ahead of Prince Charles' investiture as Prince of Wales. Over this too the Queen, at least initially, was not noticeably enthusiastic. While she had every intention of keeping her long-ago promise to present her eldest son to the Welsh people at Caernarvon, she questioned whether, with Welsh nationalists resorting more and more to violence, this was the right time for such ceremony and spectacle. To a point, her doubts were to appear justified. The twenty months leading up to the investiture were punctuated by no fewer than thirteen bomb blasts in Wales, the thirteenth of which, in Abergele on the very day of the ceremony, resulted in two would-be bombers blowing themselves up with their own bomb. The Queen was already on her way to Caernarvon when what appeared to be yet another bomb was spotted on the underside of the bridge over the River Dee which the royal train would have to cross at Chester. The train was halted and the Queen waited patiently while bomb experts investigated. The 'bomb' proved to be a hoax, a bunch of candles tied together to give the appearance of sticks of dynamite.

To safeguard the Queen, her Heir and others of the Royal Family, thousands of extra police were drafted into Caernarvon for the occasion. Police helicopters buzzed around overhead, and naval frogmen guarded the royal yacht berthed off Holyhead. Security in and around the remains of Caernarvon's ancient castle was so tight that even the Queen's sister, Princess Margaret, had her handbag checked. In the event, the investiture ceremony passed off with nothing more than a few very minor hitches. The mother in the Queen could not resist the temptation to adjust the gold clasps on the ermine-trimmed robe in which her eldest son was draped for the occasion, a gesture which television cameras transmitted to some 19 million viewers in Britain and an estimated half a billion more around the world. The American show-business magazine *Variety* summed it up satirically as 'the best commercial for the tourist trade since the coronation'. It was that too, of course, though that was not how the Queen saw it. Her earlier doubts were forgotten as her Heir took the oath of allegiance to her and she buckled on his sword and placed a princely coronet on his head. It was with a mixture of queenly pride and motherly love – and certainly no thought of possible danger – that she led him on to the balcony known as Queen Eleanor's Gate and presented him to the Welsh people as 'My most dear son'.

The bombings in Wales ahead of the investiture marked the beginning of a new and more violent era in the Queen's life. In the years ahead there would be frequent threats of assassination. Even in New Zealand in 1970, a country one does not normally associate with violence, there was a bomb threat when she attended a concert in Dunedin. She went to the concert just the same. Indeed, as though to show her contempt for threats against her, it was on that tour of New Zealand and Australia that she initiated the now famous royal walkabouts, sauntering through the crowds who flocked to see her instead of merely driving past them, pausing here and there for a few sentences of conversation. If, initially, she was slightly nervous it was more because of her inherent shyness than from fear of assassination. The experiment went well in New Zealand, slightly less well in some places in Australia where the idea of the Queen moving around on foot worried the authorities and security was on a massive scale. There was little point in such walkabouts, the Queen joked, if the only people she could talk to were those assigned to protect her.

In those days the Queen was inclined to jib against the security surrounding her, relatively light though it was at the time. So, for that matter, did Prince Philip. Both felt, as the Queen said in Australia, that it came between them and the people. But increased security was to become more and more important as the world moved into an era of ever more violence and threats of violence. The following year, back home in Britain, there would be a whole series of threats made against the Queen's life. There was a threat to assassinate her when she carried out a royal tour of Essex; another threat to shoot her during a visit to York.

There was no way of knowing, of course, whether such threats were genuine or simply hoaxes. What was known was that both occasions afforded opportunity for an assassination attempt. In Essex the Queen's car would be driving slowly along a succession of narrow, winding roads, while in York there would be a drive in an open carriage through the city streets.

With the assassination of President Kennedy very much in mind, those responsible for the Queen's security would have preferred both visits to have been cancelled. But it is not in the Queen's nature to give way in the face of threats. However, she did agree that for the tour of Essex she should have a police motor-cycle escort, something against which she had previously held out. For further safeguard extra police were stationed at crossroads and

156

other points along the route and an armed bodyguard sat beside the royal chauffeur. Unknown to the Queen, her chauffeur was also given instructions to speed up past the most likely danger spots.

For the Queen's visit to York, advantage was taken of the fact that the royal carriage would be escorted by a detachment of the Household Cavalry. The escort, on this occasion, was more than merely ceremonial. Ahead of the Queen's visit, the escorting troopers practised a special manoeuvre which would see the Queen hidden by a screen of horses and riders at the first hint of danger. In the event, both her tour of Essex and the visit to York passed off without incident.

Despite threats, the Queen made no change in her accustomed lifestyle, public or private. That was the year she went to Burghley to see Princess Anne compete in the European Eventing Championship. Passed over by the British team selectors because it was thought that she was not fully fit after a spell in hospital for the removal of an ovarian cyst, the Princess took part in the championship as an individual entry. To the delight of her mother, and doubtless the chagrin of the team selectors, she beat the officially selected riders from five countries to win the championship.

There was yet a further threat against the Queen's life just ahead of the State Opening of Parliament. Since the days of Guy Fawkes it has been traditional for the vaults beneath the Houses of Parliament to be searched prior to the opening ceremony as a precaution against another attempt to blow up Monarch and Parliament. Over the course of the more than three and a half centuries since the original Gunpowder Plot, however, it was perhaps inevitable that the search should have become little more than a quaint old British custom, a tradition observed by Yeomen of the Guard clad in picturesque Tudor costumes and armed with nothing more lethal than old-fashioned halberds. The 1971 threat against the Queen's life quickly changed all that. That year, for the first time, Tudor ruffs and halberds were supplemented by bomb experts and sniffer dogs. And in case the bomb threat was merely a ruse designed to draw attention away from planned assassination by another means and from a different quarter, hundreds of extra police, many armed, were on duty that day as the Queen, accompanied by

Prince Philip and the Prince of Wales, journeyed between Buckingham Palace and the Palace of Westminster, where Parliament sits.

Like the others, this threat came to nothing. But there is no way of knowing, even now, if that was because they were hoaxes or because would-be assassins were baulked by increased security. And it speaks volumes for the Queen's courage and dedication to duty that still less was there any way of knowing beforehand.

The spring of the following year found the Queen again in Paris, where her uncle the Duke of Windsor, who had once been briefly King Edward VIII, lay dying. Her visit to Paris was an official engagement, but she made time to visit her dying uncle and the Duchess of Windsor at their home in the Bois de Boulogne. Prince Philip and the Prince of Wales went with her. The Duke of Windsor died eight days later. His body was brought home to Britain for interment at Windsor. The Queen, as a final gesture of restitution for the long years which had so sadly divided the Windsors from the rest of the Royal Family, sent an aircraft of the Queen's Flight to France to bring the Duchess to Britain also, had her to stay at the palace for the first time in two reigns and sat beside her at the memorial service in St George's Chapel, Windsor.

That was also the year when the Queen, at the age of forty-six, celebrated her silver wedding anniversary. It came on her as 'a bit of a surprise', she confessed. Most couples share their silver wedding anniversaries with relatives and friends. The Queen and Prince Philip shared theirs also with the nation, marking the occasion with a state drive to Westminster Abbey, where they had been married, for a service of thanksgiving and by sitting down to a celebration luncheon at the Guildhall. Freed for once from the necessity to utter no more than platitudes, the Queen's after-luncheon speech would rank, in its emotional depth and feeling, with the one she made when unveiling the memorial to her dead father. It was also one of the few speeches, perhaps the only one so far, in which she has permitted herself the levity of a public quip. It was surely an occasion on which she might be forgiven for employing that overworked royal expression 'My husband and I', she joked. More seriously, she lifted the royal veil to give a brief glimpse of herself as a woman, wife and mother. 'A marriage begins by joining man and wife together,' she said. 'But this relationship, however deep, needs to develop and mature with the passing years. For that it must be held firm in the web of family relationships – between parents and children, grandparents and grandchildren, cousins, aunts and uncles.'

Though she could have no way of knowing it at the time, in another five years she would be a grandmother herself.

11 GREAT GOING, LIZ

While no one could foresee it, the Queen was about to enter upon the most traumatic part of her life and reign, a period during which the assassination threats of 1971 would come close to reality and, indeed, would become reality itself in the case of Prince Philip's uncle, Earl Mountbatten. There would be, in addition, an attempt to kidnap Princess Anne and the shock of an intruder not only getting past the Buckingham Palace security but gaining access to the Queen's bedroom. On a constitutional level, there would be the downfall of Edward Heath in Britain, a furore over the use of the royal prerogative in Australia and the antics of Idi Amin in Uganda with which to contend. On a personal level, there would be sadness over the breakdown of her sister's marriage, grief over the horrific murder of Prince Philip's uncle, Earl Mountbatten by the IRA and fears for the safety of Prince Andrew while serving with British forces fighting to retake the Falkland Islands.

All these things were hidden in the future when the Queen happily celebrated her silver wedding anniversary in 1972. Indeed, the future seemed to promise only further happiness. In addition to the public celebrations marking the occasion, the Queen's two older children, the Prince of Wales, twenty-four that same month and a sub-lieutenant in the Royal Navy, and Princess Anne, now twenty-two, clubbed together in giving a private party for their parents' silver wedding. Among those the Princess invited to the party as her personal guests was the young man with whom she had been seen conversing so animatedly in the *Royal Family* television documentary, Mark Phillips, a lieutenant in the Queen's Dragoons. They had known each other now for some four years and would be married within the space of another year. Both the Queen and Prince Philip quickly came to like Mark, and the Queen left her daughter in no doubt that she would be more than happy to give her formal consent as required by the Royal Marriage Act. That left only a small matter of family protocol to be resolved. When the mother of his intended is also Queen of the United Kingdom, it is difficult for a young man to know whether it is the mother or the father he should approach to seek the daughter's hand in marriage. Mark was gently nudged in the direction of Prince Philip in his capacity as head of family. It was Prince Philip too who acted as chef at a picnic party, a mixture of vintage champagne and barbecued chops and sausages, with which the family secretly celebrated the couple's betrothal in the hills around Balmoral.

The wedding took place on 14 November 1973, which was also the twenty-fifth birthday of the Prince of Wales. To the Queen's disappointment, there were as yet no signs of her Heir Apparent taking a bride, though there were hopes in that direction. However, any hopes the Queen may have entertained concerning her eldest son were to be dashed when his friendship with the young lady of the moment failed to blossom into love.

Princess Anne had been married only a few months when the Queen experienced the first of a series of cataclysmic shocks which were to punctuate her life over the next decade and beyond. It was March 1974. She was in Indonesia, in Jakarta, the capital, asleep in bed in the early hours of the morning, when the telephone rang. Prince Philip, who was with her, was quietly summoned to take the call. It was from London, from Princess Anne. Replacing the telephone, he woke the Queen to tell her of the horrifying attempt to kidnap their daughter as she and her husband drove back to Buckingham Palace after attending a charity film show.

Shocked though she was by the news, the Queen considered the situation calmly and logically. Her two-month tour of the Pacific and Far East had already been interrupted once. She had just arrived in Australia at the tail-end of February when events back home in Britain had obliged her to abandon her intended two-week visit to that country, leaving Prince Philip to carry on there alone. In Britain that was the 'winter of discontent' when the miners' strike forced a three-day working week upon the nation and brought down the government of Edward Heath, who had followed Harold Wilson as prime minister. Heath made the mistake of appealing to the country. In the General Election which took place in Britain on the same day that the Queen, as Queen of Australia, was opening the new Australian Parliament, his Conservative party gained fractionally more votes, but Labour, under Britain's first-past-the-post electoral system, had the victory by five seats, a slender majority which meant that the balance of power lay with the Liberals, Nationalists and other minorities who held a mere thirty-eight of the 635 seats in the new House of Commons.

The Queen had arrived back in Britain to find herself confronted by a complex situation. Theoretically, Edward Heath was still her prime minister. Equally theoretical was the Queen's power to dismiss him. No monarch had done that for more than two centuries. So the Queen could only sit in her palace and wait while Heath sought to involve the Liberals in a coalition with the Conservatives. Even had he succeeded, there was no guarantee that such a government would have survived. In the event, he failed, and the Queen, at the end of three frustrating days, accepted his belated resignation and sent again for Harold Wilson as the man most likely to restore Britain to something approaching normality.

Now, three weeks later in Indonesia, she was again confronted with the problem of whether to cut short her tour and fly home. With only two days to go and assured that Princess Anne herself was unharmed, she decided that the fulfilment of her royal obligations should take precedence over her concern as a mother. But, later, she showed her appreciation to those who had been instrumental in saving her daughter from the would-be kidnapper, awarding them decorations for gallantry from the George Cross down. Following the investiture, in the privacy of the White Drawing Room she also extended her personal thanks as a mother. 'It's almost unbelievable,' she exclaimed as she listened to their combined account of what had happened in the Mall, within a few yards of Buckingham Palace, that night in March.

Problems, official and personal, continued to crowd in upon the Queen. The following year found her intervening personally to secure the release of a Briton under sentence of death in Uganda, while in Australia the royal prerogative which she herself had refrained from using in Britain was invoked by her Governor General to dismiss the prime minister there. The Queen is not Queen of Uganda as she is of Britain and Australia, but Uganda is a republic within the Commonwealth, and it was as Head of the

Commonwealth that the Queen sought to save the life of lecturer Denis Hills when he was arrested and threatened with execution for having referred to Idi Amin, the Ugandan president, as 'a village tyrant'. Hills was, in fact, merely a pawn in the game Amin was playing at the time with the object of forcing Britain to return Ugandan exiles opposed to his regime so that they could be rendered permanently harmless. The Queen's intervention took the form of a personal letter, delivered by hand to the Ugandan president by Lieutenant-General Sir Chandos Blair, who had been Amin's commanding officer when he was no more than a sergeant in the King's African Rifles. It was in accordance with Amin's braggart nature that he should take advantage of the situation to accuse his old CO of being 'undiplomatic and disrespectful'. However, he also sent a reply to the Queen's letter in which he reiterated his demand for the return of Ugandan exiles. It was read over the telephone to the Queen, who was now staying at Balmoral. She was still considering her next move when a second letter, even more verbose than the first, was received from Amin. He no longer insisted upon the return of Ugandan exiles, but he did repeat an earlier demand that Britain's Foreign Secretary, James Callaghan, must go personally to Uganda if there was to be any question of Hills being released. Meanwhile, Amin wrote, he was postponing Hills' execution because of 'the love, confidence and respect which I and the entire people of Uganda have for you as leader of Great Britain and the Commonwealth'. The Queen was in something of a cleft stick. She was seeking to save Hills' life but had no desire to be seen as knuckling under to Uganda's puffed-up president. A way out was devised by having Callaghan go to Uganda, though not directly. He called there in passing, as it were, on his way back from visiting another African state, Zaire.

What happened in Australia was very different, but no less dramatic. The Queen herself played no direct part. It was her Governor General* who invoked the power of the Crown and

* The Queen is represented by a Governor General in those countries of the Commonwealth (such as Australia) of which she is also Queen. Time was when members of the Royal Family were despatched to serve as Governors General, but nowadays such appointments are made on the advice of the prime minister of the country concerned. However, a Governor General is not a member of the country's government and still less an agent of the British government, but represents – as was made so dramatically clear in Australia – the Crown.

wielded the royal prerogative in a way the Queen had carefully refrained from doing in Britain when Edward Heath sought to stay in office as prime minister despite a general election which had gone against him.

Governor General of Australia at this time was Sir John Kerr, son of a boilermaker and a former member of the Labour party, appointed to office on the advice of Gough Whitlam, the country's Labour prime minister. He was, many people thought, Whitlam's 'boy'. In the event, it did not turn out like that.

Labour had been in power in Australia for some eighteen months. Political scandals had brought about the resignations of two of its chief ministers. More importantly, the combined Opposition parties had gained slender control of the Senate, Australia's upper house. That power was now used – in 1975 – to block the budget. It would be passed, said Malcolm Fraser, the Liberal leader, only if Whitlam called a general election. But Whitlam was determined to serve out his three-year term of office. Lacking funds in the normal way, he turned to the banks, arranging with them for money to be loaned to civil servants and government contractors until such time as the budget might be passed.

As the representative of the Crown, the Governor General sought to resolve this clearly unsatisfactory situation by effecting a compromise between Whitlam and Fraser. But neither would give an inch. Trapped between a seemingly irresistible force and an equally immovable object, Sir John looked for another way out from a situation which was fast bringing Australia to the verge of political disaster. His options were limited in the extreme. Like the Queen in Britain, he could act, as Whitlam was quick to remind him, only on the advice of his prime minister. If that was all there was to it, Sir John reasoned, why have a Governor General at all? Finally he found what he was seeking under section 64 of the Australian constitution. Ignoring Whitlam's 'advice' to the contrary, he sought the views of the country's Lord Chief Justice, who confirmed his opinion.

Whitlam and Fraser were due to meet again on 11 November, Remembrance Day. Sir John held his hand, still hoping they would arrive at a compromise. When they did not, he asked both men to see him, summoning the prime minister at one o'clock and Fraser ten minutes later. However, Whitlam was late and Fraser early. So it was with Fraser hidden in an anteroom and his car tucked away out of sight that Sir John saw Whitlam, again asked him if he would call a general election so that the budget could be passed and, when he again refused, dismissed him from office. Then, summoning Fraser, he appointed him prime minister of a caretaker government on condition that the Senate passed the budget and there was an immediate general election.

In all this, the Queen herself was never consulted. Indeed, she knew nothing of the dramatic happenings in Australia until several hours after the whole thing had become a *fait accompli*. But what Sir John Kerr had done had been in the name of the Crown, and the rumblings of the affair can be heard still in Labour's wish to turn Australia from a monarchy into a republic. However, this cannot be done without a national referendum, and such is the popularity of the Queen and her family, her daughter-in-law especially, among the vast majority of the Australian people that any such referendum would seem to stand little chance of producing the desired Labour result in the foreseeable future.

Closer to home in a personal as well as a geographic sense was the problem of Princess Margaret's marriage, which the Queen saw ever more clearly was drifting with increasing speed towards the rocks. Indeed, a degree of disenchantment between the couple had been apparent to close relatives even before their second child was born in 1964. Whispers of disharmony had filtered through to the gossip columns, though rumours of impending separation or divorce had earlier been either jokingly dismissed by Snowdon or formally denied by the Buckingham Palace press office. By the 1970s their marriage had reached a stage of disintegration when they were sometimes not on speaking terms in private while on other occasions the growing bitterness between them would spill over in front of friends and even, on one occasion at least, break through the façade of togetherness they still tried to maintain on public occasions. For a long time the Queen continued to hope that things would blow over, that her sister and her brother-in-law would patch things up so that the marriage could survive. That hope diminished as the ill-matched couple each began to seek consolation elsewhere. Separation was now clearly only a matter of time, but the Queen urged on them the desirability of staying

165

together a little longer. She was not so much worried over the effect separation would have on the royal image as concerned for what it might do to the children. It would be better, she said, if they could hang on until the children were older and better able to stand the shock. But that became impossible when Margaret's friendship with the youthful Roddy Llewellyn became public knowledge. By 1976 separation had become inevitable.

The Queen did not seek to apportion blame, though some others of the family did. Indeed, far from blaming either party, she continued for some time to come, against the odds, to hope for a reconciliation. It was perhaps in an attempt to promote reconciliation, though more probably because she personally liked Snowdon and did not want him to think that he had incurred her displeasure, that she invited him as well as Margaret to a private party she gave later in the year to celebrate her fiftieth birthday. In any event, if reconciliation was her aim, it did not succeed, and in another two years separation would become divorce, surely an ironic twist of fate.

Constitutional and personal problems were alike forgotten by the Queen, at least temporarily, in the excitement of her Silver Jubilee. On 6 February 1977, she had been Monarch for twenty-five years, occupying the throne longer than her father, her uncle or her great-grandfather, though it would require another year to surpass the reign of her grandfather, King George V, and nearly another forty years before she could hope to rival her great-great-grandmother, Queen Victoria. The actual anniversary of her accession fell on a Sunday, and she spent the weekend quietly at Windsor Castle, as usual. The year would not be permitted to pass without due celebration, but in Britain not until the warmer weather had come.

Britain, of course, is not the only country of which she became Queen on 6 February 1952 and was not the only one to celebrate. The island of Fiji, with a population less than one-hundredth that of Britain, was the first of her kingdoms to explode into celebration when she called there in her royal yacht on her way to further celebrations in New Zealand, Australia (with a separate visit to Tasmania) and Papua New Guinea. Back in Britain, rather after the manner of the first Elizabeth, the Queen indulged in a series of royal progresses throughout various parts of the country. Unlike

166

her Tudor predecessor, however, she was anxious not to overstrain the resources of those who hosted her and kept down costs by using the royal yacht and the royal train as mobile hotels. The royal train with its ten air-conditioned coaches was a new one built specially for her Jubilee, and she and Prince Philip, with some help from Sir Hugh Casson, had the pleasant task of choosing the fittings and furnishings for her personal saloon. If British Rail could equip her with a new train, the Society of Motor Manufacturers and Traders was equally eager to provide her with a new Rolls Royce, custom built at a cost of £60,000. However, the giving of this gift was rather marred by the fact that the car was not finished until the following year, due to one of the many disputes which have held back British industry in the postwar years. As at the time of her Coronation, the Queen, in her Silver Jubilee year, was inundated with gifts, loyal letters of goodwill and cards of congratulation, over a hundred thousand in all. The largest of the cards measured a colossal ten feet by five feet and required a five-strong team to carry it through the palace gates.

London, that year, was again awash with tourists drawn from all parts of the world. Celebrations in the capital included a thanksgiving service in St Paul's Cathedral, two royal tours of the London boroughs, a waterborne progress along the River Thames and a banquet at Buckingham Palace at which the Queen played host to heads of state of the Commonwealth. As was to be expected, the Birthday Parade that summer with its spectacular Trooping the Colour ceremony drew even larger crowds than usual. 'GREAT GOING, LIZ' said a banner in the crowd. There were many other such small instances of the heart-warming affection the British have for the Monarch, and many occasions on which the Queen's emotions were sent swinging from one extreme to the other. There was, for instance, a moment during her celebration walkabout in the City of London when she laughed aloud with joy, a rare thing for her to do in public, and another, only minutes after, when she had visible difficulty in holding back tears.

The IRA virtually dared her to go to Northern Ireland as part of her Jubilee celebrations, with threats of what would happen to her if she did. It is not in the Queen's nature to sidestep such a challenge. 'I was crowned Queen of the United Kingdom,' she said. 'Great Britain *and* Northern Ireland.' She was obstinately

167

determined to visit those of her subjects who has 'suffered and courageously borne so much'. Of course, it was not possible for her to progress through the terror-torn province with anything like the same degree of freedom that she enjoyed in England, Scotland and Wales. The risk of assassination was too great, as the murder of Earl Mountbatten would subsequently prove. So strict security hemmed in her visit. The royal yacht served as a secure offshore base from which the Queen was ferried back and forth by helicopter, perhaps the only form of travel of which she is still rather nervous. As good as its word, the IRA marked the visit by stepping-up its terrorist campaign. Bombs exploded in Belfast and Crossmaglen, and elsewhere there was a shoot-out with the security forces. There was an attempt to keep the Queen from visiting the new University of Ulster at Coleraine by warning that another bomb had been planted there. The Queen not only visited the university just the same, in company with Prince Philip, but, on the second day of her visit to Northern Ireland, exhibited further defiance of the IRA by taking Prince Andrew ashore with her. He was seventeen at the time.

Frederick Mulley, the Secretary of Defence, might snatch forty winks while sitting beside the Queen at a Jubilee display by the Royal Air Force. The Queen herself could hardly do the same, either there or elsewhere. In consequence, though she found the nationwide celebrations joyful, they also tired her. In Britain alone she travelled a total of seven thousand miles and, before it was over, the strain was showing. But there were other of her queen-doms which had still to celebrate her twenty-five years of mon-archy, and she was not about to disappoint them. So, the cel-ebrations in Britain over, off she flew to Canada, the Bahamas, Barbados and elsewhere.

Punctuality is the Queen's watchword. She does not like to be kept waiting – given the crowded itinerary of the average working day, her life would be chaotic if she was – and will not willingly keep others waiting. So for those attending a royal investiture at Buckingham Palace on 15 November 1977, it came as a surprise when the ceremony did not begin promptly on time. The Queen, though those awaiting knighthoods and medals did not know it until later, had been delayed by a last-minute telephone call. It was Princess Anne calling from St Mary's Hospital to give her mother the heart-warming news that she was now a grandmother.

Even royal duty was forgotten for once as the Queen chatted delightedly with her daughter, asking those questions grand-mothers always ask. *A boy – how lovely. What weight?* Seven pounds nine ounces. *How are you both doing?* 'Fine,' said the Princess. The Queen was beaming with delight when she finally made it to the investiture ten minutes late and bursting to tell someone her good news. So she told the whole of the assembled company. 'My daughter has just given birth to a son.'

The Queen was fifty-one when her first grandchild, Peter Phillips, was born. More than twenty-five years of reading the small print of state documents had weakened her eyes to a point where it was necessary to resort to glasses both for tackling the contents of her Boxes and for her speeches, which she invariably reads. She was wearing them for the speech she made the following year in West Berlin.

For the Queen, it was an unusual and remarkably outspoken speech. Unlike Prince Philip, whose speeches not infrequently verge on the political and arouse controversy in consequence, the Queen is usually concerned to be non-political and non-controversial. That speech she made in West Berlin stands as a unique departure from royal custom. If less dramatic than the *'Ich bin ein Berliner'* pronouncement of America's ill-fated President Kennedy, the Queen's speech equally reflected the determined spirit of the western democracies.

'Your city has compelled our sympathy and admiration,' she told the estimated 25,000 Berliners who packed one of the city's squares to hear her. 'You have kept burning the flame of freedom. In Berlin we test the peaceful intentions of others. We have lived through difficult and dangerous times together. My Government and my people stand beside you. My soldiers and airmen stationed in Berlin embody the British commitment to defend your freedom for as long as need be – until the divisions in Europe and in your city can be healed.'

As if to underline that commitment of which she spoke, she personally ordered the Trooping the Colour ceremony to be carried out by British troops stationed in Berlin. The ceremony was held in that same Olympic Stadium where Adolf Hitler once ranted of a Reich that would endure for a thousand years – the first time since the Queen ascended the throne that it had been executed outside Britain.

That 1978 visit to West Berlin was the forty-third royal tour of her reign. Over the course of twenty-six years she had visited seventy-nine different countries, islands and such remnants of Britain's imperial past as Gibraltar and Hong Kong. The major Commonwealth countries of which she is also Queen she had visited many times. She had, for instance, toured Australia and New Zealand each on five occasions, and been to Canada eleven times. Even in 1964, the year Prince Edward was born, there had been a trip to Canada. Only once, in 1960, the year of Prince Andrew's birth, had the Queen permitted herself a year's sabbatical from overseas travel. And in 1979 came one of the strangest trips of her reign, a tour embracing the Gulf States of Kuwait, Bahrain, Saudi Arabia, Qatar and Oman, with her Arab hosts finding it more embarrassing than she did herself. At times they found it seemingly impossible to reconcile the fact that the visiting monarch was a woman with their traditional Islamic belief in the inferiority of women. To the Queen's amusement, they endeavoured at times to resolve the irreconcilable by apparently pretending that she was not a woman at all but a male of high standing, even down to speaking of 'he' instead of 'she'. For her part, out of deference to her hosts and their Islamic attitude, the Queen's wardrobe for the tour was yet more modest than usual. Even her day dresses were of ankle-length, with her neck, arms and legs effectively hidden from the lecherous gaze of men.

The oil-rich heads of the Gulf States loaded her with jewels to add to her already almost fabulous collection. There was a three-strand choker of pearls from the Emir of Kuwait, a diamond and sapphire necklace with matching ring and ear-rings from Sheik Rashid in Dubai, another mouth-watering necklace from the favourite wife of Sheik Zaid, head of the United Arab Emirates, and from others diamond-studded watches, a ruby brooch, a gold handbag, gold goblets, gold coffee-pot, a gold fruit bowl, a lapis lazuli fruit-stand adorned with gold horses, a gold table centre and what can only be described as a pinafore except that it was worked in gold chainmail and studded with sapphires and amethysts. A million pounds would probably not have bought the lot.

Another royal tour that same year was to revive the old question

170

as to how far Britain's prime minister can go in advising the Queen over something in which she is involved in her capacity as Head of the Commonwealth. At issue was a four-nation African tour embracing Tanzania, Malawi, Botswana and Zambia. The Commonwealth Conference that year was to be held in Zambia, in Lusaka, the capital. The Queen sees it as part of her duty as Head of the Commonwealth to 'sit in' on such conferences, not attending the actual sessions but exerting a soothing behind-the-scenes influence by meeting and talking with each Commonwealth leader in turn. 'A sort of problem-solving umpire', she has been termed. The difficulty in 1979 was that there was fighting not far from Lusaka, with guerrillas based in Zambia striking across the border in attempts to topple the regime of Bishop Muzorewa in Zimbabwe and troops from Zimbabwe invading Zambia in efforts to destroy the guerrilla bases.

Margaret Thatcher was now in power in Britain, the eighth prime minister of the Queen's reign, and she was not alone in querying whether it was wise for the Queen to visit Zambia in the circumstances. Some other Commonwealth leaders also felt it unsafe. But Mrs Thatcher was the only one among them who, because the Queen is normally in Britain, has a regular weekly audience with the Monarch. She was also in no doubt that, as Britain's prime minister, it was for her to advise the Queen whether to go or not and for the Queen to accept such advice. The Queen, who does not see things in quite the same light when her role as Head of the Commonwealth is involved, told the prime minister that it was her 'firm intention' to go. She would accept and act on advice to the contrary only as 'a last resort'. Mrs Thatcher's case was perhaps slightly weakened by the fact that she planned to go to Lusaka herself for the conference. Just as King George VI saw no reason why he should not sail with his troops on D-Day if Winston Churchill did – though, in the end, neither did – so the Queen saw nothing to keep her from going to Lusaka if it was safe enough for her prime minister. Mrs Thatcher's view was that it was for her, as prime minister, to be satisfied that 'all possible arrangements have been made for the Queen's safety'. To this end, she sent a team of security men to Zambia to check on things. They reported back that the possible danger was no greater than the Queen had faced in Northern Ireland in her Silver Jubilee year

171

and probably less. The situation was further defused when Joshua Nkomo promised that his guerrilla forces in Zambia would not mount another strike into Zimbabwe until after the Queen's visit. However, his announcement did not prevent Zimbabwe troops again striking across the border at guerrilla bases in Zambia at a time when the Queen was already in Tanzania and due in Lusaka the following week.

Told of the Zimbabwe raid, the Queen still insisted that she would go to Lusaka as planned. And to Lusaka she went, again – as in Northern Ireland – showing her contempt for possible danger by having Prince Philip and Prince Andrew with her. She also had with her, though she did not learn about this until later, a dozen members of the SAS for additional security. Her biggest threat, as it turned out, came not from a Kalashnikov rifle or a Sam 6 missile but in the form of a tirade from Simon Mwema, Mayor of Lusaka, to which she was obliged to listen. He ranted on at some length about what he termed the 'war of liberation' being waged against an administration set up 'to protect the interests of less able whites'. Invited to reply to this curious speech of welcome, the Queen declined to do so.

Her four-nation African tour over, the Queen went to Balmoral that summer as usual to rest and relax. But the atmosphere of violence which had clouded recent years of her reign was to follow her even there. It was Bank Holiday Monday, 27 August, when she received the heart-rending news that Prince Philip's uncle, Earl Mountbatten, had been murdered along with one of his grandsons, Nicholas Knatchbull, and a young deckhand named Paul Maxwell when their boat *Shadow V* was blown up off the coast of Ireland by an IRA bomb. Others of the boating party, Mountbatten's daughter Patricia, his son-in-law Lord Brabourne, another grandson, Nicholas's twin brother Timothy, and Lord Brabourne's widowed mother had all been seriously injured, Brabourne's mother so badly that she too died soon after.

The news came in the form of a telephone call from the prime minister's office at 10 Downing Street. The Queen was deeply shocked. While Earl Mountbatten was Prince Philip's uncle, he was also related to her through their joint descent from Queen Victoria. The Earl's grandmother, Princess Alice, who married the Grand Duke Louis IV of Hesse, was sister to the Queen's great-grandfather, King Edward VII. But the relationship in recent years had been deeper than that. Despite Mountbatten's initial indignation in 1952 when the Queen revived her father's name of Windsor for the purposes of monarchy, he had, over the years since, become more and more a father-figure to her, just as he was an 'honorary grandfather' to Prince Charles. So it was personal grief and affection rather than mere duty which saw the Queen heading the mourners at the funeral of the murdered Earl, in his lifetime an heroic and flamboyant figure who had been, by turns, skipper of the famous destroyer *Kelly*, Allied Supreme Commander in South East Asia, the last Viceroy of India, First Sea Lord and Chief of the Defence Staff.

12 GRANNY
QUEEN

Among the visitors to Balmoral that tragic summer of Earl Mountbatten's murder was Lady Diana, youngest of the three daughters of Earl Spencer. She did not actually stay with the Royal Family but with her sister, whose husband, Robert Fellowes, is one of the Queen's Assistant Private Secretaries. The Queen has known Earl Spencer since the days when she was a Princess and he was one of her father's equerries, and Diana since she was a baby, born the year following the birth of Prince Andrew. As children, the two of them, Andrew and Diana, had sometimes played together, and in 1979, when they were respectively nineteen and eighteen, the Queen saw Diana as being an eminently suitable feminine companion for her second son. To her surprise, it was her eldest son, the Prince of Wales, thirteen years older than Diana, who was to be more and more drawn to the girl in the months to come.

That Charles was attracted to Diana was also a relief to the Queen. In his thirty-first year, the Prince of Wales was now of an age when mothers begin to worry about their sons – when they will marry, who they will marry and, indeed, whether they will ever marry at all. To the Queen, with her sense of dynasty, it was important that the Heir Apparent should marry and have a child to carry on the royal line. Princess Anne had already done this, of course, but her small son was a Phillips, not a Windsor, and ranked only fifth in the line of succession after his own mother and her three brothers. A child fathered by the Heir Apparent, on the other hand, would be not only a Windsor but – because the line of succession descends vertically in the first instance – automatically the next but one King or Queen. But before that could happen, the Prince of Wales had first to find himself a wife acceptable to the nation as its future Queen, and not all the young ladies with whom he had associated since reaching the age of sexual awareness had come into that category. If the Queen, over the years, had sometimes shuddered at the possibility that her eldest son might make an unwise choice it was surely understandable. Always there, at the back of her mind, was the spectre of that earlier Prince of Wales, her Uncle David, and all that had happened because he fell in love with a woman Britain would not accept as its Queen.

Lady Diana was at Balmoral again the following summer, again staying with her sister, though no longer seen by the Queen as providing suitable feminine company for Prince Andrew. It was the Prince of Wales who was constantly seen at her side as the Royal Family pursued its holiday itinerary of walking, stalking, grouse shooting, fishing and barbecue picnics amidst the heather. But if the Queen hoped that the romantic atmosphere of her hideaway castle in the Scottish Highlands would persuade the young couple to plight their troth, as she and Prince Philip had done there nearly a quarter of a century before, she was to be disappointed. Still, she remained hopeful as she set off that autumn on yet another royal tour, this time embracing the North African countries of Tunisia, Algeria and Morocco. As far as Morocco was concerned, it was to prove the most wretched tour she had ever undertaken or is likely to undertake.

The Arab rulers of the Gulf States who had hosted the Queen the previous year, though they found it embarrassing that the visiting Monarch was a mere woman, had never been less than courteous and gracious to her. King Hassan of Morocco was not. From the moment she arrived in Morocco, it was as though he set out deliberately to put her down. He absented himself from the welcome luncheon in order to play golf. When he eventually condescended to receive her in his palace at Rabat, he summarily dismissed her two accompanying ladies-in-waiting from his presence. There was an on-off-on again state banquet which had the Queen not knowing whether to dress for dinner or not. And when she did, she was kept sitting outside in her car for half an hour. A planned visit to Fez was peremptorily cancelled by the King. There was a desert picnic at the foot of the Atlas Mountains when the King disappeared for an hour into the comfort of his air-conditioned caravan while the Queen and Prince Philip were left kicking their heels – in fact, the Queen began foot-tapping, a sure sign that her patience is wearing thin – in the stuffy heat of a dusty, if colourful, tent. To crown it all, the King was fifty-five minutes late for a farewell banquet in his honour given aboard the royal yacht *Britannia*. All this, with a steel contract worth several million pounds hanging in the balance, the Queen was obliged to take. Royal aides would subsequently mouth platitudes to the effect that no, of course the Queen was not offended, but the truth was that there were times during the tour when she was as angry and indignant as she had not been since she was a young Princess and swept out of a private ball in dudgeon because someone spoke of her as 'horsey'.

She returned to Britain to find her eldest son still no closer to proposing to Lady Diana than he had been at Balmoral, either unable to make up his mind or, if his mind was already made up, to brace himself sufficiently to utter the words of proposal. Of these alternatives, it seemed to be the latter, a fear of possible rejection, which was causing him to hold back. In an attempt to help out, the Queen gave a private party at Sandringham that November to celebrate his thirty-second birthday, with Lady Diana as the only non-family guest. But it was not until after Christmas, when the Queen was again at Sandringham, that Charles came to her with the news that he had finally proposed and been accepted. She was delighted to hear it, delighted too to learn from Princess Anne that she was again pregnant. The baby, a daughter this time, to be named Zara at the suggestion of the Prince of Wales, was born the following May.

The wedding of the Prince of Wales and Lady Diana Spencer was six weeks in the future – and the murder of Earl Mountbatten not yet two years in the past – when the Queen, wearing the customary riding breeches under her black skirt as protection for her legs, the skirt surmounted by the tunic and tricorne of the Welsh Guards, rode side-saddle from the Palace to play her traditional role in the annual ceremony of Trooping the Colour. It was Saturday 13 June – the day selected that year as the Queen's official birthday, the weather likely to be finer and warmer in June than on her actual birthday in April. She was riding Burmese, a mare given to her by the Royal Canadian Mounted Police and specially trained not to react to the blare of military bands or the loyal cheering of the

176

crowd. The clock was coming up to 11 a.m. as she turned Burmese in the direction of Horse Guards Parade. Suddenly a succession of shots rang out – four or five, perhaps six. So sudden and shocking was the incident that no one, afterwards, was quite sure. Burmese shied and the Queen's face drained of colour as she struggled to control her mount. Prince Philip, behind her, rode quickly forward to help and protect her. On the fringe of the crowd, only feet away, loyal subjects were struggling with a seventeen-year-old youth, Marcus Sarjeant. A corporal in the Scots Guards, Alistair Galloway, grabbed the pistol Sarjeant was holding. Leslie Smith, a special constable, and John Heasman, an ambulanceman, also grappled with him. A police sergeant, a constable and an American tourist, Michael Maude, waded in to help. There were shouts of 'Lynch the bastard' as the pistol was wrested from Sarjeant's grasp and he was manhandled away.

The weapon turned out to be a replica, and the shots no more than blanks, but the assassination attempt would have been real enough had Sarjeant succeeded in his original intentions. He had earlier tried to obtain real bullets to fit his father's revolver. Failing in that, he had then tried to buy a pistol by mail order. Not having a firearms certificate, he failed in that too. 'I have little doubt,' Lord Lane, the Lord Chief Justice, said later, in sentencing him to five years' imprisonment, 'that had you been able to obtain a real gun or live ammunition for your father's gun, you would have tried to murder Her Majesty.'

In any event, the Queen, at the time, had no way of knowing whether the shots were real or not, whether or not there had been an attempt on her life. Burmese under control again, she glanced quickly round to ensure that her husband and eldest son, who was also with her, were unharmed. Satisfied that no one was hurt, she gave Burmese a reassuring pat and, with a considerable show of dedication and courage, continued with the traditional ceremony of Trooping the Colour as though nothing had happened.

Sarjeant's idea of shooting the Queen, it emerged at the court hearing later, stemmed from reading about the assassination of President Kennedy, the murder of Beatle John Lennon and the attempt on the life of President Reagan. Violence, in today's world, was more and more begetting violence, it seemed, a fact which worried those whose duty it is to safeguard the Royal Family. The

177

Queen herself, with her somewhat fatalistic attitude, was less worried. She had by no means forgotten the incident by the time she arrived back at the Palace after the ceremony, but she had adjusted to it and was said to be 'totally relaxed'.

Publicly, the Queen has never been heard to reveal her attitude to the danger of assassination which, these days, is always there. Her Heir has. 'If you are going to worry about it,' the Prince of Wales said once, 'you might as well give up.' Clearly the Queen shares that view. Equally clearly, she has no intention of giving up, and not even the incident at the Trooping the Colour could persuade her to alter arrangements for public appearances more than fractionally. She declined to entertain a suggestion that, on the occasion of the royal wedding the following month, she and the Prince of Wales should each travel to and from St Paul's Cathedral in a closed carriage. But she did agree that armed bodyguards, decked in footmen's livery, should ride on the backs of their open carriages. Other precautions against the possibility of an assassination attempt more professional than that of young Marcus Sarjeant were also taken. Sewers beneath the processional route were checked for possible bombs, and while the uniformed troops lining the route still faced inwards in ceremonial fashion, the police did not. They now faced outwards so that they could watch people in the crowd undistracted by the passage of the bride, bridegroom and others. It was all very different from the Queen's own wedding day thirty-four years before. In those days the idea of assassination had been unthinkable. In the 1980s it was not.

There was another small difference indicative of how times had changed since the Queen was married. She, for all that she was a royal princess and destined to become Queen, had promised to love, honour and *obey* the man she married. Her new daughter-in-law, reflecting the more independent, more equal attitude of womanhood in the 1980s, saw no reason to promise obedience. But if the wedding ceremony was different in this respect, there were also similarities to the Queen's own wedding to bring back memories – a wedding ring fashioned from the same nugget of Welsh gold, a teasing remark, 'I remember *your* wedding', from the Queen Mother; a first night spent in the same Mountbatten residence in Hampshire, and in the same bedroom, where the Queen and Prince Philip had spent theirs.

To the Queen's joy, her new daughter-in-law was to be as quickly pregnant as she had been herself. More quickly, in fact. The Queen had been married just three days short of a full year when her first child was born. Her next grandchild would be born when the Prince and Princess of Wales had been married little more than forty-seven weeks.

Before and after the wedding, the Queen was alive to the strain royal life imposed on the new member of the Royal Family and quick to protect her. She reacted angrily to a newspaper story that her future daughter-in-law might have anticipated the wedding date by spending a night with the Prince of Wales aboard the royal train, denying it utterly. When the Princess became pregnant, and unnerved by the seemingly ever-present photographers and reporters as pregnancy ran its course, the Queen summoned national newspaper editors to her Palace. 'She can't even go to the village shop to buy wine gums in peace,' she protested to them. And when Barry Askew, editor of the *News of the World*, asked 'Why can't she send a servant?', the Queen rounded on him quickly. 'That, if I may say so, is an extremely pompous remark,' she told him. She expressed herself as 'shocked and disgusted' when two newspapers, the *Sun* and the *Daily Star*, published pictures of a pregnant and bikini-clad Princess of Wales on holiday in the Bahamas. 'Tasteless behaviour', she labelled the publication of those pictures, as angry as she has ever been in her life.

That was in February 1982, shortly before Argentina invaded the Falkland Islands. In the weeks following the Argentinian invasion, as a British task force set about the business of regaining the islands, the Queen was concerned as both Monarch and mother. Her concern as a mother stemmed from the fact that she had a son, Prince Andrew, twenty-two now and a helicopter pilot in the Royal Navy, with the task force. A monarch of less determined character, lording it over some less democratic nation, might well have taken advantage of her position to ensure that her son remained safely behind when the task force sailed. Such a thought did not for a moment enter the Queen's head, though the son concerned was, at that time, second in the line of succession. But he was also 'a serving officer and there is no question in her mind that he should go', said one of the Queen's aides.

Life was further complicated for her at this time by the fact that

179

Canada required *its* Queen to be on the other side of the Atlantic, to append her formal 'Elizabeth R' signature to a royal proclamation which, after a space of 115 years, would finally free Canada from the overlordship of Britain's Parliament in London and bring it to full nationhood. The Queen, as she signed the proclamation, must surely have thought back to her very first visit to Canada, as a young, not-long-married Princess in 1951. She had gone there then with worry over the failing health of her father very much on her mind. Now, in 1982, at the age of fifty-six, a mother and a grandmother, she was worried for her son, Prince Andrew, facing danger in the South Atlantic. Throughout her visit to Canada a hot-line linked her with Margaret Thatcher's prime ministerial office in Downing Street. But there was no such line, in either Canada or Britain, which could link her directly with her son aboard HMS *Invincible*. So she could reply only, 'I hope he is all right', when someone asked her about him during a royal visit to Manchester. Like thousands of other mothers and wives at that time, she could only hope and pray and wait.

Then, the evening before Royal Ascot, the telephone rang in her sitting-room at the Palace. Answering it, she was surprised and overjoyed to hear Andrew's voice coming to her from some seven thousand miles away, from aboard a Royal Fleet Auxiliary anchored in Stanley harbour. She already knew that the fighting in the Falklands was over, of course, but it was a relief to be talking to Andrew himself, alive, well and apparently full of beans. Nor, in her delight as a mother at hearing her son's voice, did she forget that she was also the Queen. She asked him to pass on a personal message from her to all those who had fought so bravely to free and regain the Falkland Islands. 'Tell them how proud I am of them,' she said, 'and that it has been a marvellous operation.'

Prince Andrew was still serving aboard HMS *Invincible* when the Queen's third grandchild, to be named Prince William of Wales, was born on 21 June 1982. With the birth of this very special grandchild, the firstborn son of her firstborn son, succession to the throne in direct line was assured into another generation. Eager to see the newborn baby who would one day follow her and the Prince of Wales as Monarch, she drove the following day to St Mary's Hospital in Paddington. The Prince of Wales, who had been with his wife for the birth of the baby, was waiting to receive

180

his mother. He escorted her to the hospital elevator but, in his excitement, somehow pressed the wrong button so that they descended to the basement before eventually reaching the right floor. There was the inevitable discussion between grandmother, father and mother as to whom the baby took after. If all three did not necessarily agree on that, there was complete agreement, parents and grandmothers being what they are, that he was 'the prettiest baby in the world'. He also proved himself 'a good speechmaker', or so the Queen joked when her newest grandchild, at his christening ceremony, protested loudly that it was time for his next feed.

Between these two happy family events, the birth of Prince William and his christening ceremony, the Queen was to experience another traumatic shock. It was just after seven o'clock in the morning on Friday 9 July when she blinked into wakefulness as the curtains screening the tall windows of her bedroom were drawn back and daylight flooded into the room. Normally it is the duty of one of the Queen's dressers to tiptoe into the royal bedroom at eight o'clock in the morning and draw the curtains before going into the adjoining bathroom and dressing-room to run the Queen's bath and lay out her clothes for the day. But, awakening on this particular morning, the Queen was astonished to see not one of her dressers fiddling with the curtains but a man. And not Prince Philip, who had been up early and left for Windsor to practise carriage-driving, the new sport over which he is so enthused,* but a complete stranger, an intruder, dishevelled and shoeless. He crossed the room and sat on the Queen's bed, blood dripping from a cut thumb.

A curious – and worrying – combination of circumstances had enabled Michael Fagan, a thirty-one-year-old unemployed labourer with an obsessional regard for the Queen, to gain access to the royal bedroom, a sanctum which not even palace pages and footmen are normally permitted to enter. Circumstance one was that elsewhere in the palace a housemaid on early duty had opened a window to let in some fresh air. It was through this window that Fagan scrambled into the palace after removing his shoes and clambering up a drainpipe. In doing so, he triggered the alarm

* Prince Philip took up carriage-driving when he was obliged to stop playing polo in 1971 because of arthritis in his right wrist.

system, but the man on duty in the palace police station (circumstance two) thought it was a case of the alarm being 'on the blink' and simply switched it off. Having gained entrance to the palace, Fagan wandered along the crimson-carpeted corridor in search of the Queen. In the course of his wanderings he was seen by a servant who, despite the fact that he was without shoes (circumstance three), assumed he was a workman. In his hunt for the Queen, Fagan went first into at least one other room. It was in there that he broke a glass ashtray and cut his thumb in the process. Circumstance four, enabling him to obtain access to the Queen's bedroom, was the fact that the armed police officer who stands guard outside her bedroom door throughout the night had gone off duty at 6 a.m. Circumstance five was that the duty footman was out in the palace grounds, walking the corgis, and circumstance six that Prince Philip was up and away early, leaving the Queen on her own in their second-floor private apartment.

It was not the first time an intruder has succeeded in invading royal privacy. Fagan, on his own admission, had entered the palace once before, though on that occasion he left again without finding the Queen. He did, however, find a bottle of wine, some of which he drank. King George V, years ago, entered his study on one occasion to find a workman seated at his desk, writing home on a sheet of scarlet-crested royal notepaper. The Queen Mother, in wartime, discovered an army deserter hiding in her bathroom. She talked to him in her quiet, persuasive fashion and prevailed upon him to surrender to the authorities.

The Queen, in 1982, reacted with equal coolness to Fagan's intrusion into her bedroom, though circumstances continued to work against her. Twice, on the pretext of getting some cigarettes for her unwelcome guest, she telephoned in the hope of help. Despite the strangeness of her request – a Queen who has never smoked suddenly asking for cigarettes to be sent to her bedroom at seven o'clock in the morning – nobody seems to have cottoned on immediately to the fact that it was really a cry for help. Still on the pretext of getting Fagan some cigarettes, the Queen finally managed to attract the attention of Elizabeth Andrew, a chambermaid at work in the next room.

If the chambermaid's language on seeing the dishevelled and bleeding Fagan was hardly the sort one normally uses in the presence of royalty, it was surely understandable. 'Bloody hell, Ma'am,' she exclaimed. 'What's he doing here?'

Between them, Queen and chambermaid persuaded Fagan out of the bedroom and into a small room on the other side of the royal corridor which is used by the duty footman. The footman on duty that day, Paul Whybrew, arrived back with the corgis. At the Queen's request, he fetched the cigarettes she had promised Fagan. Then, with the help of Elizabeth Andrew, he manœuvred Fagan into yet another room where he was also given some whisky. It was at this point that the palace police arrived belatedly on the scene. The Queen greeted them – understandably, surely – with the sort of rich comment for which Prince Philip is better known.

The incident shook the Queen far more than the blank shots fired during the Trooping the Colour ceremony had done. If she was not safe in her palace home, where was she safe? With that strength of will which is part of her character, she forced herself, on the very day of Fagan's intrusion, to carry out an investiture ceremony already arranged and, later that same week, mingled as usual with guests invited to a royal garden party. But she was not her old self. Indeed, for several weeks after, she was as strained and tense as she has ever been.

However, composure and confidence were alike restored by the time she crossed the Atlantic in 1983 to visit President Reagan at his Californian ranch. She enjoyed herself thoroughly despite the torrential storms which plagued her visit and was highly delighted with the President's gift of a computer into which the bloodlines of her thoroughbreds could be programmed. She was less well pleased with America's President later that same year when US marines stormed ashore on the tiny island of Grenada to prevent its becoming a second Cuba off the American coast. The fact that other Commonwealth countries in the Caribbean had connived in the invasion, indeed had perhaps instigated it, did nothing to assuage her regal indignation that it had all been done without her knowledge or consent. She is Queen of Grenada just as she is Queen of the United Kingdom, and she felt that her sovereignty had been violated. Margaret Thatcher, her prime minister, promptly denounced the invasion of Grenada almost as though it was on a par with Argentina's invasion of the Falkland Islands the previous year. Only the future publication of her prime ministerial memoirs may reveal to what degree Margaret

Thatcher's comments at that time reflected the Queen's indignation rather than her own attitude.

In 1944, as an eighteen-year-old Princess, the Queen had accompanied her father in conditions of utmost secrecy to watch a rehearsal of the planned D-Day assault on Hitler's Europe. Forty years later, in 1984, as a woman of fifty-eight, she stood in the town square at Arromanches in Normandy, one of the focal points of the 1944 invasion, to take the salute at an anniversary parade of Britain's D-Day veterans. The parade in Arromanches came towards the end of what was, for the Queen, a long and tiring day of ceremonies, at Caen and Bayeux and on the sandy stretch still known by its 1944 code-name of Utah Beach, where she was one of eight national leaders – the others were America's President Reagan, Pierre Trudeau of Canada, President Mitterand of France, King Baudouin of the Belgians, Queen Beatrix of the Netherlands, King Olav of Norway and Grand Duke Jean of Luxembourg – who had gathered there to mark the fortieth anniversary of D-Day. The march-past at Arromanches, however, was a uniquely British occasion. It had been anticipated that it would be a small, short ceremony in which only a few hundred veterans would take part. In the event, three thousand turned up to march, limp or be pushed in wheel-chairs past the saluting base on which the Queen stood, singing as they passed her. The song they sang was the soldier's version of the 'Colonel Bogey' march. At the time no one quite knew how many were taking part or when the parade would end. 'I'll stand here all night if need be,' said the Queen at one point.

The speech she made in Arromanches that day ranks with her earlier speech in West Berlin as among the most stirring of her reign. 'There are only a few occasions in history when the course of human destiny has depended on the events of a single day,' she told those veterans of D-Day. 'June the Sixth, 1944, was one of those critical moments. Those taking part were mostly young men. None wished to die. But they knew that unless they established a bridgehead on the shores of France there was no prospect of an end to Hitler's war which had already cost so many millions of lives and so much suffering throughout the world.' She spoke of sacrifice and freedom and democratic ideals, and her speech over, in company with Prince Philip, walked among the veterans, pausing here and there to talk with them of those eventful days of forty years before when they were young soldiers and she was a girl of eighteen.

If the Queen is known to dispute the right of her (British) prime minister to advise her on the subject of her Commonwealth travels, there is no such argument when it comes to visiting foreign countries. Except for very rare private visits, such as that to Kentucky in 1984 to plan her future thoroughbred breeding programme, she goes where the Government of the day wants her to go and does not visit those nations with which Britain does not see eye to eye. So it was in the interest of foreign relations that, also in 1984, she accepted an invitation to visit Jordan's diminutive and British-educated King Hussein. Over his years of monarchy King Hussein has several times come closer to being assassinated than ever the Queen has, and from the moment the visit was pencilled in on the Queen's engagement calendar, there was concern for her safety. Fears increased when there was a bomb blast outside the Intercontinental Hotel in Amman, the Jordanian capital, and two further bombs were discovered and defused in the nick of time. The Queen, as always, was reluctant to call off her visit on the grounds of personal safety. The Prime Minister was more hesitant, and it was only a personal telephone call from King Hussein to Mrs Thatcher which finally decided her not to advise cancellation of the visit.

The substance of the King's telephone call was to give the Prime Minister his personal guarantee that the Queen would be safe. Guarantees are, of course, only as good as the steps taken to implement them. In consequence, the security measures taken by both the British Government and King Hussein to ensure the Queen's safety were the most stringent to date. The British Airways Tristar in which the Queen flew to Jordan was specially fitted with missile-deflection equipment. As a further precaution, she flew by a roundabout route designed to avoid the more volatile trouble spots of the Middle East. By the time she arrived in Jordan the area around Amman airport had taken on the appearance of an armed camp, with machine-guns stationed at every crossing point and armed guards ringing the airfield. The arrival ceremony was brief. In minutes the Queen had been ushered into a bullet-proof car in the middle of what was tantamount to an armoured column and was being whisked the eight miles to King Hussein's palace at almost breakneck speed. The result was a considerable disappointment for a small group of British youngsters who had gathered at one point along the route in the hope of seeing her. Characteristically, when she learned what had happened, the Queen insisted on going to their school to see them. King Hussein himself drove her there in his bullet-proof car. The visit – indeed, the entire few days the Queen spent in Jordan – passed off without incident.

By now the Queen knew – in fact, the whole world knew – that her daughter-in-law was again pregnant. In this respect too, times had changed since the Queen was a young wife and mother. Even when the Queen was pregnant with Prince Andrew, the official announcement said no more than that she would be undertaking no further public engagements. The 1984 announcement concerning the Princess of Wales was more frank and open: the Princess was pregnant but would continue to undertake public engagements for as long as possible, with the baby expected in September.

Britain's newspaper editors had apparently taken the Queen's earlier strictures to heart, with the result that her daughter-in-law was far less harassed by photographers and reporters during the period of her second pregnancy. The Queen was on holiday at Balmoral when the baby, another boy, was born on 15 September 1984, and did not get to see him for another week when, following her return to London, she drove to Highgrove, the country home of the Prince and Princess of Wales. Harry, as he is known to his royal grandmother, though christened Henry Charles Albert David, was her fourth grandchild but, as the second-born son of the Heir Apparent, third in line of succession to the throne after his own father and his elder brother, Prince William.

Two days after seeing her latest grandchild, the Queen flew out from London on yet another royal tour of Canada, and it was as though the gremlins which had tampered with previous visits to that country, notably in 1959 when she was secretly pregnant with Prince Andrew and in 1964 when there was rioting in the streets of Quebec, again flew with her. This time they took advantage of the fact that the tour had been originally planned for July but postponed because prime minister John Turner had decided to call a snap election (which he lost disastrously) and the Queen had no desire for a royal tour to be linked with electioneering. Postponement necessarily involved altering dates and times of the various functions planned for the tour and considerable extra expense in re-printing invitations and programmes – estimated to have cost Ontario alone an additional $200,000 – all of which caused a degree of grumbling in some quarters. It also meant very different conditions of light and weather, with outdoor events sometimes fading into evening gloom and reduced crowds shivering in the autumnal chill instead of basking in summer sunshine.

None of this was the Queen's responsibility, and the blame can hardly be laid at her door. She was doing only what Canada had asked her to do. Indeed, in small ways she did more than was asked of her. Her first meeting with the country's new prime minister, Brian Mulroney, had been scheduled to last only ten minutes. But they had much to talk about, and she allowed it to run for half an hour. Similarly there was a reception aboard the royal yacht for which no receiving line had been planned. By her own wish the Queen nevertheless greeted personally each of the two hundred guests invited aboard. But such small gestures went unnoticed in the criticisms thrown at her in Toronto newspapers which variously described her as 'dowdy' and 'looking bored'. The *Globe & Mail* further criticized her use of cosmetics, while the *Sun* thought her clothes old-fashioned, her hats 'awful' and her hairstyle looking as though she had 'just got up'. Prince Philip too came in for his share of criticism for his 'tart, unpredictable tongue'. The *Star*, more objectively, queried Canada's need for a 'panoply of monarchs' in this day and age.

The criticisms of the Toronto newspapers were not shared by newspapers elsewhere, most of which were more than enthusiastic about the Queen's visits to their localities, and the new Prime Minister did his best to set the record straight with his speech at a farewell banquet in Manitoba. 'You have carried out your difficult and onerous duties with a warmth and charm which have endeared you to Canadians everywhere,' he told Canada's Queen. 'The monarchy is a central feature of our national life and parliamentary democracy.' Nevertheless, what was printed in Toronto had been hurtful, and it was with a silent sigh of relief that the Queen crossed into the United States for the first holiday she had enjoyed outside Britain in seventeen years.

Unlike her children and her sister, Princess Margaret, the Queen is normally content to spend her holidays at Balmoral or Sandringham, as Britain's monarchs have done for five generations An exception came in 1977 when a tour of the Pacific and West Indies was punctuated with private stop-overs at a number of islands, among them Mustique, where Princess Margaret has a holiday home. The Queen's 1984 visit to America's blue-grass state of Kentucky was similarly exceptional, similarly private, though to more purpose. For twenty years on and off she had been shipping mares to Kentucky to be mated with American stallions. In selecting suitable stallions, she had hitherto had to rely upon photographs, bloodlines and details of racing performances. Now, in pursuit of her long-time ambition to breed a racehorse which would win the Derby for her, she had come to see for herself. She stayed at the Lexington home of William Farish, one of America's leading breeders, from where, in the company of Lord Porchester, her racing manager, and Michael Oswald, who looks after the royal stud, she journeyed around to inspect the available stallions. Her only public appearance during her stay was at the local race-track where she witnessed the first running of the Queen Elizabeth II Challenge Cup and personally presented the winning owner with the cup she had taken from London with her.

From Kentucky the Queen travelled to Wyoming to spend a few days on a ranch near Big Horn. Her stay there coincided with the Conservative conference and the IRA attempt to assassinate Margaret Thatcher and members of her Cabinet. News of the Brighton hotel bombing, in which four people died and others were seriously injured, shocked and outraged the Queen, as did the news soon after of the assassination of Mrs Gandhi, whom she had visited in India only the year before. The world had become so violent that not even a monarch as phlegmatic as the Queen could any longer be certain that no one could possibly wish to kill her. Indeed, intelligence sources picked up a rumour that the IRA planned to assassinate a member of the Royal Family 'by Christmas'. Security, especially for public occasions such as the visit to London of President Mitterand of France, the state opening of Parliament and the Remembrance Day service at the Cenotaph, was further stepped up to a scale unthinkable in those days of the 1950s when the Queen first ascended the throne. Yet the radiance of her smile, as she drove to open Parliament yet again in 1984, was as brilliant as when she first performed that particular duty in

The Queen walking with her corgis in the grounds of Windsor Castle.
In March 1991, she needed three stitches after breaking up a fight between her
dogs and two belonging to the Queen Mother

The Queen received a warm welcome when she went walkabout in Bracknell
in April 1990

As Colonel-in-Chief of the Welsh Guards, the Queen inspected the ranks at
Buckingham Palace in May 1990 and presented them with their new colours

40 years a Queen. At the royal banquet held in honour of President Lech
Walesa of Poland

1952 and an enterprising photographer captured a picture of a fresh, young Queen which went round the world.

In the event, Christmas came and went with no more violence around the Queen than the playfulness of her other grandchildren, Prince William and Princess Anne's pigeon pair, Peter and Zara, at the christening of her latest grandchild, Prince Henry. The christening ceremony, held privately at Windsor four days before Christmas, was exactly that combination of family occasion and royal tradition which the Queen enjoys most. The baby's christening robe was the same one in which the Queen herself had been swaddled over half-a-century before – indeed, the same one used for royal christenings right back to the days of Queen Victoria. The font too dated from Queen Victoria, designed for her by her consort, Prince Albert. Film clips of the family, shot before and after the christening ceremony, were included in 'The Queen Show', as Prince Philip jokingly labels his wife's traditional Christmas Day telecast.

> The happy arrival of our fourth grandchild gave great cause
> for family celebrations [the Queen told the millions who
> watched her on television]. But for parents and grandparents
> a birth is also a time for reflection on what the future holds for
> the baby and how they can best ensure its safety and
> happiness.
>   To do that, I believe we must be prepared to learn as much
> from them as they do from us. We could use some of that
> sturdy confidence and devastating honesty with which
> children rescue us from self-doubts and self-delusions. We could
> borrow that unstinting trust of the child in its parents for our
> dealings with each other. Above all, we must retain the child's
> readiness to forgive, with which we are all born and which
> it is all too easy to lose as we grow older. Without it, divisions
> between families, communities and nations remain
> unbridgeable.

Andrew, the 'afterthought' baby born in 1960, was now almost the age the Queen herself had been when she first succeeded to the throne. Even Edward, the youngest of her royal brood, would soon be as old as his mother had been when she married his father.

A week after Edward's twenty-first birthday in March 1985, she journeyed to Cambridge to see him playing a variety of roles in a student revue, a gala performance specially staged as a Mothering Sunday treat for her and other mums. In keeping with her own role as a mother rather than the Monarch, the Queen sat that evening not in the customary royal box but some seven or eight rows back in the University theatre. Princess Margaret was with her, making her first appearance in public since undergoing exploratory surgery for lung cancer.

While the elder of the royal sisters has never smoked, the younger had been an increasingly addicted cigarette smoker from the age of nineteen, when she flamboyantly flourished the first of the long cigarette-holders which have since become almost a trade mark with her. Even the sad example of their father, whose heavy smoking resulted in arteriosclerosis, lung cancer and the coronary thrombosis from which he died, could not persuade her to give up smoking. However, family fears that she too might have contracted lung cancer were allayed by a medical bulletin stating that tests on tissue taken from her left lung had shown it 'to be innocent' (meaning non-malignant). If the elder sister saw fit to lecture the younger on the perils of smoking, as she had lectured her on so many less important topics in childhood, Margaret took not an iota of notice. Within weeks of leaving hospital she was back on cigarettes.

As she entered upon her thirty-fourth year of monarchy, it must surely have seemed to the Queen that the hardy annuals of royal life, such as Trooping the Colour and the distribution of the Royal Maundy, came round more quickly than ever, just as Christmas seems to come round more quickly with the years for all of us. When she first handed out the Royal Maundy (which takes the form of specially-minted coins contained in thonged purses) as a new young Queen in 1952, there had been only twenty-six recipients of each sex. In 1985, because tradition decrees that the number of recipients should correspond with the years of the Monarch's age, this figure had more than doubled. There were other signs too of the passage of time, among them a state visit to Portugal, with its memory of that earlier visit of twenty-eight years before which had reunited her with Prince Philip and ended rumours of a rift between them.

The pattern of her 1985 state visit to Portugal differed little from all the other state visits she has made over the years. There was the customary state banquet (at which she joked about the part port wine may have played in the long friendship between the British and Portuguese), a reciprocal banquet aboard her royal yacht, the laying of a wreath on the tomb of the national poet, the unveiling of a bust of her great-grandfather, Edward VII, in the Lisbon botanical gardens, visits to the National Assembly, the cathedral at Evora and the university at Oporto. And because royal visits these days are designed to boost trade as well as fly the flag, her royal yacht, while she was sight-seeing ashore, also served as a showcase for the display of British technology to Portuguese businessmen.

Another visit that year was to prove rather less harmonious. The Queen's secondary role of Head of the Commonwealth is dear to her heart. She is as fiercely proud of the title as her great-great-grandmother, Queen Victoria, was at being styled Empress of India. But it is also one which was to call upon all her reserves of diplomacy and tact when she went to Nassau for the 1985 Commonwealth conference.

At issue was the question of whether the countries of the Commonwealth should institute sanctions against South Africa. With Britain obstinately opposed to such a move and most other Commonwealth countries firmly in favour, the conference became the scene of bitter acrimony, and only the Queen's diplomatic behind-the-scenes influence averted what could have been a decisive split.

Nor was that the end of the matter. The pot may have gone off the boil temporarily, but it continued to simmer ominously, bubbling up again and again, feelings running so high at times as to threaten the disintegration of the Commonwealth. Though the Queen had attended every Commonwealth conference since she was first invited in 1973, she had until now always steered clear of playing an active part, confining herself to private off-the-record talks with the leader of each country. But now, alarmed by the growing disharmony between member states, she decided that the time had come when she must speak out.

'I have visited every one of the now forty-nine member countries,' she said in a speech made aboard *Britannia*, her floating headquarters for yet another Commonwealth conference, held this time in

191

Malaysia, 'and I know that each, however small, has its individual contribution to make to the Commonwealth partnership.'

Having thus clearly underlined her position as Head of the Commonwealth, she went on to tell its leaders that they must listen as well as talk to each other, respect each other's point of view and learn to disagree without falling out. 'The Commonwealth', she said, 'is an experiment in living and working together which has been proved and could be the way of the future. If anything, the world needs the Commonwealth more now than ever before.'

Her speech had the effect she intended. Britain and others might still disagree over the South African question, but the Commonwealth would remain intact.

The Queen was as active as ever in 1986, the year of her sixtieth birthday, fit enough to ride her mare Burmese at the annual ceremony of Trooping the Colour, though it would be for the last time. For such ceremonies in future she would use a carriage. And not only fit and active, but busy too, carrying out 430 engagements at home and a further 170 on tours overseas, twice as many as her daughter-in-law, the Princess of Wales, for all that the Princess, with her youthful freshness, continued to enjoy a larger share of newspaper space.

And now there was also another daughter-in-law to share the headlines, Prince Andrew's bride, Sarah Ferguson. If the Queen has a favourite among her four children it is surely Andrew . . . 'The baby,' friends say, 'she had for herself.' Certainly she is intensely proud of him and had earlier selected photographs he had taken of her as official portraits to mark her sixtieth birthday. She was 'overjoyed' – Andrew's own word – when he sought her permission to marry. Perhaps also a shade relieved that her second son, after so many headline-making episodes, had finally at the age of twenty-six decided to settle down. She marked her pleasure by bestowing on him the title of Duke of York, a royal title last borne by the father to whom she was so deeply attached. Following Andrew's wedding she would also dig down into her personal fortune to provide the newlyweds with a luxurious country residence, said to have cost between £2 million and £5 million according to which newspaper you read.

Still cherishing that longtime ambition to emulate her great-grandfather, Edward VII, by winning the Derby, earlier that year

192

she had made another trip to the 'blue grass' horse country of Kentucky. Since her previous visit two years before, a number of her mares had been shipped over to be mated with selected American stallions. Her 1986 visit afforded an opportunity to inspect the offspring of these pairings as well as select further stallions for future breeding. 'The odds are against someone breeding their own winner,' said her racing manager, Lord Porchester, 'but we still hope.'

Later that same year there was a state visit to China, a royal gesture of goodwill made to mark the agreement to hand Hong Kong back to the Chinese in 1997. The handing back of Hong Kong, however inevitable, was always a matter for doubt, but at the time all seemed relatively harmonious and the horrifying massacre in Tienanmen Square was still in the future. The Queen requested several changes to the itinerary originally proposed, with China's Communist leaders giving way far more gracefully than they would subsequently do over questions affecting the future of Hong Kong. All things considered, the visit went off well, though it is doubtful how many of China's vast population knew anything about it. The Queen saw the Forbidden City, the Great Wall, the tombs of the Ming emperors and the tomb of Chin Shi Huang in Xian with its army of terracotta soldiers, some 6,000 of which had been unearthed and restored at the time of her visit. An important sideshoot, which had more and more become a part of the Queen's overseas tours during the previous few years, was a trade exhibition and seminar held aboard the royal yacht, moored in Shanghai while the Queen herself was in Beijing, which resulted in the signing of more than a dozen multi-million pound contracts in the fields of telecommunications, steel production, transportation and suchlike.

With the Queen now a grandmother in her sixties, with her eldest son and Heir Apparent not far short of forty, it was perhaps inevitable that from time to time there should be speculation as to whether she might abdicate in his favour in similar fashion to queens of the Netherlands. The Queen, in a speech she made in Canada around this time, appeared to be saying that she does not necessarily see things in the same light. 'I am happy to give you my assurance', she told her Canadian audience, 'that I will serve Canada for as long as the compact between the Crown and the people continues.' And in case there should be any lingering doubt, a

Buckingham Palace spokesperson would state categorically soon after: 'The Queen has no intention of abdicating.'

But while the Queen may have no intention of abdicating, her style of monarchy will surely change. She has travelled further and more frequently than any previous monarch in British history. She has carried out more – far more – Commonwealth tours and state visits than any monarch before her. Very occasionally the strain shows. It is only natural that she may be expected to tire more easily and more often as she progresses through the second half of her sixties and into her seventies. But tours, state visits and public engagements, at home and abroad, are no more than the icing on the royal cake. There is no reason why they should not be delegated more and more to the Prince and Princess of Wales, the Princess Royal and other younger members of the family, as indeed has already begun to happen, leaving the Queen free to devote more of her time and energy to the constitutional aspects of monarchy. This, surely, is the part of her role which really matters and which she is now, after so many years on the Throne, more than ever qualified to fulfil.

The Queen was back from China, relaxing at Sandringham after Christmas, when she first learned that her youngest son, Prince Edward, now nearly twenty-three, was having second thoughts about his career as a Royal Marine. 'There will be nothing special laid on and he will have to meet the standards of any other Royal Marine officer,' his commanding officer had said when he signed on in September 1986. Edward had previously undergone a two-week course at the Commando Training Centre at Lympstone and three years of part-time training, but the tough full-time regime was to prove not to his liking. After only four months he had already decided that enough was enough and drove to Sand-ringham to discuss things with his parents. He would seem to have left his father at least with the idea that he might soldier on, but a subsequent telephone call from the son would finally shatter that hope, much to the disappointment and embarrassment of Prince Philip in his role as Captain General of the Marines.

A year later Edward would opt for a theatrical career, starting as a production assistant with Andrew Lloyd Webber's Really Useful Company. Before that, however, he became briefly involved in organizing a royal version of the crazy television game show titled

It's A Knockout. He was supported in the venture by three others of his royal generation, brother Andrew, sister-in-law Sarah and, somewhat surprisingly, sister Anne, whom the Queen had recently elevated to the status of Princess Royal in recognition of, among other things, her sterling work for the Save The Children Fund.

That a big change was taking place in royal attitudes and outlook was never more clearly seen than on that day when three of the Queen's children and one of her daughters-in-law donned mock mediaeval costumes and romped around for the benefit of television cameras, while some 150 miles away, at Windsor Castle, the Queen herself was installing former prime minister James Callaghan as a Knight of the Garter, Britain's highest order of chivalry. The romping was done with the best of intentions, in the cause of charity, but there were those who thought it all a bit undignified. As Peregrine Worsthorne was to write in the *Sunday Telegraph* 'No self-respecting nation is long going to remain content with having the family from which its Head of State is drawn turned into the stuff of soap opera.' Or, as Godfrey Talbot would say in a television documentary entitled *Royal Pursuits*, ' . . . although it was to raise money for charities, I'm not sure that that was sufficient excuse for what went on and I'm not sure that a great deal of harm was not done in the world to the image of the Royal Family.'

But if royal attitudes and outlook were changing, so were those of the Queen's subjects. The former Lord Altrincham, a generation before, had been slapped in the face, and Malcolm Muggeridge had had a newspaper contract cancelled for airing views similar to those published in the *Sunday Telegraph* and spoken on television. As far as is known, neither Peregrine Worsthorne nor Godfrey Talbot suffered a similar fate, while the Queen, whose own attitude and outlook have changed hardly at all, who has never sacrificed royal dignity in pursuit of popularity, was to be concerned, hurt, even angered on one occasion, by the amount of criticism and gossip to which her children and even herself would be subject over the next few years.

However, the birth in August, 1988, of a daughter, Princess Beatrice, to the Duke and Duchess of York was hailed with national jubilation, even by the tabloids. The Queen, receiving news of the baby's birth while on a visit to Paisley, beamed with pleasure at the shouts of 'Congratulations' which greeted her from crowds in the market square and was delighted when someone gave her a toy rabbit as a gift for this latest addition to her family. Yet within weeks there was to be controversy and criticism because the Duchess opted to leave baby Beatrice behind while accompanying husband Andrew on a tour of Australia. That particular spate of criticism must surely have brought a wry smile to the Queen's face as she recalled how she, as a babe of eight months, had been similarly left behind – and for much longer – in the 1920s, and how she herself had left baby Charles behind in the 1940s in order to be with her husband in Malta.

In relatively close succession the Queen found herself entertaining both Mikhail Gorbachev, president of the Soviet Union, and an old friend, Ronald Reagan, now succeeded by George Bush as president of the United States. The Gorbachev visit was very much a full dress state affair, with a guard of honour from the Coldstreams on parade at Windsor Castle, a tour of the castle's main rooms with the Queen herself acting as tour guide – 'It's a big house,' she joked – a luncheon party for thirty-four guests, including Britain's then prime minister, Margaret Thatcher, in the state dining room, and two leather-bound volumes of the book *Royal Heritage* for President Gorbachev as a parting gift. It was during luncheon that the Soviet president, through an interpreter, invited the Queen to visit his country. She accepted the invitation and will go there, as she said, 'in due course'.

Ex-President Reagan's visit, in contrast, was very much a private, informal affair, during which, as he said on leaving Buckingham Palace, he was 'greatly honoured' to have been appointed an honorary Knight Grand Cross of the Order of the Bath. 'Honorary' because he is not a British subject. It was for the same reason that he was not knighted at an investiture in traditional fashion. Instead, the Queen presented him with the insignia of the Order in the privacy of her own apartment with only Prince Philip and Mrs Reagan to witness the small ceremony.

At the time of the Reagan visit the Queen already knew, had known for some three months, that newspaper gossip concerning her daughter's marriage was founded in fact. Princess Anne had told her mother earlier in the year of her decision to separate from her husband, Mark Phillips, after nearly sixteen years of marriage.

It was news which 'deeply saddened' the Queen. But it was not until that August, shortly after Anne's thirty-ninth birthday, that newspaper gossip was confirmed by an official announcement. The delay was caused by the difficulty of arranging a satisfactory financial settlement between husband and wife, with the Queen herself peripherally involved as the owner of one of the two properties making up the couple's country estate.

As with most families, there were swings and roundabouts in family life. In March, 1990, with the birth of another daughter, Eugenie, to the Duke and Duchess of York, the Queen, now within nodding distance of her sixty-fourth birthday, became a grand-mother for the sixth time and it was a delighted granny who popped into London's Portland Hospital a day or so later to see her latest grandchild. There were several other reasons for special celebration that year, the Queen Mother's ninetieth birthday, Princess Margaret's sixtieth birthday and Princess Anne's fortieth, all in August. But celebration was held over until December when a party for all three, and some eight hundred other guests, was held in the picture gallery at Buckingham Palace.

A week later found the Queen striking a far from celebratory note when her annual telecast was video-taped ready for transmission on Christmas Day. With war clouds gathering over the Gulf, she spoke of Saddam Hussein's invasion of Kuwait as 'an example on an international scale of an evil which has beset us at different levels in recent years - attempts by ruthless people to impose their will on a peaceable majority.' She spoke also of IRA terrorism in Northern Ireland, saying, 'We have suffered once again during the past year from the scourge of terrorism, its disregard for human life and its efforts to dress its crimes in political clothes.'

The situation in the Gulf, where British forces were joined with the Americans and others in the operation known as Desert Shield which, in turn, would become Desert Storm provoked yet another spate of newspaper criticism and public controversy, with the *Sunday Times* and other newspapers indicting the Royal Family, its younger members in particular, for failing to give sufficient moral support to Britain's armed forces.

As it happened, the very day after the *Sunday Times* spearheaded this critical attack, the Prince and Princess of Wales were to be found at Plymouth, bolstering the morale of the wives of sailors serving in the Gulf, the Princess Royal was on her way to Germany to visit three regiments of which she is Colonel-in-Chief, the Duke of York was on duty aboard HMS *Campbeltown* and arrangements were in hand for his Duchess to visit the Royal Naval Air Station at Portsmouth the following day. Royal visits not being arranged overnight, all except possibly the last of these must surely already have been in motion when the first critical headlines hit the news-stands.

That this fact was not immediately apparent to the man and woman in the street was revealed by the findings of a public opinion poll conducted later that week. This showed that while 69 per cent of those interviewed were perfectly satisfied with the support the Queen herself was giving to the armed forces, 68 per cent were similarly satisfied with the Princess of Wales and 63 per cent with both the Prince of Wales and the Princess Royal, the same reasonably high figures did not hold for all members of the family. For Prince Philip the satisfaction figure dropped to 54 per cent and went lower still for the Duke of York (50 per cent), the Duchess (35 per cent) and Prince Edward (27 per cent). More disturbing still were some of the poll's other findings, with 38 per cent of those interviewed apparently considering the Royal Family 'an expensive luxury', and a staggering 73 per cent of the opinion that the Queen should pay income tax on her private monies.

Whether or not the Queen summoned others of the family to Windsor to give them a piece of straight talking, as the *Sunday Times* advocated, it was noticeable that thereafter the number of Gulf-related royal visits to military establishments and suchlike took a distinct upward turn, though such visits, of course, may also have been in the planning stage earlier. And the Queen herself took the decision to appear again on television and speak of her pride in Britain's armed forces, the first such broadcast since those made by her father half-a-century before during World War II. She prayed, she said 'that their success will be as swift as it is certain and that it may be achieved with as small a cost in human life and suffering as possible.'

If the Queen was 'angered', as was said, over this particular outburst of criticism, she can hardly have been pleased by a magazine survey purporting to give estimates of her wealth which, according to the magazine, was now in the region of £6.6 billion and increasing at the rate of £1.6 million a day.

Any estimate of the Queen's wealth must necessarily be regarded with caution. Twenty years ago the size of her personal fortune was being variously estimated at £3 million, £50 million and £100 million. At that time the then Lord Chamberlain, Lord Cobbold, told a Parliamentary Select Committee that suggestions that the Queen's wealth ran as high as £50 million or more were 'wildly exaggerated', while in what appeared to be an inspired 'leak', John Colville, a director of Coutts & Co., where the Queen banks, offered to 'eat my hat' if she had more than £2 million. As in 1971, so in 1991, with the magazine's figures labelled 'a gross distortion' by an unofficial royal spokesperson.

All that can safely be said is that the Queen is very, very wealthy and quite probably the richest woman in the world.

More reliable were the figures given in a report issued by the Royal Trustees, though the report, of course, dealt only with what might be termed her official finances, not with her personal wealth. Nevertheless, it afforded an intriguing glimpse into how the Queen's Civil List stipend is expended. Of the £5.9 million the Queen received in 1990, slightly over £3.4 million went on staff salaries, £200,783 on what were termed 'kitchens' (presumably food and cleaning materials), £71,250 on wines, £180,557 on furnishings, £63,700 on laundry and, £37,950 on flowers. Livery cost £88,100, newspapers £13,532, garden parties £213,650, horses and carriages (purchases and upkeep) £165,025 and cars (purchases, hire and upkeep) £73,317.

There was, in addition, office equipment to be purchased and maintained, stationery to be bought, insurance paid and donations made. All these things the Queen pays for out of her Civil List monies. These were increased to £7.9 million in 1991, a figure which will no longer be increased annually to allow for inflation but will remain fixed for ten years.

Civil List emoluments for others of the family have also been increased to an annual total of £1.89 million. 'Why should the taxpayer be handing out large sums of money to the Queen and all the hangers-on at the Palace?' Labour's Dennis Skinner wanted to know when the increases were announced in the House of Commons.

199

In fact, of course, the taxpayer will be contributing rather more than that to maintain the monarchy. In addition to payments to the Queen and others of the family, the cost, on the basis of the 1990/91 Parliamentary estimates, would include £25.7 million for the up-keep of palaces and other royal residences, £9.3 million to maintain the royal yacht, £6.7 million for the Queen's Flight and £2.3 million for the royal train. Altogether, a total of close on £54 million, including the Civil List. Nevertheless, Margaret Thatcher, prime minister at the time of the announcement, was probably right when she asserted, 'The overwhelming majority of people are agreed that the Royal Family is the greatest asset the United Kingdom has.'

Though no longer prime minister, Mrs Thatcher was to find her words echoed in America when the Queen went there again in 1991, progressing from Washington to Florida (where she bestowed an honorary knighthood on General Norman Schwarzkopf, chief architect of the Allied victory over Iraq) and on to Texas. In Washington, addressing a joint session of Congress, she joked – a rare thing with her – that she hoped everyone could see her, a sly reference to the fact that a bevy of microphones had obscured her face earlier when responding to President Bush's words of greeting. Commented the *Washington Post*: 'She's not our Queen, but before we're through with her she'll probably think she is. Two centuries after George III lost the colonies, Elizabeth II is in danger of winning them back.'

As the Queen drew towards the fortieth anniversary of her reign, perhaps three things – money, criticism, security – served to emphasise the way life had changed for her over the years. In 1952, when she first succeeded to the Throne, her Civil List emolument was £475,000, a figure which would remain unchanged for the next nineteen years. Now it is £7.9 million, over sixteen times as much. Criticism in the early days of her reign was limited to such occasional trivialities as to whether her two small children, Charles and Anne, should have ice creams bought for them on a Sunday. Today newspaper gossip and criticism has grown out of all pro-portion. Security in the days when she was Heir Presumptive was of so little moment that her personal detective, on the occasion of a house party, could be despatched to the kitchen to help with the washing-up. Now she is hemmed in by electronic devices at home, shadowed by SAS-trained bodyguards wherever she goes, and her new royal train has had to be armour-plated against the possibility of rocket attack.

Yet over those same forty years, to a truly remarkable extent, she has somehow accomplished the seemingly impossible task of being nearly all things to nearly all people. She has managed to be – and is – regal without being pompous, dutiful without being dull, idealistic without seeming prudish, and deeply religious without being priggish. She has even been down-to-earth, upon occasion, without any loss of royal dignity.

If she does not exude the same degree of emotional warmth as the Queen Mother and lacks the bubbling nature of her daughter-in-law, the Princess of Wales, it is partly because it goes against both her nature and early training to display her emotions in public and partly because her role is different. Elizabeth II is not a Queen Consort, as her mother was, and as her Spencer daughter-in-law will one day be. She is Queen in her own right.

These days, of course, the Monarch no longer has political power. But she does have influence. And she does have experience. After all, she has been forty years in the job. Daily during those forty years she has studied and digested the contents of her Boxes. Weekly, in exercise of what is perhaps her sole remaining royal prerogative – to be kept informed, to encourage or to counsel caution – she has received the prime minister of the day in Audience.

No one can know how far words of encouragement or caution uttered by the Queen in the privacy of her Audience Room at Buckingham Palace may have influenced the nine British prime ministers who have so far served her though we do know that her private alphabetical-order talks with national leaders at Commonwealth conferences have more than once smoothed out differences and helped to restore good relations. But almost certainly she has achieved far more than is realized, while her true value as Queen may yet lie in the future.

BOOKS CONSULTED

In writing this book we have necessarily drawn to a small degree upon some of our earlier books, in particular *The Crown & The Ring* (published 1972), *The Queen's Life* (1976) and *Monarchy & The Royal Family* (1979). While these are now out of print, copies can still be obtained on loan through the public library system.

Other works we have consulted and found helpful include:

Thatched With Gold, MABEL, COUNTESS OF AIRLIE (Hutchinson)

Queen Mary, SIR GEORGE ARTHUR (Butterworth & Co)

The King's Daughters, LADY CYNTHIA ASQUITH (Hutchinson)

Chips: The Diaries of Sir Henry Channon (Weidenfeld & Nicolson)

The Little Princesses (Cassel) and *Queen Elizabeth II* (Newnes), MARION CRAWFORD

HRH Prince Philip, JOHN DEAN (Robert Hale)

George & Elizabeth: A Royal Marriage, DAVID DUFF (Collins)

Edward VIII, FRANCES DONALDSON (Weidenfeld)

George V, JOHN GORE (John Murray)

Silver & Gold, SIR NORMAN HARTNELL (Evans Brothers)

The Crown Jewels, MARTIN HOLMES (HMSO)

How The Queen Reigns, DOROTHY LAIRD (Hodder & Stoughton)

Tides of Fortune, *Riding The Storm* and *Pointing The Way* – the memoirs of HAROLD MACMILLAN (Macmillan)

The Crown & The People, ALLAN A. MICHIE (Secker & Warburg)

The Work Of The Queen, DERMOT MORRAH (William Kimber & Co)

The Queen's World Tour, L. A. NICKOLLS (Macdonald & Co)

King George V, HAROLD NICHOLSON (Constable & Co)

Queen Mary, JAMES POPE-HENNESSY (Allen & Unwin)

Buckingham Palace, H. CLIFFORD SMITH (Country Life)

Thirty Years A Queen, GEOFFREY WAKEFORD (Robert Hale)

King George VI, JOHN WHEELER BENNETT (Macmillan)

The Labour Government 1964–70, Sir Harold Wilson (Weidenfeld & Nicolson/Michael Joseph)

The Heart Has Its Reasons, The Duchess of Windsor (Michael Joseph)

A King's Story, The Duke of Windsor (Cassel & Co)

Princess Margaret, Christopher Warwick (Weidenfeld & Nicolson)

Elizabeth & Philip, Louis Wulff (Sampson Low)

Double Exposure Gloria Vanderbilt and Thelma, Lady Furness (Frederick Muller)

Time & Chance, Peter Townsend (Collins)

Philip – An Informal Biography, Basil Boothroyd (Longman)

King George V, Sir Arthur Bryant (Peter Davies)

INDEX

Abdication (of King Edward VIII),
1, 3, 46–9, 50–1, 197

Act of Settlement, 50, 52, 82

Adams, Marcus, 35

Aga Khan, 20

Airlie, Dowager Countess of, 38, 67

Aitchison, Sir David, 134

Albert, Prince Consort, 17, 20–1, 85,
102, 125, 153, 189

Alexander of Tunis, Earl, 129

Alexandra, Princess, 23

Alexandra, Queen, 31

Alice, Princess (née Battenberg) – *see*
Andrew, Princess of Greece

Alice, Princess, Countess of Athlone,
99

Alice, Princess, Dowager Duchess of
Gloucester, 23

Alice, Princess, Grand Duchess of
Hesse, 58, 172

Althorp, Viscount – *see* Spencer, 8th
Earl

Altrincham, Lord – *see* Grigg, John

Amin, Idi, 163

Andrew, Prince, 22, 168, 172, 174,
175, 195, 196, 197, 198
birth, xii, 146
Duke of York, 192
education, 152
(in) Falklands, 179–80
marriage, 192

Andrew, Prince of Greece, 58, 90

Andrew, Princess of Greece, 30, 58,
89, 90, 153–4

Andrew, Elizabeth, 182–3

Anne, Princess Royal, 160, 195, 198
birth, xii, 106
childhood, 134
children, xi, 2, 168–9, 176
European Eventing Champion, 157
health, 157
kidnap attempt, 161, 162
marriage, xii
name, 124–5, 126, 146
separation, xii, 196–7
wedding, 93, 161

Anne, Queen, 197

Aosta, Duchess of, 96

Armstrong-Jones, Antony – *see*
Snowdon, Earl of

Armstrong-Jones, Lady Sarah, 2

Ascot racecourse, 19

Askew, Barry, 179

Athlone, Earl of, 99

Attlee, Clement, 85, 109, 118

Auriol, Vincent, President of France,
108

Avon, Earl of, 15, 118, 136, 137, 139

**Baden, Margrave and Margravine
of**, 96

Badouin, King of the Belgians, 184

Bagehot, Walter, 129, 197

Baldwin, Stanley, 48

Balmoral Castle 6, 14, 20–1, 43, 56,
61–2, 83–4, 101, 128, 137, 151,
163, 174–5, 184

Barcelona, Count and Countess of, 96

Beatrice, Princess, xii, 195–6
Beatrix, Queen of the Netherlands, 184
Bernhardt, Prince of the Netherlands,
    96, 108
Bevin, Ernest, 85
Blacker, Sir George, 27
Blair, Sir Chandos, 163
Boyd Rochfort, Captain Cecil, 132
Brabourne, 7th Baron, 172
Brabourne, Lady – see Mountbatten,
    Patricia, Countess
Brabourne, Dowager Lady, 172
Britannia HMY, 134, 135, 145, 176
Brooke, Sir Basil, 61
Buckingham Palace, 6, 13, 32, 52–3,
    74–5, 89–90, 126–7, 168, 181–3
Bush, President George, 196, 200
Butler of Saffron Walden, Baron, 139

Callaghan, James, 16, 163, 195
Cambridge, Lady Mary – see Whitley,
    Lady Mary
Carnarvon, Earl of, 79, 188, 193
Casson, Sir Hugh, 166
Charles I, King, 19
Charles II, King, 195
Charteris, Lord, 115, 116
Child, Sir Hill, 63
Churchill, Sir Winston, 15, 50, 71, 98,
    118, 119, 125, 126, 127, 133, 135,
    140, 149
Civil List, 199–200
Clarence, Albert Victor, Duke of, 1
Clarence House, 103–5
Clarendon, Earl of, 119
Clynes, John Robert, 38
Colville, Sir John, 95–6
Connaught, Arthur, Duke of, 32
Coronation of Elizabeth II, xi, 128–32
Crawford, Marion, 5, 41–2, 43, 59,
    60, 81, 83
Cromwell, Oliver, 129
Crookshank, Harry, 118

**Dalrymple-Hamilton, Sir
    Frederick**, 59

Dean, John, 115, 116
Diefenbaker, John, Prime Minister of
    Canada, 145
Dionne quintuplets, 111
Douglas-Home, Sir Alec – see Home,
    Lord
Duke of York Camps, 40, 61

Ecgbert the Great, 119
Ede, Chuter, 86
Eden, Sir Anthony – see Avon, Earl
    of
Edward the Confessor, 19, 123
Edward VII, King, 20, 126, 173, 191,
    192
Edward VIII, King, 1, 2, 3, 22, 25,
    28, 29, 33, 39–40, 46, 50, 126,
    136, 137, 197; as Duke of
    Windsor, 54, 129–50, 158
Edward, Prince, xii, 22, 148, 152,
    189–90, 194–5, 198
Eisenhower, Mamie, 145
Elisabeth of Luxembourg, Princess,
    96
Elizabeth I, Queen, 7, 55, 195
Elizabeth II, Queen
    Abdication of Edward VIII, 1, 3, 5,
        47–9
    accession, 3, 9–10, 114–17,
        118–22
    ancestry, 200–201
    appearance, 6, 76
    assassination threats, 156–8, 167–8,
        190
    ATS, 73–4
    audiences, 11
    Australia, 11, 134, 156, 166, 170
    baby, 31–5
    betrothal, 84–5, 86, 88–91
    birth, xi, 24, 26–30
    Birthday Parade – see Trooping the
        Colour
    Canada, 11, 109–11, 142, 144–5,
        148–9, 168, 170, 179–80, 186–7,
        193
    ceremonies, 18–19

character, 5, 6–8, 13, 43, 44–5, 63,
  65, 67–8, 73, 77–8, 127, 130,
  147, 157, 178, 195
childbirth, 101–2, 146
childhood, 35–49
China, 193
christening, 32
Christmas, 20, 22–3, 43, 65,
  111–12, 128, 139, 191
clothes, 6, 13–14, 45, 54, 63, 67,
  76–7, 78, 92–3
coming of age, 88
Commonwealth Tour 1953–54,
  133–5
confirmation, 67
cooking, 13, 99
corgis, 12, 14, 44
coronation, xi, 128–32
coronation of King George VI,
  53–4
cosmetics, 8, 128
Counsellor of State, 70–1
courtship, 68–70, 79–86
criticisms of, 101, 140, 141–2,
  186–7
D-Day, 72, 184
early reign, 123–8
education, 40–3, 55–6, 57
Elizabeth of York, 23, 24–49
engagement ring, 90
finances, 52, 99–100, 193, 198–200
Germany, 151, 169–70
Girl Guide, 56–7, 65
grandmother, 168–9, 180–1, 186,
  189, 195–6, 197
habits, 5–6, 43, 190
handbag, 12–13
Head of the Commonwealth,
  10–11, 16–17, 162–3, 170–1,
  183, 191–2, 201
health, 5–6, 8, 103, 127–8, 143,
  144, 192
height, 14
Heir Presumptive, 1, 3, 5, 19, 48–9,
  50–113
holidays, 10, 20–1, 37, 56, 187–8

honeymoon, 98–9
horse racing, 20, 56, 78, 132, 135,
  185, 188, 192–3
in-laws, 100, 151, 154
jewellery, 44, 63–4, 134, 170
Jordan, 185–6
Kenya, 113–17
King George V, 34, 36, 37–8, 44,
  46
King George VI, 40, 53, 55, 70, 78,
  98, 109–10, 122, 127, 129
knitting, 47
leisure, 18, 20–1
lifestyle, 5–7, 18, 20–1
luncheon parties, 12–13
Malta, 105–6
married life, 21–2, 99–100, 103–6,
  138–9, 152
meals, 6, 9, 12, 14, 18
mimicry, 65
mock assassination, 176–8
Monarch, 9–12, 14–15, 139–40,
  147–8, 161–2, 163–5, 185–6,
  193–4, 201
monarchies, xi
Morocco, 11, 175–6
mother, 102, 103, 104–6, 123–4,
  146, 179–80, 184–5
names, x, 1, 15, 31, 34, 124–5,
  145–6
New Zealand, 11, 134, 156, 166,
  170
Northern Ireland, 76, 77, 167–8
palace intruder, 181–3
pantomime, 65–6, 69
powers, 14–15, 139–40, 147–8
pregnancies, 99–101, 144–5, 148,
  186
prime ministers, 14–17
Prince Philip, 9, 12, 17–18, 55,
  58–60, 68–9, 79, 129–30, 153 (see
  also 'courtship' and 'married
  life')
Prince of Wales, 143, 152, 155,
  196
Princess of Wales, 179

207

Elizabeth II, Queen – *cont.*
  Princess Margaret, 39, 43, 44, 45,
    54–5, 61–2, 64–5, 71, 93, 132–3,
    136–7, 165–6
  Privy Council, 11–12
  public appearances (as Princess), 35,
    41, 53, 57, 67, 71, 76, 77, 81, 90,
    94, 104
  Queen Mary, 34, 36–7, 43, 119,
    130
  Queen Mother, 9, 20
  racing colours, 20
  radio broadcast, 66
  Rhodesian situation, 151–2
  riding, 5–6, 18, 37, 41, 65
  Sea Ranger, 69
  security, 149, 155–8, 168, 178,
    181–3, 185–6, 188, 200–1
  Silver Jubilee, 88, 166–8
  Silver Wedding, 158–9, 160
  South Africa, 86–8
  speeches, 71, 88, 120, 137–8, 143,
    158–9, 169, 186, 189, 191–2, 197,
    198
  stalking, 78
  swimming, 47
  succession to the throne, xii, 1,
    28–9
  televiewer, 18
  television, 22, 142–3, 154, 189, 197,
    198
  tennis, 56
  titles, xi, 120–2
  Peter Townsend, 132–3, 136–7
  travels (other than those listed
    separately), 5, 10–11, 101, 147,
    161, 166, 167, 170, 187, 190–2
  Trooping the Colour, 8, 19, 41,
    108, 109, 169–70, 176–8
  USA, 11, 111, 141, 183, 188,
    192–3, 200
  walking, 5–6, 18
  wedding and wedding gifts, xi,
    92–8, 104
  weekends, 18
  Windsors, 149–50, 158

  World War II, 61–75
  work, 9–13, 14–17, 18–19, 192
Elizabeth, the Queen Mother, Queen
  birth, xi
  character, 17, 25, 62
  coronation (King George VI), 54
  courtship, 25–6
  Duchess of York, 23, 25–6, 33
  health, 46, 49, 153
  names, x
  Queen Consort, 49, 182, 196
  Peter Townsend, 131, 133
  wedding, 24
  wife and mother, 31, 35, 39, 41,
    52–3
  Windsors, 149–50, 150–1
  World War II, 61, 62, 67
Elphinstone, Lady, 32
Eugenie, Princess, xii, 197
Euston, Earl of, 79

Fagan, Michael, 8, 181–3
Farish, William, 188
Fellowes, Robert, 174
Ferguson, Sarah – *see* York, Duchess
  of
Fraser, Malcolm, Prime Minister of
  Australia, 164–5
Furness, Thelma, Lady, 2

Galloway, Alistair, 177
Gandhi, Indira, 188
Gandhi, Mahatma, 93
Garter, Most Noble Order of, 19
Georg of Hanover, Prince and
  Princess, 96
George II, King, 7, 40
George II, King of the Hellenes, 70,
  83, 85
George III, King, 25
George IV, King, 40, 133
George V, King, xi, 1, 23, 24, 25, 26,
  27, 29, 30, 31–2, 33, 34, 36,
  37–8, 39, 42, 44, 45, 46, 126,
  166, 182
George VI, King

Abdication of Edward VIII, 1, 3, 5,
49
accession, 1, 3, 5, 49, 50–2
character, 24, 25, 26, 39, 51, 86–7
coronation, 53–4
death, x, 3, 114, 190
Duke of York, 23–6, 28, 29, 33,
46
Elizabeth, 21, 40, 49, 53, 55, 68, 70,
74, 78–9, 82, 94–5, 98–9, 101,
112–13
funeral, 122–3
health, 87, 101, 103, 107–9
King, 49, 50–113, 126
Margaret, 78
Philip, 60, 66–7, 70, 84, 91, 93,
94–5
World War II, 61, 67, 171
Gibbs, Sir Humphrey, 151
Gloucester, Henry, 1st Duke of, 28,
29, 50, 92, 118
Gloucester, Richard, 2nd Duke of, 97
Gorbachev, President Mikhail, 11,
196
Gottfried of Hohenlohe-Langenburg,
Prince and Princess, 96
Grigg, John, 140, 141, 195

Halliday, Edward, 124
Halsey, Admiral William, 79
Harewood, 6th Earl of, 27
Harewood, 7th Earl of, 16, 27, 28, 29,
133
Hartnell, Sir Norman, 13, 92, 128
Hassan, King of Morocco, 11, 175–6
Heasman, John, 177
Heath, Edward, 16, 161–2, 164, 198
Helen of Romania, Queen, 96
Henry VII, King, 31
Henry of Wales, Prince, xi, 186, 189
Hicks, Lady Pamela, 113
Hills, Denis, 163
Hitler, Adolf, 72, 169
Home, Lord, 16, 147–8
Hussein of Jordan, King, 185–6
Hussein, Saddam, 197

Investiture of the Prince of Wales,
154–5

Jagger, Walter, 27
James I, King, 83
James II, King, 38, 82
Jean, Grand Duke of Luxembourg,
96, 184
Jefferies, Timothy, 185
Joyce, William, 61
Joynson-Hicks, Sir William, 27
Juliana, Queen of the Netherlands,
108

Kennedy, John F., U.S. President,
148, 157, 177
Kent, George, 1st Duke of, 28, 29,
50, 51, 55, 66, 72
Kent, Marina, Duchess of, 66, 81, 96,
101
Kerr, Sir John, 164–5
Knatchbull, Nicholas, 172
Knatchbull, Timothy, 172
Knight, Clara, 31, 36, 53, 63

Lander, Mabel, 41
Lane, Lord Chief Justice, 177
Lang, Dr Cosmo, Archbishop of
Canterbury, 32, 37, 67
Lascelles, Sir Alan, 124, 125, 132
Lascelles, Hon. Gerald, 27, 28, 29
Lascelles, Viscount – see Harewood,
6th Earl of
Learmouth, Sir James, 107, 123
LeBrun, Albert, President of France,
53
Legh, Sir Piers, 124
Lennon, John, 177
Lightbody, Helen, 104, 126
Linley, David, Viscount, 2
Llewellyn, Roddy, 166
Lloyd Webber, Andrew, 194
Louis of Battenberg, Prince – see
Milford Haven, 1st Marquess of
Louis IV, Grand Duke of Hesse, 58, 172
Louise, Queen of Sweden, 30

MacDonald, Margaret, 36, 39, 53, 71, 93, 95, 115, 116, 124
Macleod, Iain, 148
Macmillan, Harold – *see* Stockton, Earl of
Major, John, 15
Margaret, Princess, 93, 97, 155, 190
  birth, xi, 38–9
  character, 45, 64, 78
  childhood, 39, 45, 46, 48–9, 51, 54–5, 64–5, 78, 82
  children, 2
  divorce, 21
  health, 192
  marriage, 146–7, 165–6
  names, x
  Peter Townsend, 80–1, 87, 131–2, 136, 137
Marten, Sir Henry, 57, 61, 65
Mary, Princess Royal, 21, 27, 28, 29, 30, 32
Mary, Queen, 1, 24, 25, 26, 30, 31, 32, 34, 36–7, 41, 42, 43, 45, 46–7, 51, 53, 55–6, 66, 67, 77, 90, 102, 119, 127, 130, 150
Mary of Modena, 50
Maude, Michael, 177
Maxwell, Paul, 172
Milford Haven, 1st Marquess of, 58
Milford Haven, 2nd Marquess of, 59
Milford Haven, 3rd Marquess of, 97
Milford Haven, Dowager Marchioness of, 30, 58, 89
Mitterand François, President of France, 184, 188
Montgomery of Alamein, Viscount, 129
Mountbatten of Burma, Earl, 59, 83, 86, 106, 118, 124, 125, 152, 154, 168, 172–3
Mountbatten, Edwina, Countess, 86, 106
Mountbatten, Patricia, Countess, 172
Muggeridge, Malcolm, 141–2, 195
Mulley, Frederick, 168

Mulroney, Brian, Prime Minister of Canada, 187
Muzorewa, Bishop, 171
Mwema, Sam, 172

Nkomo, Joshua, 172
Nkrumah, Kwame, 147
Norfolk, 16th Duke of, 119

Olav, King of Norway, 184
Oswald, Michael, 188

Parker, Eileen, 139
Parker, Michael, 100, 101, 113, 114, 115, 139
Parliament, State Opening of, 6, 19, 108, 123, 157–8
Peter, King of Yugoslavia, 70
Philip, Prince
  accidents, 93–4
  antecedents, 58–9, 82–3
  betrothal, 84–5, 86, 88–91
  birth, 1–2, 58–9
  boyhood, 59
  carriage driving, 181
  character, 21, 141
  Consort, 17–18, 124–5, 126, 142, 153, 157, 158, 161, 196, 198
  constitutional position, 17
  courtship, 68–70, 79–86
  education, 21, 59, 151
  Elizabeth, 55, 59–60, 66–7, 68–9 (*see also* 'courtship' and 'married life')
  finance, 100
  George VI, 84
  habits, 13, 90
  honeymoon, 98–9
  husband and father, 100, 101–2, 103, 104, 124–5, 136, 141, 152, 161, 194 (*see also* 'married life')
  married life, 99–102, 106, 138–9
  name, 86, 87
  naturalization, 82–3, 87
  naval cadet, 58–60
  naval career, 21, 79, 105–6, 109

polo, 106, 144
Regent, 126
religion, 94
shooting, 84
sisters, 59, 85, 96, 100, 151
television, 142, 154
titles, xii, 94–5, 139
travels, 10, 104, 109–11, 138, 144, 168, 172, 175, 184
wedding, xi, 92–8, 104
World War II, 66
Phillips, Captain Mark, xii, 2, 146, 160–1
Phillips, Peter, xi, 2, 168–9, 189
Phillips, Zara, xi, 2, 176, 189
Piccadilly, no. 145, 34–6, 39–40, 41–3
Porchester, Lord – *see* Carnarvon, Earl of
Powell, Enoch, 148
Privy Council, 11–12, 111, 137

Reagan, Ronald, U.S. President, 177, 183, 184, 196
Reagan, Nancy, 196
Remembrance Day, 19
Richards, Sir Gordon, 132
Roberts, Granville, 115
Roosevelt, Franklin D., U.S. President, 57
Royal Ascot, 19–20
Royal Family (TV documentary), 154, 160
Royal Lodge, 40–1, 48, 62
Royal Marriage Act, 16, 25, 133, 137, 160–1
Royal Maundy, 19, 123, 190
Rutland, Duke of, 79

Salisbury, 5th Marquess of, 140
Sandringham, 6, 14, 18, 20, 33, 37, 43, 46, 56, 62, 111, 122, 128, 139, 143, 176
Sarjeant, Marcus, 177, 178
Scargill, Arthur, 198
Schwarzkopf, General Norman, 200
Seymour, Captain Reginald, 27

Simon, Sir John, 52
Smith, Ian, 10, 151–2
Smith, Leslie, 177
Snowdon, Earl of, 146–7, 165
Sophia, Electress of Hanover, 83
Spencer, 8th Earl, 84, 174
Stimson, Sir Henry, 27
Stockton, Earl of, 7, 15–16, 139, 145, 147, 148
Strachey, Lady Mary, 71
Strathmore and Kinghorne, 14th Earl, 24, 32
Strathmore and Kinghorne, 16th Earl, 141
Strathmore, Countess of, 25, 26
Succession to the Throne, 28–9, 38, 133, 174, 180, 186, 202

Talbot, Geoffrey, 195
Tanner, Hubert, 65
Thatcher, Margaret, 15, 16–17, 171, 183–4, 185, 188, 196, 200
Townsend, Group Captain Peter, 55, 80–1, 87, 131–2, 136, 137
Treetops (Kenya), 113–14
Trudeau, Pierre, Prime Minister of Canada, 184
Truman, Harry S., U.S. President, 111
Tryon, Lord, 124
Turner, John, Prime Minister of Canada, 186

Victoria, Queen, 32, 55, 58, 83, 85, 102, 126, 128, 130, 153, 166, 189, 191
Victoria Eugenie, Queen of Spain, 96

Wales, Charles, Prince of, 157, 158, 160, 180, 197–8
birth, xi, 101–2
childhood, 23, 102–3, 104, 131, 134
children – *see* William of Wales and Henry of Wales
courtship, 174–5, 176
created Prince of Wales, 143

211

Wales, Charles, Prince of – *cont.*
  education, 140–1
  Heir Apparent, 196
  investiture, 154–5
  names, xi, 102
  titles, xi
  wedding, xi, 96–7, 178
Wales, Diana, Princess of, 197–8
  character, 7
  children – *see* William of Wales and
    Henry of Wales
  courtship, 174–5, 176
  pregnancies, 179, 186
  wedding, 93, 97, 178
Watts, Maurice, 124
Whitlam, Gough, Prime Minister of
    Australia, 164–5
Whitley, Lady Mary, 73
Whybrew, Paul, 183
Wilhelmina, Queen of the
    Netherlands, 108

William IV, King, 40, 126
William of Wales, Prince, xi, 180–1,
    189
William of Gloucester, Prince, 97
Wills, Mr and Mrs John Lycett, 137
Wilson of Rievaulx, Lord (Harold),
    15, 16, 99, 133, 149, 152, 161,
    162
Windsor, Duke of – *see* Edward VIII,
    King
Windsor, Duchess of, 2–3, 48, 136,
    137, 149–50, 158
Windsor Castle, 6, 18, 20, 27, 30, 41,
    62–4, 65–6, 135–6, 166
Woolton, Lord, 118
Worsthorne, Peregrine, 195

York, Duchess of, xii, 192, 195, 196,
    197, 198
York, Duke of – *see* Andrew,
    Prince

212